FINDING ELEVATION

FINDING ELEVATION

FEAR AND COURAGE ON THE WORLD'S
MOST DANGEROUS MOUNTAIN

LISA THOMPSON

GIRL FRIDAY BOOKS

Published by Girl Friday Books™, Seattle
www.girlfridaybooks.com

Produced by Girl Friday Productions

Development & editorial: Devon Fredericksen
Production editorial: Bethany Davis
Project management: Devon Fredericksen and Mari Kesselring
Design: Paul Barrett

Cover photo © Daniel Benitez, Branded Films

ISBN (hardcover): 978-1-954854-67-3
ISBN (e-book): 978-1-954854-68-0

Library of Congress Control Number: 2022909672

First edition

For Sara, because you *have always been the strong one.*

I want to be all I am capable of becoming.

—Katherine Mansfield

Partway up K2's Black Pyramid, 23,000 feet above sea level, I become aware of how slowly I'm climbing, and I don't like it. I don't like the self-doubt it awakens. Now is not the time. My chest heaves as I force frigid air into my lungs twice, then tilt my head down to search for the next logical place to put my clunky boot. Strapped to my boots are crampons, which add to their clunkiness—twelve metal spikes meant to aid my travel on steep ice. When I look down between my legs, I see the striated flow of the Baltoro and Godwin Austen Glaciers, reaching toward Pakistan's desolate plains. I trace the line where the glaciers converge 7,600 feet below me. Just beyond their meeting point, the earth rises sharply in a twisted mass of rock and ice to this precarious point where I now hang, suspended by the artificial safety of rope and metal, on the side of the second highest mountain in the world.

I scan the rock at my feet again for options. It's black and slick from melting snow and looks more like a cobble of rock remnants than a solid mountain. The best I can hope for is a chunky protrusion deep enough to support my crampon's one-inch-long steel front points. I find a small bump of wet stone and trust the narrow points with my body weight. A little at first. Then a committing amount. As my foot moves to the protrusion, I simultaneously slide the ascension device in my right hand higher up the climbing rope. On a 28,251-foot-tall mountain, I've just gained four inches. In ten minutes. I consider that maybe I am beyond my limit. In this moment, I do not feel capable of delivering what this deadly mountain demands, and the potential that I am disrespecting her with my impotence smacks in my throat and twists my lips.

Why am I doing this?

I've carried this question with me to every mountain I've climbed since Everest; searching for the answer both haunts me and pushes me forward.

In retrospect, my decision to climb K2 feels haphazard. Climbing the second highest mountain in the world didn't start as a distant hypothetical idea or as a childhood dream that percolated into reality. Summiting K2 fell into my consciousness on an icy weekend in 2014 while hiking in the Cascade mountains near my Seattle home.

It was the kind of February day that provokes even the most intrepid Pacific Northwesterners to shield themselves with Gore-Tex and retreat to anyplace warm and dry—the kind of day where we wonder aloud if we will ever feel the sun's warmth again, if we'll ever wear tank tops again. Instead of sheltering myself that day, however, I'd intentionally put myself face-to-face with Mother Nature to hike Mailbox Peak. While I carefully descended a steep, rocky trail encased in an inch of new ice, my boots searched for traction underneath me, moving in cartoonish slides and skids as I hiked down. I'd forgotten to bring a trekking pole, which would have created an additional point of contact with the ground, bringing more stabilization to the situation. Without it, I devised a cumbersome method of sliding downward from tree to tree, using each burly trunk to catch my fall before sliding into the next. The trees were mostly Douglas fir, their long, straight trunks rising toward the gray sky with sways and groans—audible protests against the weight of the ice wrapped around their highest branches. *Rime ice*, it's called, created when water droplets in the air touch a frozen surface and become locked to it, frozen instantly. The firs' motion occasionally sent showers of ice pellets down on me, each time bouncing off my jacket and scattering to the frozen ground like tiny crystals.

I don't recall exactly when during my icy descent K2 crept into my consciousness that day. I just know that it landed there, not as a question to be contemplated but as a fact. I knew that I would attempt K2 just as clearly as I knew that I would slide into the next tree. But at that point in 2014, I still hadn't done enough research to understand that for every four people who attempt to summit the world's second highest mountain, one will die, or that for women, the stats are even grimmer: of the first six to reach the summit, three lost their lives on descent.

Most of what I knew about K2 consisted of details from a 2008 *Seattle Times* article that described the deaths of eleven climbers in a tragic accident. When I read and reread the article from my patio that summer, I wondered what it was like for those climbers to realize they were stuck in the dark at 27,000 feet on a precarious slope in Pakistan without the means to safely descend. I was a neophyte climber in 2008, and though their perseverance and strength fascinated me, I didn't want a personal experience with such a deadly mountain. Yet I'd folded the article into quarters, slid it into a manila folder labeled *Mountains,* and tucked it away in a desk drawer. K2 would remain dormant in my consciousness after that, like a seed waiting for the right conditions to sprout and take root.

Something about that wintry descent in 2014, on a mountain I'd hiked for years, cultivated that seed. In the following months, I casually studied K2's routes, history, and risks. Studying a mountain brings it to life for me, gives it character, forging a relationship between us and making me feel like I am getting to know it and its challenges. Most importantly, studying my next climbing objective allows me to determine whether my ability and ambition are aligned with the mountain. As I devoured books and blogs during the summer of 2014, a persona of K2 quickly formed. It's not fun and approachable Mount Rainier, easily summited in a day or two if you're up for it. It's not austere and icy Denali, which demands a slow, steady uphill slog. Not even close. Although K2 is 778 feet shorter than Mount Everest, it is not even in the same league as the highest mountain in the world in terms of danger or difficulty.

K2 is 28,251 feet of unforgiving rock and ice on the Pakistan-China border that dares humans to fuck with it. It is treacherous exposure. It is unrelenting steepness from the first step beyond Advanced Base Camp. It is untrustworthy rock holds and unpredictable storms that snatch climbers off the mountain in the blink of an eye. Unlike on Everest, there is no tent at base camp acting as an emergency room; there are no commercial helicopters available to whisk injured climbers to safety. I knew that K2 would ask more of me than I could imagine. But still, that tiny seed nudged me to devise a hypothetical timeline of mountains to climb and skills to attain to meet K2's demands.

My timeline for climbing K2 was private. In my circle of mountaineering friends, we dreamed of and discussed the possibility of climbing Mount Everest and other Himalayan peaks, but our public ambition stopped there. I was also uneasy when it came to sharing mountaineering goals because I didn't want to risk the embarrassment of reeling it back in once it was out there. And I'd rather privately plan and surprise my fellow climbers with success than disappoint all of us with failure.

It was 2015 when I summoned enough courage to share my plans with a climbing partner while we slogged up Mailbox Peak, the same mountain where K2 had first planted itself into my awareness a year earlier. It wasn't icy this time, but the steep, meandering trail was slick with mud and loose rock that had dislodged itself in a recent rainstorm. My climbing partner was updating me on the first solo winter summit of Denali. I liked these training hikes together because his stories distracted me from the hours of uphill torture and my backpack's unforgiving weight. We were so comfortable with each other from years of climbing and training together that we could also let our conversations pause and move together in quiet mindlessness for hours, communicating only with grunts and hand gestures.

"You see he tied a tree trunk to his waist so he wouldn't fall in a crevasse?"

"Yeah, seems brutal," I said, economizing my words and breath as I struggled up the rocky hillside, trying to imagine climbing a mountain with a tree trunk strung to my waist.

"He's tried like four times."

"Intense."

When he and I had summited Denali together three years prior, we'd experienced the summer version of North America's tallest mountain, which pinned us down for six days in an endless white expanse of blowing snow at 17,200 feet before conditions became safe enough to venture from our tents and climb higher. I tried to comprehend the brutality of a Denali January.

"No way I'd do that in winter," he confirmed. "You think you'll ever climb Everest?"

"I don't know, maybe. I feel like I need to summit another Himalayan peak first," I said, giving him a glimpse into my plans.

I didn't tell him that technically this hike was training for climbing my first Himalayan peak—that I'd stuffed fifteen extra pounds of lead bricks in my backpack.

He shifted the conversation. "Jesus, what do you do after summiting Denali in winter?"

"K2."

"Yeah, right," he said with a huff.

I kept trudging up the steep mud behind him in silence—until he planted his trekking pole, stopped, whipped his head around, and looked at me with wide eyes and raised eyebrows. I looked up at him, deadpan, and shrugged my shoulders casually. We shared the type of bond that develops from mutual struggle toward a common goal. He knew me well enough to correctly interpret my silence as a plan. But he mercifully said nothing, not forcing me to justify or explain my scheme.

I hadn't told anyone about my future climbing objectives even though I had carefully constructed a two-year climbing plan in a pink notebook with shimmery purple ink and butterfly stickers. Connecting the dots between each goal seemed straightforward within the safe realm of my notebook's lines, but verbalizing my plan—especially to male climbing partners—stymied me. I wanted to shield myself from their doubt, which I knew would follow. I wasn't ready for their curious stares and raised eyebrows, wanting to prolong the comfort of secrecy. I wasn't ready to defend myself, to prove that I knew what I was doing, that I wasn't reckless. I didn't know whether the goal of climbing K2 positioned my ambition above my ability. Maybe it did—but that was how I'd started climbing big mountains in the beginning: blind ambition. And a lot of defiance.

CHAPTER 1

75 FEET

When I had sat cross-legged and scattered the bright, glossy catalogs from colleges like Stanford and the University of Illinois across my twin bed in high school, I'd had zero idea where to focus my studies. I liked science, mostly struggled with math, and primarily desired a high-paying job that would take me far away from the tiny farm town in central Illinois that had raised me. For some reason, I chose to major in biomedical engineering, based on an illogical appraisal that it was a balanced combination of my mom's profession as a nurse and my dad's as a janitor and therefore the best major for their eldest daughter. I recall thoughtfully explaining the inept rationale behind my choice during my college entrance interview. The interviewer sitting across the table looked back at me blankly with tight, pursed lips, glanced down at my application, and asked why I didn't want to study English.

When I arrived at the Milwaukee School of Engineering in the fall of 1991, it became swiftly and painfully obvious that I was no longer one of the smartest kids in the class. I'd never heard of differential calculus, or integral calculus—or even plain old calculus. And, in a continuation of my overachieving tendencies, I thought it'd be a good idea to study Japanese, too. As the entrance interviewer likely knew, I was in over my head—way over. A scene that would repeat emerged for the first time that autumn: I'd reach too high, which would lead to overwhelm, and my only remedy for the impending embarrassment of failure would be hard work. I hoped that I could study my way to decent grades; I could not abide the shame of quitting or lessening my major (though I would drop Japanese when I couldn't fathom verbs at the ends of sentences).

My college roommates seemed to effortlessly comprehend complex lecture material, apply it in labs, sum it all up in a tidy double-spaced paper at the end of the week, and still have time to test their fake IDs at the bars that surrounded MSOE's urban campus. I, on the other hand, would stare at exotic equations and hope I could apply them cleverly enough to earn Bs when it mattered. Feeling guilty about considering blowing off studying to join my roommates one Thursday night, I sat instead at my dorm-room desk, ate three giant chocolate-chip cookies, and created a schedule that allowed only for study, classes, and sleeping.

Somehow, after the requisite four years, I made it out with an above-average GPA, a degree in biomedical engineering, and a job as an engineer with the Hewlett-Packard Company. I spent my twenties and early thirties in Saint Louis, Missouri, fumbling to figure myself out, desperately trying to keep up with some imaginary ideal of what a young professional woman should do, act like, and be. Would a young professional woman wear business suits or dresses? Pantyhose? Should she live in Clayton or University City? Drink merlot? Smoke menthols? Learn golf? I amassed embarrassing piles of credit-card debt in an attempt to prove that I was successful and independent, even though that meant using cash advances from credit cards to pay rent.

I did not, in my twenties or thirties, dabble much in the outdoors, though when I was twenty-six I did eagerly agree to a multiday backpacking trip with my adventure-seeking redheaded boyfriend. Traveling together from infinitely flat Saint Louis to the Hoh River trail in the westernmost thumb of Washington State felt like blasting into adulthood. There, we would navigate, cook our own food, and ward off wild bears.

This being my first backpacking experience, shopping for gear was required. I studied the summer 1998 Campmor catalog for sleeping bags, backpacks, socks, bear vaults (whatever those were), and fancy pants with zippers that circumnavigated my thighs. When the giant box arrived, large enough for me to sleep in, it was missing only one key item: footwear. For that, I visited a local discount shoe warehouse, the kind that carried past-season styles that weren't sold at department stores.

As I wandered through the towering aisles in the industrial, perfectly square building, the platform mules and flip-flops quickly distracted me. But, on the highest shelf, I spied what I was looking for: hiking boots. The leather kind with green laces and lug soles beefy enough to tromp through the Hoh River trail. These hiking boots, though, were specially equipped with an added feature: steel toes. *Even better*, I thought, rationalizing that my toes wouldn't get squished if a rock or tree rolled on them. Most importantly, my toes would still look cute in those platform flip-flops after the trip. I reached up to grab them from the top shelf before someone else did. The kit for my first backpacking trip was complete.

I made a pit stop in eastern Washington to visit my aunt Carol and uncle Mike before venturing into the forest. My aunt and uncle had always been examples of stability in my life. As a kid, I'd escaped a chaotic home in Illinois for summers at theirs in the mountains, and I'd cried at the airport each time I left them. My aunt bought me fancy face creams at the Bon Marché, and my uncle taught me to drive, with important tips like: "Don't touch the radio for the first six months." So I arrived at their house now proud of my hefty backpack and specially equipped hiking boots. My uncle Mike took one look at the purple backpack hulking above my head, snickered, and said, "That thing weighs more than you."

In a whirl of gear and chuckles, he immediately halved the contents of my backpack. No consultation, just surgical elimination.

"You'll thank me next week," he said with confidence and admonishment as I tallied the exiled pile: wool sweaters, books, a hunting knife, travel-sized shampoo bottles.

"Do you actually know what to do with a hunting knife, city girl?"

Whatever, I thought. Normally I played along with his sardonic humor. But I didn't have time now. I was going to cook my own food. In the wild. With bears.

I failed to understand that the Hoh River trail is in the Hoh Rainforest. And that rainforests are . . . wet. Always.

Aside from leaky tents, pervasive mud, and rare glimpses of sunshine, one memory stands out: barely one day into the seventeen-mile trek, I realized the error in my boot purchase. Steel, it turns out, should be reserved for boots worn in environments where your foot might actually get squished. Like construction or logging. Those protective steel plates wore blisters into my tender city toes. As I stood at the side of the trail, leaning on a giant mossy tree while popping the blisters on my shriveled feet, a blur of men passed by on the trail. They moved nimbly, confidently, barely noticing my discomfort and unwieldy backpack. Their packs, curiously smaller than my purple behemoth, were hung with helmets and strange metal axes with sleek, curved heads and pointy, glistening picks, along with neat coils of rope draped over the tops.

"Are they mining coal somewhere?" I asked, half serious, between blister pops.

"They're climbing Mount Olympus," my boyfriend explained.

"Like, a mountain? *Why?*"

I hadn't grown up with stories of Sir Edmund Hillary or Maurice Herzog. I'd grown up with Abraham Lincoln and sports heroes like William Perry. Not only had mountain climbing not been in my lexicon, but I also hadn't known it was a thing people did. For fun.

None of it made sense to me. But, from my damp spot against the mossy tree, I was drawn to those men. They resonated blithesome strength and capability—in their non-steel-toed boots.

Waterlogged backpacking trips aside, my outdoor forays revolved around drunken camping trips with friends from work. When one skinny-legged, fine-haired guy with round lips offered to share his tent, I felt the flush of friendship bloom into more. I hadn't been treated with admiration or respect by a guy before. At the office I was used to being overlooked, ogled, or treated like one of the guys. Reverence was new. He didn't flinch when I couldn't sleep because the laundry wasn't folded and put away. "You let me be me," I told him months later, snuggling under a pile of sleeping bags, watching a Midwest sunset fade into night. Plus, there was a hint of sadness behind his blue eyes that I wanted to ease.

We wrote long, achy love notes to each other and slipped them into pockets or books for the other to find later. We reconfigured work trips to be together, spending long, lazy weekends in the backwoods of Maine. I even baked. Finally, we painfully and abruptly ended other relationships, and he and his dogs drove to my house, which eventually became our house. Our life was simple then, in our twenties. I'd only just signed my first mortgage. Our only responsibilities were our dogs and staying true to our yearning to explore.

My professional responsibilities at Hewlett-Packard grew, and, through mergers and spin-offs, I landed my first management job at Philips Healthcare in 2007. With my soon-to-be husband, I moved to Seattle. Though I'd visited the Pacific Northwest many times as a kid, it felt unknown and unexplored. And now, I had a partner to discover it with. Together we attended orienteering seminars, studied maps of lost mining towns, attended avalanche-awareness courses, and spent every weekend in the mountains.

On my first hike on Mount Rainier's Muir Snowfield—still unaware of the importance of proper fueling—I became so calorie depleted that after the hike I collapsed in the snow near the Paradise parking lot, my electrolyte-starved legs jackhammering.

"Come on, I know you can make it to the car," he encouraged.

"I don't know if I can," I said, staring at my twitchy legs through half-open eyelids.

"We've got this. I'll help."

Together, we trudged down the last bit of snow, and he drove as fast as Rainier's windy roads would allow to the first open restaurant, where he coaxed me into eating a whole plate of french fries. I felt cared for then, looked after, like I had a partner in this world who wasn't canine.

The Philips office where I worked in Seattle was drab. An oily-looking trail meandered up the center of the matted gray carpet that defined each aisle. Industrial "furniture" panels interlocked at hard right angles to create small cubes that failed at creating privacy. Which was why, on a particular June morning, I already knew that my cube neighbor Derek and his girlfriend had just gotten a German shepherd puppy, and that she was sweet but also systematically destroying their furniture, room by room, like a furry tornado, and that they therefore needed to TiVo *Dancing with the Stars* that night so they could go to IKEA for a replacement dining room table before Derek's sister arrived on Thursday.

While privacy was superficial at the office, hierarchy was not. The vice presidents—all men—sat in cookie-cutter square rooms along the building's perimeter, their offices dank, too, despite windows. Rippled inward toward the center of the building from the VPs were rows of subordinates of decreasing rank. I was situated one row in from the VPs, directly across from the one I reported to. The configuration was convenient for me because I could spring from my chair when he yelled "*Liiisssaaa!*"

My official job title was field operations manager, and I was the first to hold this newly created position. My days were filled, like a bottomless garbage can, with orphaned projects and chronically broken processes that no one else wanted to fix.

One Monday morning, I sat at my desk, fighting to morph data into meaningful conclusions before the first *Liiisssaaa!* of the day summoned me to recite the current status of our team's metrics. But a hallway conversation between three guys distracted me.

"Dude, I don't believe we pulled that off," said the skinny one.

"*You* didn't pull anything off, loser; it wasn't supposed to be epic," the tall one reminded him, breaking into laughter and snide snorts with his friend at the skinny one's expense. Their camaraderie sparked a column of envy to rise from my core.

The mean one jumped in. "Maybe if you learned how to walk in crampons you could keep up next time."

"Not my fault, man, we don't have mountains in Minnesota," said the skinny one in a squeaky voice, defending himself with a puffed chest.

In recent months, from my dingy cube, I'd listened with growing jealousy to their convivial stories about fording wild, icy rivers on Glacier Peak and navigating whiteout snowstorms on Mount Baker. Their chumminess didn't just exist on mountains and in hallways;

it slipped into meeting rooms, too, like a thick fog that I could not penetrate. And I tried, ending sentences with *man*, pretending I knew how to smoke cigars at the office Christmas party, accepting the worst assignments, and spending so many late nights working alone at the office that I knew the cleaning crew personally. But, unlike in college, working hard and masquerading weren't enough to gain acceptance within the masculine culture at my first job with *manager* in its title.

Although the promotion to this position moved me from the Midwest to more progressive Seattle, I still worked for a conservative medical-device company. And when I looked to my right and to my left, and even above and below me on the org chart, I saw very few people who looked like me. In meetings, I was often not only the lone woman but also, at thirty-five years old, the youngest person at the table. Without any professional role models, I struggled to define my persona. I felt deeply that I couldn't be too feminine, so I wore mini versions of men's suits and practiced lowering my voice two octaves. I also urgently wanted to compensate for my youth and meager management experience, so I devoured stacks of business books at night that instructed me to use masculine words like *believe* instead of *think* or *feel*.

Yet my attempts to convey counterfeit competence failed, and at an annual planning meeting, a barrel-chested, gregarious man from Los Angeles repeatedly addressed me as *kiddo*. No one seemed to notice but me, and during the million times since that I've replayed that day in my head, I always responded with a witty quip that promptly put him in his place and made him humbly realize that he was undermining my credibility.

"You can call me 'kiddo' if I can call you 'old man,'" I retorted in my made-up world.

"Oh, sorry, Lisa," he'd reply, tail tucked between his legs to retreat. "I didn't realize how insensitive that was."

But, sitting at that long wooden table, I'd done nothing. I'd taken it. And I could feel my tenuous veneer of perfection fracturing.

Slowly, the pride in my academic and professional accomplishments was supplanted by overwhelm and insecurity, as if I'd been pushed out of the nest too soon. One weekend, I turned from business books to my family tree for guidance. I sat cross-legged on the floor of my tiny suburban apartment and sorted 1970s-era photographs, thinking surely someone had crossed this bridge before me. But no; my lineage was thick with generations of men and women who had served their countries, reared children, mopped floors, driven tractors, and labored in assembly lines. Despite their hard work and resilience, none of them had earned a college degree or held a corporate job. I was the first. My family was proud of my accomplishments, I knew, but I could see something else in their distant faces: suspicion. I was the aloof, hy-percompetitive sister/cousin/daughter who couldn't find satisfaction in farming or parenting or the entire state of Illinois. As I searched for professional direction, I realized my path had distanced us.

Since my only tangible examples of corporate environments were the soap-opera episodes I'd watched with my mom—her from her sewing machine and me from a clandestine position behind the nubby green couch in my childhood living room—I didn't yet have the faculty or the courage to provoke change or to stand up for myself in the of-fice. But even though my soap-opera lessons had left me with a mostly inaccurate impression of how the corporate world worked, I knew the way I was being treated wasn't right.

One day in the office, my eavesdropping spiked. "What about Rainier, man?" I heard the skinny one ask his friends.

Truthfully, I hadn't previously harbored any interest in climbing a mountain; barely five feet tall, I was not athletic, and I didn't even know what a crampon was. Being lost in a blizzard didn't match my definition of "fun," either. Looking back, I realize that my emotions were complex. I was on the outside, observing my male colleagues bond over shared mountain experiences. Being included would have meant that they viewed me as smart, strong, and capable. But hard work had been my only trick to accomplishing that, and it was proving ineffective. I wanted to be taken seriously. I wanted the same oppor-tunity as everyone else. Without it, and lacking the courage to assert myself, my envy and indignation threatened to boil over. I needed a relief valve. In that second, when I returned to my keyboard, some-thing changed. I was no longer satisfied fulfilling the role of the quiet, hardworking girl. There was some invisible but mighty part of me that knew I would never join their club by working hard. Because what separated us wasn't workplace accomplishments; it was this female body and this female mind. I was done letting men define my boundaries as a woman.

So I decided to climb my own damn mountains.

CHAPTER 2

14,410 FEET

While intellectually I understood that defiance could only get me so far, I didn't really understand its limitations until I climbed Mount Rainier when I was thirty-seven, a year after my office cohort's chumminess provoked me.

Mount Rainier is the highest mountain in Washington State, occupying almost 400 square miles of wild forest, pristine rivers, and glaciated snow, and is only sixty miles from Seattle's city center. It's not just Mount Rainier's untamed beauty that inspires climbers and sea-levelers alike; it's also her elusiveness. One community survey estimates that the mountain is only visible from Seattle eighty days per year. Leaving us to wonder what she's up to the remaining 285 and eliciting the phrase *the mountain is out* whenever even a sliver of her slopes is visible from afar.

My relationship with Mount Rainier changed after I haphazardly decided to start climbing. I no longer stared at her in casual awe from I-5 on the days she revealed herself. Now, my pulse quickened, and I wondered how the hell I was going to get up there. And back. My naive determination spawned a late-night internet search habit, prompted me to relinquish large portions of my paycheck to REI, and motivated me to run on the wooded trails near my suburban house.

My first attempt to summit Mount Rainier, in 2008, ended at 11,200 feet, more than 3,000 feet and many hours from the summit. Still carrying that giant purple backpack, I'd been relieved when high winds on the upper mountain had ended the climb. By the time I descended to the Paradise parking lot, relief had been replaced by the certainty that I'd try again. Rainier had shown me enough that I knew I needed to reassess how I would prepare for my next attempt.

Over the winter, I traded gardening books for climbing memoirs. I sat in the front row of mountaineering lectures, mesmerized by the burly men at the lectern. I studied Rainier's climbing routes and sat cross-legged on the couch reading *Mountaineering: The Freedom of the Hills*, underlining passages and writing in the margins like it was a textbook. I practiced tying climbing knots on my backyard deck. I quickly learned that I needed a new training plan, too. Hiking a few miles on the weekend and random runs wouldn't be enough this time. So I cobbled together a list of exercises to perfect, elevations to gain, and miles to run.

By the time I stepped onto the trail from the Paradise parking lot in 2009, I had said goodbye to the purple backpack, my quads no longer fit into my business-suit pants, and I could tie a figure-eight knot with my eyes closed.

It was during this attempt that I began to feel the pull of mountains take root in my soul. Ascending from Mount Rainier's highest camp in the predawn hours of a July morning, I felt an incomprehensibly vast expanse around me, like I was on the mountain but also a tiny part of the mountain. My brain could not reconcile the immensity that I felt around me with the only thing that I could see: the tiny circle of light that my headlamp illuminated on the snow in front of me. This was the most I'd flirted with my physical and mental limits, and I was scared. I wasn't sure whether I was capable of summiting and returning safely, and I wasn't sure if I would even know how to tell.

My headlamp scanned the snow. All around me, the glacier had cracked from the pressure of its constant downward slide. Some of these crevasses were deeper than my headlamp's light, and I found it unimaginable that I could be walking on snow that deep. There was twenty feet of rope between me and the climber in front of me, enough to ensure that if one of us fell into a crevasse, the other would have enough time and distance to stab the glacier with an ice axe and arrest the fall. But in this distance, I felt utterly alone.

Everything was unknown. I didn't yet recognize the metallic pings above me as ice axes clanked against porous volcanic rock. I'd read in books that the snow would be much steeper above me, that there would be overhanging ice blocks, but my brain had no point of reference for these wonders. Every time I inhaled, my lungs protested the cold, anemic air that I was forcing into them.

This was a new feeling for me, this sense of excelling in suboptimal physical conditions. All my life I had tried to control everything, to create just the right environment to pass the test, to get the job, to impress. Tenuously standing thousands of feet above Seattle forced me to release control. Not to lose it, but to release it to a mountain that would always be bigger and fiercer than me. With control out of the way that morning, I felt its counterbalance: freedom.

I moved forward, walking with bulky steps on steep, hardened snow. The muscles in my legs ached, and my shoulders hurt from an ill-fitting backpack, but there was no part of me that wanted to turn back. I knew that in the dark above me lay more steep snow and ice, steeper than this. I had no idea what challenges those slopes would present, or if I would be able to overcome them. But I did not want to quit.

Over my right shoulder the bright orange of a summer morning was just beginning to split the dark sky from its horizon. I didn't know that colors this rich existed. I was watching Mother Nature work, observing the silent transformation of night into day, and I felt connected to her in a way that I hadn't realized was possible.

The pace of my rope team quickened. The resulting pain in my lungs distracted me until I realized that we'd sped up to pass another rope team. I was in the middle position of my team, my primary job to maintain the right amount of distance between me and the lead climber. Too much distance and he would drag me forward, too little and I would slide farther than necessary down the mountain if I fell. I was determined to keep my short legs moving on pace with the men on my rope team. The members of the slower team sped up to prevent our passing but eventually could not maintain the quickened pace and stopped. As I stepped around their climbing rope in the snow, I noticed their gasps and pained exhalations, thick puffs of vapor in my headlamp's light. I studied the anguish on their faces.

"*Oh, a girl,*" I thought I heard one of them say as I passed by. I felt the sting of the bar being lowered for me, but I was too overtaken by adrenaline to care. Until that moment, I hadn't known that I could be that strong.

On a steep snow slope at 13,000 feet, our little team stopped in the dark so the lead guide could assess our desire and ability to safely continue higher. He methodically spoke to each person in short, stoic sentences with a Scottish accent.

"You need to focus on your footwork, Mark. Clean it up."

"Looking strong, Robert," he said to another.

"I think this is your high point tonight, Jack—sorry, man," he said to the man standing next to me.

I was anxious about what I'd hear from the guide, mentally comparing my performance to the climbers he had turned around. *Was I moving slower than them? Faster? Did I need more breaks than them?* I wished for a second chance to prove my readiness.

"You're going to the top," he said to me brusquely, then moved on to the next climber.

Pride swirled with fear and uncertainty in my oxygen-deprived brain. I hadn't known that I could be this capable.

Hours later, when we neared the summit, the sun had transformed the mountain. I was flanked by crevasses of clear blue ice and massive blocks of compressed snow called *seracs* that are as fragile as glass and as ominous as thunder. A falling serac would release hundreds of tons of snow and ice, devouring with deadly force everything in its path. The contradictions of this mountainous place were a wonder. I heard the ice groan as I climbed, sulfur gas pricking my nose—a reminder that this volcanic mountain was alive with motion, always shifting, always in control. Near the Columbia Crest, Mount Rainier's highest point, I sat in volcanic sand and removed my gloves to sign the register: Lisa, 2009, first summit.

Mount Rainier gave me an indelible sense of accomplishment and reinforced my studious temperament. It's true that I committed to climbing my first big mountain out of defiance, as a way to prove myself. Even though I'd had no idea what climbing Mount Rainier entailed, I'd been acutely aware that I'd set an audacious goal. I knew others had doubted me. I had doubted myself. Just like at the office, fear of failing had provoked me to work hard to rise to the demands of the mountain. I could not name it then, but standing at 14,410 feet in the frozen sunshine that day, for a moment—just a moment—I no longer felt underestimated; I felt like an equal member of a strong team. I felt capable.

CHAPTER 3

591 FEET

Summiting Mount Rainier made me feel capable in a permanent, unfamiliar way. I felt my feet lift easier and my back rise a little higher when I returned to the Paradise parking lot that day, and, weeks later, I spoke about my summit with quiet confidence. "Yes, I did summit," I said with an easy, calm voice at the office. It was possibly the first time in my life that I'd felt the self-assurance that comes from stretching just beyond what I believed I was capable of. Earning a college degree hadn't done it; advancing my career hadn't. But standing in compact snow at 14,410 feet, looking out across vast glaciers dusted and striped brown with volcanic sand, I had wondered how much farther I could stretch.

This feeling—that I could set and achieve a goal bigger than I'd ever imagined—was novel. I'd been raised by a family of stoic, hardworking Midwesterners who hadn't encouraged their children to exceed expectations or to push boundaries or to wonder what else might be possible.

My younger sister, Sara, and I grew up in modest houses with tidy lawns tended to by do-it-yourselfers. Our furniture had been handed down, our Halloween costumes homemade. Our school clothes were purchased on layaway. We ate thick slices of government cheese after school. Road trips bookended our vacations. We had summer jobs in cornfields and variety stores. We envied the rich kids because they had swimming pools. My parents didn't speak about opportunities for their daughters beyond our county's square boundaries.

My parents' marriage, built on the tenuous foundation of an unplanned pregnancy, crumbled when I was eight. As a teenager, I'd ricocheted between thinking that my parents' divorce was my mom's fault, then believing the nasty things my mom said about my dad, blaming him instead. When I was old enough to realize that I'd been an unwitting parental pawn, and that blame for a failed marriage couldn't be absolute, my vacillations stopped. However, like the hands of a broken clock, they got stuck pointing blame at my mom, at which point my relationship with her began to erode. By this time, I was old enough to compare my home life to that of my friends, and I resented my mom for the difference. I couldn't see then that she was taking any shift she could at the local hospital to make ends meet. I wanted her to greet me with snacks after school and show me how to blend eye shadow, how to prevent constellations of pimples from erupting on my forehead. Instead, after my parents' divorce, Sara and I were mostly in the care of teenage babysitters. We concocted microwave dinners from raw egg noodles and butter and sat cross-legged on the shaggy carpet watching *Remington Steele* on the console TV while the babysitter had sex in my mom's bed in the adjoining room. As a teenager, I rebelled by disappearing, bouncing from school activities to friends' houses to avoid my own.

During a high school basketball game, sitting high on glossy wooden bleachers, I explained my teenage rationale to my skeptical uncle.

"I get that," he said, "but she's your mother."

"I know, and I'm her *daughter*" was my snippy reply. He let it drop.

I knew even then that his intentions were to prevent a rupture in our family—one that I would painfully regret as an adult. What I couldn't articulate to him then was that I'd waited for her acceptance since I was a child. I'd tried every trick I could. Cutting out the filmy Butterick sewing patterns perfectly along their thick black lines hadn't worked. Sitting obediently at my mom's office hadn't worked. Neither had straight As. During my teenage years, I found the acceptance I craved in other places: from friends with access to their parents' liquor cabinet, from boys with cars and large back seats, from neighborhood men who wanted to trade moist kisses for one-pound Hershey's bars and twenty-dollar bills, and from chemistry teachers who recognized a nascent combination of curiosity and intelligence.

I compensated. When my mother failed to pick me up from my first day of high school, I asked a blond girl in the hallway if she could drive me. "I live close," I lied to convince her.

I tidied and covered up the blemishes to maintain my family's fragile veneer of normalcy.

When Dad passed out in the shady strawberry patch behind the house, I covered him with a blanket, hoping the neighbors would think he was napping. When there wasn't money on hand, I stood in the school lunch line anyway. When there wasn't anyone to escort me across the track at senior night, I walked anyway. When I didn't understand something, I faked it. I smiled when it hurt. I lied. I wanted it to be enough. I got good at it.

Like the kids of most divorced families, Sara and I were shuffled between relatives, babysitters, and parents in an elaborate puzzle of childcare. Whether the result of scheduling snafus or boredom or lack of concern, I remember summer afternoons with my dad in taverns. He'd drive his aged yellow pickup truck into the gravel parking lot, positioning it among familiar vehicles there, and I'd scoot across the bench seat's hot vinyl to exit the truck on his side. We'd walk into the one-room concrete building, me ahead of him, his hands resting on my shoulders, and I'd feel the heavy metal door clang shut behind us and separate me from the sunshine and humidity outside. The first time I joined him, the tavern's dark, cool interior was a relief, but eventually I learned to dread the stale air and cigarette smoke that came with it. Being inside felt dirty, like I was breaking the rules by hanging out with the wrong kids. Dad would lift me onto a black barstool, the kind with a high back that swivels from side to side until its curved arms touch the bar top. My legs, bare below my shorts, would stick uncomfortably to the barstool's tacky vinyl.

Midwestern taverns in the 1980s were occupied by men—men

with deep voices and foul mouths that rarely spoke flattering words about women, or each other. I don't remember them being unkind to me; I remember feeling welcome and novel. Still, I recall the pungent smell of layers of alcohol on their breaths, their unshaven cheeks, their slurred words, and a deep desire to bolt for the metal door and escape to the freedom of outside. I'd pass the time drinking Shirley Temples with extra cherries, hoping the men wouldn't talk to me, and organizing the paper coasters, creating tidy stacks of matching beer logos on the glossed wooden bar. Eventually, my novelty would wane, my dad and his friends would talk about the things that men talk about in taverns, I'd run out of coasters to stack, and the light sneaking through rectangular windows near the room's flat ceiling would shift to dusk.

Dad and I exited the tavern the same way we'd entered, him walking behind me with his hands on my shoulders.

"We good, Lis?" he'd ask slowly. I knew we weren't. I always knew.

I'd sit close to him on the truck's bench seat, my knees bent under me so I could sit on my feet and gain a few more inches of visibility over the dusty dashboard. I couldn't untangle disappointment and helplessness from fear then. And it wouldn't have mattered anyway. I ignored all the uneasy feelings in my belly and tried to be helpful, tried to measure the distance between our truck and curbs, our truck and parked cars. I watched our rearview mirror for police and kept an eye on the speedometer as we drove down the residential streets from the tavern to Dad's house. I wanted it to be enough.

There were days when my dad wasn't plagued with alcohol and I'd follow him around our wooded yard, wearing overalls and a flannel shirt like him. He'd assign me tasks like stacking wood or gathering fallen apples. At the end of the day, we'd stand at a pile of dry leaves, and he'd trust me to start the fire with a long match from the living room fireplace. "That's right, Lis," he'd say, "stick it right in there," as I cautiously extended a skinny, shaky arm toward the leaf pile.

Dad, like many of the men in his bloodline, was a laborer. He'd hop from one job to the next, pouring concrete at a nuclear power plant or laying viscous bitumen on cracked roadways. I thought his jobs were exciting, and I liked studying his friends in the garage, where they'd sit in folding lawn chairs and drink Pabst Blue Ribbon beers and smoke cigarettes on weekends. Dad was the shortest of the group but made up for his stature with long, animated stories. It was enthralling, the way they held their cans of beer, the way they taunted one another and laughed at things I didn't understand, the way Dad sucked beer foam off his red mustache.

Before the divorce, family time had seemed perfunctory. We went to church together on Sundays. At home, we sat at a round laminate table and ate tuna casserole with crushed potato chips on top. Our family time lacked the fervor of those nights with Dad's friends in the garage, and I couldn't make out why. Many nights, after Sara and I were in bed, the mood in our house shifted and was often loud, my parents arguing downstairs about drinking too much and things called *affairs* that I didn't understand. It felt like Mom was perpetually mad at Dad, but from my view, I couldn't understand what he'd done wrong. As a woman, I can understand my mom's madness.

I don't know if I ever felt the kind of love I needed as a kid. It wasn't that my parents were incapable of giving love to Sara and me. They showed love in a way that I was incapable of understanding; there was a mismatch. I yearned to be seen by my parents, to know that I took up sacred space in their hearts. In the corner of my adolescent bedroom there was a record player that, over and over again, played the lyrics from a record I got at church camp, declaring that I was full of possibility and potential.

I wanted to know that they believed it, too.

As an adult, I didn't spend much time in my hometown of Lincoln, even though I lived just a few hours away in Saint Louis. In my early thirties, though, I agreed to travel back home to help my mom and stepfather move from the house where I'd spent most of my high school years to an upgraded version a few blocks away. The move was easily accomplished, given the short commute—no need to meticulously wrap fragile dishes in newspaper or to carefully bundle tchotchkes in Bubble Wrap.

"Sure," I told her out of obligation when she asked, "I'll take Friday off and drive up."

When I arrived at the new house, I was promptly assigned newhouse-cleaning duty with Sara. There was something extra distasteful about cleaning a stranger's food splats and forgotten dust bunnies, but we rolled up our sleeves, blared seventies rock music from a tinny speaker, and got to work anyway.

"Oh, Sara! I wanted you to clean the kitchen cabinets with the orange-oil cleaner instead," Mom said when she returned from shopping with friends, hours into our cleaning efforts.

"Really? Oh, OK," Sara said, and let out an uncertain chuckle.

I knew that laugh; it was the one I relied on, too, to mask hurt and discomfort.

"Yeah, thanks." And Mom shuffled through the kitchen with friends and crisp shopping bags in tow.

She doesn't get to treat us that way just because she's our mother, I reminded myself.

Sara dutifully placed the dirty rag on the counter, fetched the correct cleaner, and began scrubbing the cabinets again, wiping in wide strokes and angling the fingernail of her thumb to exactly trace their grooved fronts.

In her wake, Mom left shame and disgrace in that kitchen, a room that I would never visit again. I let the shame fall this time and didn't pick it back up. I couldn't carry it anymore.

"Fuck this," I said to Sara, and put my own dirty rag on the floor.

I cocked my head toward the door, and together we walked out.

CHAPTER 4

56 FEET

That my family didn't understand my ambitions in the mountains didn't deter me. Instead, it fueled a fervor for more. I traded business-acumen books for climbing memoirs. My friend circle split into two spheres, one climbing, one not. I gave up happy hours with nonclimbing friends to hear accomplished mountaineers speak. I picked airplane seats based on the best view of the volcanoes that dot the West Coast between Washington and California. With my husband, I took weekend-long mountaineering classes, climbed everything local within my capability, and remortgaged our house to afford international climbing trips.

Each climb became a case study. Afterward, I'd note areas for improvement in my journal. When the underside of my nose blistered because I'd wiped away layers of sunscreen from blowing my nose, I devised a mental reminder to smear SPF lip balm under it after every wipe: *Wipe, then swipe.* When rigid mountaineering boots rubbed raw my bony ankles, I duct-taped hydrocolloidal bandages to them. When base-camp food was leftover lunch meat that had been buried in the glacier for a year, I didn't care. It was fuel. I struggled to outsmart two things: greasy hair and moving quickly with a heavy backpack.

. . .

By 2014, I had summited the highest mountains on five continents. From those peaks, I'd gained the ability to adapt to difficult situations, I'd discovered the importance of taking care of myself to be a stronger team member, and I'd realized that I could survive nineteen days without a shower. As important: I could also survive my partner not showering for nineteen days.

I began planning the next climb before the current one was complete, and I detailed my future expeditions in a pink notebook that sat on the top shelf of my office bookcase. Its next entry read: Manaslu—autumn 2015. In high-altitude mountaineering there is a magical altitude threshold of 8,000 meters (26,247 feet). This elevation is special because there are just fourteen mountains in the world that rise this high, most of them held within the Himalayan mountain range that traverses Asia. Of these hallowed peaks, Manaslu, in central Nepal, is considered an entry-level 8,000-meter climb. Its snowy slopes lack technical ice climbing and, at 8,163 meters, barely make the 8,000-meter cut.

There was just one little problem, though. Although he'd given me for Christmas five paperback journals with matching bookmarks for each climb in my pink notebook, my husband didn't share my excitement.

"I could think of a lot of other things to do with that money," he said. "We could travel for months. We could buy a new boat."

"But this is my *thing*," I pleaded. "We went on a cheaper climb last year."

"Why is your *thing* so expensive? You realize it costs us double, right? Since there's two of us."

"Maybe we could get a discount since we'll share a tent?" I tried.

I was undeterred. I was also starting to sense that I needed climbing more than he did.

And I was overwhelmed. I knew by now that refusing to be dissuaded by what others thought I was capable of would not be enough to get me up and down a Himalayan peak. I also knew that trail runs and hiking on local mountains with a backpack full of kitty litter would be insufficient to prepare me for the physical and mental challenges of the Himalayas. I needed to up my game.

At the beginning of 2015, I tentatively sent an email to Scott Johnston asking him to coach me. I had recently devoured his book about mountain training, adding sticky notes to important pages and highlighting key physiological facts. When I say that I emailed Scott, I really mean that I email-stalked him until he returned my messages. Even so, I was not sure why a coach and climber as experienced as he would agree to take on a mountaineering neophyte with modest aspirations to climb her first 8,000-meter peak. But he did. I didn't sense hesitation in his voice during our first phone call, just the matter-of-factness that I'd come to expect from seasoned mountaineers. Yes, he would coach me, he said. Yes, he thought I could be ready in time.

Though he coached me remotely, everything about Scott felt firm and exact; there wasn't any room for casualness, and there wasn't a lot of patting on the back, which was fine with me. Training felt serious this time, and it became my part-time job. With Scott's guidance, I retired my cobbled-together training plan from Mount Rainier. I began to understand my heart-rate zones. I realized the importance of building both strength and endurance. Every workout was intended to move my body and mind incrementally closer to meeting the demands of Manaslu. Scott thoroughly answered each question about physiology and endurance-training strategy, and he often shared books or articles, which I highlighted and marked up just like I had with his book.

With Scott's guidance, I coaxed my body to accomplish things I'd never thought possible. I could run ten miles of muddy trail—without stopping! I squatted nearly my body weight and cut tens of minutes from my hiking time on familiar peaks. The Pacific Northwest gloom and frigid rain didn't hinder me; I had a job to do. Scott's comments in the online training program that we shared were direct: *add more weight, you need to recover, that's a good pace.* His pragmatic approach felt supportive, the kind of support that I hadn't had before. I felt invested in.

When I wasn't training for Manaslu, I was thinking about it. I read every blog I could find, studied photos of the route, and hammered wooden stakes into the muddy hill of a neighborhood park to practice efficiently moving between the anchors of a fixed rope. On weekends, I tested myself in the mountains, scrambling up rocky summits like Silver Star or pushing myself to ascend Mount Rainier's familiar Muir

Snowfield faster and faster, then doing it twice in a day. With help from friends, I learned how to efficiently pack my backpack, how to build reliable snow anchors, how to descend steep, sliding rock called *scree*, and how to pee while wearing a harness. My threshold for discomfort grew and my body and mind began to look and perform like an endurance athlete. My body had never felt so strong or resilient.

One brisk morning, I took a break from a family visit to meet Scott at a wooded park in Winthrop, the half-cowboy, half-athlete hamlet in Washington's North Cascade mountains. I fiddled with the plastic buttons on my flannel shirt while I waited at a picnic table shaded by pine trees—this was our first in-person rendezvous.

Scott shared wild stories from an era when climbing was part of the counterculture. I asked endless questions and wished I'd brought a notebook to record his insights. Somewhere in the middle, Scott referred to me as a high-level athlete. A *high-level athlete*! This woman who'd barely made the junior high volleyball team was now a high-level athlete.

CHAPTER 5

85 FEET

One rainy February morning—the kind of morning when I wished it could just be ten degrees colder in Seattle so the sky would deliver brilliant snowflakes instead of dreary rain—I drove to a routine mammogram before work. I was annoyed, not just at the rain but at the inconvenience of a doctor's appointment keeping me from a growing mound of work at the office. It seemed unnecessary, at forty-two, to endure a mammogram.

Thanks to working for medical-device companies for many years, I'd spent enough hours in the imaging departments of hospitals to become comfortable with the people, noises, and machines. Still, being a patient made me feel vulnerable and needy. So I dressed quickly after my mammogram, exchanging the thin cotton robe and gown for a wool dress and blazer, and sat in the exam room's thickly cushioned chair, scanning my email for emergencies. Those years working for medical companies had also taught me the normal flow of imaging exams. I expected the technician to pop into the exam room and wish me a cheery farewell. "Everything looks great; see you in a year, Lisa," I imagined she'd say.

But it wasn't the technician who entered the exam room next;

it was the radiologist. My heart sank before she looked at me—Dr. Acheson, the same gentle, slight woman with a faint Germanic accent who had meticulously scanned my breasts a year ago and declared finally that I just had dense breast tissue. "Nothing abnormal," she'd confirmed as she put the probe back in its holder on the ultrasound machine. "I'll see you again in a year."

Now, she walked quietly toward me and sat slowly in the chair matching mine. I didn't care about checking my email anymore, or whether the rain would ever turn to snow. Dr. Acheson explained that she'd seen concerning calcification patterns in my left breast. I would need a biopsy to be certain that this chain of calcifications wasn't harmful.

"Can we do it today?" I asked.

Two weeks later, Dr. Acheson called to confirm what I already knew: I had cancer.

I thought I had considered every scenario in my pink-notebook plan. I'd thought through contingencies for money and work commitments, but cancer was not in my mental lexicon. Even so, I wasn't mad at cancer or myself or soy or the mosquito repellent sprayed from the back of a giant truck while I'd chased lightning bugs in the street as a kid. I didn't want to know why those cells in my left breast had decided to make up their own rules and deviate from the program that we had all been cohesively adhering to for the past forty-two years. I just wanted them the fuck out of my body. I was an athlete. I ate organic vegetables. I flossed my teeth. I didn't get cancer. The longer cancer found a cozy spot in my body, the more my identity—and health—was threatened.

After my phone call with Dr. Acheson ended, I sat, alone, in my home office, doodling on a presentation I'd been drafting for work the next day. I wrote the words *ductal carcinoma in situ* over and over in block letters. I needed a plan. Walking upstairs to my husband's office, I stood in the doorway until he turned to acknowledge me. I wanted him to know without saying it. I didn't want to say it.

"I have it. I have cancer."

The words hung there, between us. I was still too in denial to cry.

"OK," he said.

I didn't know what I was looking for, what I needed in that moment. To be seen, maybe. To be held and told that everything would be OK, that *I* would be OK.

I had wanted this man so badly in my twenties. When I couldn't be with him, the ache had consumed me until I'd spent hours lying on the hallway floor of my house crying. When I had cancer, I needed him to be the strong one, like that first time on Rainier. I needed to know that he didn't care if I had boobs or not, that I was beautiful anyway—always. I'd soon learn we're all entitled to come to terms with cancer in our own way, and that being the role of supporter is not an easy one. I, like anyone who has heard the word *cancer* directed at them, felt lost and vulnerable. I knew my husband wasn't exempt from those emotions, either, but just this one time, I needed him to take the lead.

I didn't know if, amid the fog of cancer, it was possible that I could be both strong and vulnerable. No person is just one thing, I realize now. We're all a mosaic of light and dark. Of strength, vulnerability, pain, and joy. At the time, I didn't believe I could be both a cancer patient and an athlete; I felt like I had to give up one for the other. So I did my best to euphemize the tumors in my left breast as just a group of misbehaved cells. I had biopsies and rushed back to the office to stand in front of a boardroom of people with a bra full of ice and a freshly punctured left breast. I ran farther and pushed myself harder in preparation for Manaslu, until I couldn't pretend anymore. Cancer wasn't going away, no matter how far I ran. Dr. Acheson had confirmed that I had it. Now, I needed to find someone to get rid of it. For the next two weeks, time compressed. Work meetings were supplanted by meetings with doctors and insurance companies.

The day I met Dr. Lee, she strode into the exam room and closed the door behind her without shifting her smile from my direction. Everything about her signaled efficiency: her wrap dress, her stylish yet unfussy short, sandy hair, casually tousled. She assuredly extended a hand to me and made firm eye contact.

"Hi, Lisa. I'm Dr. Lee."

Sitting in the stark hospital exam room, wearing my own hospital-issued and far less stylish version of a wrap dress, not knowing the outcome of this conversation, I felt exposed and tiny. But that tininess quickly folded into her confidence, and I felt safer. Still uncertain, but now protected. I'd interviewed a half dozen surgeons in the past two weeks and was prepared to present Dr. Lee with the compendium of questions I'd methodically asked each of the others, but my list seemed immaterial now. When I looked down to see her turquoise toenail polish, I knew she was my surgeon. Even before she explained she'd once run a marathon with a broken arm despite her husband's wishes, I knew that she would understand me.

On a rainy Tuesday several weeks later, Dr. Lee and I were back in the same exam room, formulating a plan to eradicate cancer from my body. She explained the results of my most recent biopsy. She sat very close to me, our knees almost touching, the exam room feeling bright but cold.

"The tumors . . . chains . . . ends"—my brain was too foggy to process more than fragments of what she was saying, even though I knew it was important, and she was speaking slowly and deliberately. I was stuck on one word: *tumors*.

I didn't want to have tumors. *Cancer* seemed like a nondescript thing, whereas *tumors* seemed specific and menacing. And apparently these tumors, which I could no longer minimize as just unruly cells, were marching their way across my left boob toward my armpit.

The room felt impossibly bright now. The tile too white, the light too harsh. I felt small and slight again, as though cancer—no, *tumors*—were sucking up my constitution. The space under my chair seemed like a cozy place to curl up and protect myself. But instead, I remained upright. And then I felt a rise of heat in my chest and my throat tightened and my eyes watered. My head threatened to wobble.

Do not cry, I berated myself.

I wanted Dr. Lee to know that I was a strong woman, not someone who cried every time she heard the word *tumor*. I was an athlete; cancer was just this little thing that was happening right now.

I managed to cobble together enough syllables to ask her if surgery could be postponed seven months until after I traveled to Nepal to climb Manaslu. The rational part of my brain, which was rapidly shrinking, knew that prioritizing climbing over my health landed somewhere between reckless and insane. But the part of my brain that had trouble accepting reality wondered how much those tumors could grow in seven months.

Dr. Lee had the rare ability to balance compassion with savage honesty.

"I think that'd be foolhardy," she said.

My eyes met hers.

"Aside from the heartache, what concerns you about postponing your climb until next year?" Her voice was buoyant but serious. And I started to cry.

Only a million things, but primarily stubbornness and denial, I wanted to tell her. But the tears blocked my words, and I just nodded my head with slow intention. Mostly, I didn't want cancer, or *tumors,* to dictate my life. That pissed me off.

"Let's do it as soon as you can," I told her.

I could no longer withhold what was happening with my body from my coach, Scott. Two months after I'd started training with him, I sat at my desk and wrote and rewrote that week's update to him, but the sentences didn't capture my emotion, the combination of powerlessness and strength making the words feel clunky. After an embarrassing number of rewrites, I opted for candor.

I have breast cancer, and will have a bilateral mastectomy next week. I don't know what my body will be capable of after, but I intend to climb Manaslu in August and would like more hands-on coaching from you to get me there.

I closed the message with a little table of data to prove my current fitness level, just in case he was unsure of my commitment or ability.

hike 1,000 vertical feet with 20 percent of my body weight: 32 minutes 44 seconds

pull-ups in 60 seconds: 12

box jumps in 60 seconds: 34

Talking about my boobs with my climbing coach was awkward. Plus, I believed that after he read my email, he would abruptly end our coaching relationship, having confirmation that girls were a pain in the ass to coach and shouldn't be climbing mountains to begin with. Instead, he wrote:

I am sorry to hear about your plight. Glad to hear you are keeping your head up and focusing on moving forward.

I have a saying: "Never allow others to impose their limitation on you."

Six weeks after I was diagnosed with cancer, I walked into Swedish Health Services with my husband. He held my hand, and it comforted me. I didn't want to be alone that day. It was early morning and light hadn't yet crept across the April sky. Everything outside was damp and dark, while inside the hospital was bright and welcoming—more like a hotel lobby than a hospital. My aunt and uncle were there to support me, too. And everything, even the homey upholstered furniture, was doing its best to be comforting. I appreciated the efforts, but they didn't match my mood, and I felt awkward. *Shouldn't I feel happy? This is the last day that cancer gets to maintain residence in my body.*

That morning, I'd woken up at four o'clock to complete a fitness test, repeating the familiar sequence of exercises and recording the results, noting that I ranked *good* on Scott's scale. In one final act of defiance, I'd clipped a ten-pound weight to my climbing harness and recorded myself completing three chin-ups. I thought that I was thumbing my nose at cancer. But really, I was scared—*terrified*—of what might happen next. My body's capabilities after cancer felt obscure and unknown. *Would I be able to wear a backpack? What would running feel like? Has anyone climbed above 26,000 feet after a mastectomy? Would I need chemotherapy?* That morning, I'd wanted proof that I was once strong.

I didn't have to wait long before the nurse called me to the pre-op area. My vitals were recorded, and a radioactive dye was injected into my arm to identify which lymph nodes my cancer would spread to first. I said a little prayer that it hadn't already gotten there.

My family joined me eventually, looking out of place in the clinical room with their jeans and rain jackets. They put all their efforts into optimism. When Dr. Lee joined us, I sensed genuine confidence. She made the whole room feel buoyant.

"What are we doing today?" she asked.

Getting cancer the fuck out of my body, I wanted to say, but I knew that I had to say the words: "A nipple-saving bilateral mastectomy without reconstruction."

Three days ago, I'd spoken those words out loud for the first, awkward time, during a pre-op phone call. At work, I'd ducked into a meeting room and quickly closed the door behind me for privacy. In slow, clear sentences, the nurse on the other end of the phone asked for the same confirmation as Dr. Lee. I'd said the words, stopping midway to swallow tears. Then I'd hung up, dropped my head to the conference table, and cried, in body-shaking spasms. The words were simple, but there were so many irrevocable decisions wrapped up in them. Though I outwardly appeared competent and confident and had access to incredible healthcare, I had no idea what I was doing, if the decisions I was making—which would change my body forever—were the right ones. *Should I keep the cancer-free breast? What about my nipples?*

In the pre-op room, my uncle opted for distracting me with future climbing plans. He and I had summited Mount Rainier together, in 2009, and the Grand Teton in Wyoming after that.

"We can do the north ridge of Baker next month," I suggested.

He gave me the same incredulous wrinkled-eyebrow face that he'd given nearly two decades ago when he'd dumped the contents of my giant purple backpack onto his living room floor. In that second, his I-don't-think-you'll-be-ready look ignited my defiance.

A nurse pulled back the curtain. "Lisa, we're ready for you in the OR. Are you ready?"

"So ready," I said.

On the morning that I returned home from the hospital, my psyche craved nature. Before I allowed myself to crawl into bed and rest, I needed to feel my body move again in the moist spring air. I wanted to reconnect with something that was real, something elemental that wasn't sterilized or controlled like the hospital I'd just come from. As I took my first cautious steps, my body felt the difference of no longer carrying breasts. I felt unbalanced, like my center of gravity had moved without my permission. The morning of my surgery, I'd done thirteen pull-ups in a minute and hiked 1,000 feet in elevation in thirty-two minutes while carrying 20 percent of my body weight. Now, after a few dozen steps across my flat driveway, I was out of breath and woozy. I wanted only to walk 100 feet to the mailbox and back. The mailbox! I wanted to walk far enough to look out past the houses and remember that the natural world still existed, and that I was still a part of it. I wanted to remember that everything—the wet maple leaves underneath my feet, the swaying firs, the breeze pricking my skin—was connected.

I didn't know how, exactly, but I felt in my core that I needed this connection with nature to begin healing.

My closest friends, Jeri and Kara, became a key ingredient, too. We'd initially met in that dingy Philips office; now they made me gooey macaroni and cheese and girl-power playlists. They took turns walking with me on wooded trails and took me shopping for prosthetic boobs. They reminded me that life would return to normal.

Four days after I returned home from the hospital, my husband and I stood in the bathroom and removed the bandages covering my boob scars. I raised my arms as high as I could, and he gingerly peeled back the soiled bandages.

"They look OK," he said.

I wrinkled my forehead. I wanted this to be a private moment. I wanted to start the relationship with my new body alone. I leaned forward, tentatively, toward the mirror and rotated from side to side. I didn't know what I'd expected. I'd thought my chest would just be flat, and it was, from a distance, when clothed. But up close, it looked concave, wrinkled, and contorted. My stomach protruded farther than my chest now. Somehow, my posture seemed off, too. And if I held still and looked in the mirror very closely, I could see my chest pulse with each beat of my heart. I wasn't ready to accept my new body; I wasn't even ready to think about it. Denial felt the simplest.

I shifted my focus to what my body could do. During my hospital stay, I'd measured my time to walk around the floor my room was on, aiming to reduce it each time. When I returned home, I walked farther each day, eventually graduating to a brisk walk on an elevated treadmill to bring my heart rate to pre-mastectomy levels. After each workout, I slowly inspected my chest in the mirror, gently running my index finger over the thick scabs that extended from armpit to nipple and wondering if they would ever go away.

One day a week after I returned home from the hospital, Kara arrived at my house, ready to escort me on a trail walk. She was in a cheery mood, her hair bouncy with blond curls. I met her at the door in yoga pants and a form-fitting long-sleeved shirt.

"I'm embracing my newly flat chest!" I said, part warning, part declaration.

"I support that," she said with a nod.

We walked side by side in the spring sunshine, up my neighborhood hill to the regional park where I had gone on runs pre-surgery.

"I just don't want to cover up with bulky sweaters anymore."

"Why'd you change your mind?"

"I don't really know." I shrugged. "It just feels important to appreciate my new anatomy."

Our paces slowed as we walked up the steepest part of the hill, past the mailbox hand-painted with flowers, past the fallen cedar carved long ago into a bench.

"How's everything healing, by the way?"

"Dr. Lee says everything looks fine."

"Shocker, since you haven't exactly been taking it easy," she scolded.

I couldn't deny that I hadn't completely followed the doctor's orders since I'd been home. I'd elevated the treadmill settings before I should have, delicately stuffing the drain bulbs collecting fluid from the cavities where my breasts used to be into the pockets of my running tights. I'd cautiously moved my body into yoga poses to force my brain through mental blocks about what my body was capable of. Every time I felt a pang of pain in my body or a tingle of doubt in my brain, I pretended I was shooting it with a pink glitter gun.

"I'm getting used to the incisions, and I felt like I shouldn't hide anything. This is my body now, you know?"

I glanced at Kara sideways as we crested the hill and stepped into the park's crunchy gravel parking lot. Kara nodded. Horse trailers lined one side of the lot, and mountain bikers readied their gear on the other.

"I mean, it's wrinkly and scabby."

"And deflated," she interrupted, repeating a description I'd used earlier.

"Hopelessly deflated," I laughed. "But to me those scars say, 'Fuck you, cancer.'" My voice broke and I sniffed back tears.

"I love you, LT," Kara said.

In four years, I would learn that I carry a gene mutation. The checkpoint kinase 2 gene sends cells instructions for making proteins that prevent damaged DNA from dividing. My checkpoint kinase 2 gene is damaged. And, without the quality-control function that it triggers, cells that contain damaged DNA, like cancer cells, are allowed to grow, unchecked.

Walking alone on a beach in California after a blood test confirmed the mutation, I let this new cancer chapter begin to unfold. Immediately, all of the uncertainty and fear bubbled over. Like it had been there the whole time, placidly waiting. I stopped walking to watch the sun roll into the ocean. *I'll never check the cancer box,* I thought. *And that is OK. This is who I am.* With this new familial knowledge, I pledged that I would pick up the fight again. I would always fight it. I would fight with the choices I made, the foods that I ate, the stress that I wouldn't let accumulate, the care I gave my body. *As long as this potential exists within me, I will fight you, cancer.*

After my mastectomy, I didn't yet know about my gene mutation. At that point, my primary focus after surgery was rebuilding and trusting my body. Eventually, how I felt about losing 222 grams of breast tissue would become situational. As an athlete, it felt phenomenal not to deal with those things flopping around when I ran. It was simpler not to wear a sports bra, or any bra—ever. As an athlete, I wasn't upset about my newly flat chest. My boobs were trying to kill me, and they had to go. Both of them. But as much as I wanted to defy the cultural construct of femininity, I missed them in social settings. I stared at other women's boobs; I wanted to wear a tight tank top and look curvy, too. And the thought of being intimate with two shriveled-up scars where my boobs used to be was a vulnerability I wasn't ready—might never be ready—to examine. So I made plans to replace them after Manaslu.

. . .

A few weeks after surgery, I had a follow-up appointment with Dr. Lee. With a confident yank, she removed the tubes circling the cavities where my breasts had lived for forty-two years. As she worked, I watched the fluid movement of her hands—hands that had been inside of me, touched places I could only visualize.

"Feeling ready for that mountain in Nepal?" she asked.

"Getting there. I'm planning to climb Baker next month. We'll see how that goes."

"Nothing's going to stop you, is it?" She chuckled and shook her head.

"I hope not."

"Please," she'd say to me years later, "call me Chris." Even then, I wouldn't feel comfortable removing her doctorly designation. Doing so would feel too casual for the intimate role she played in my life.

With the tubes removed, I was officially clear to exercise, even though Dr. Lee and I both knew I'd bent that rule a little. Now, preparing for Manaslu became a refuge for me, a bastion from which I could ignore a crumbling marriage and a damaged body. Training was the one thing that motivated me to move forward when all I wanted to do was sit in a dark room with a giant bowl of popcorn and a bottle of red wine and feel sorry for myself. Up until then, my drive had been spurred by the fear of failing. But now, more than anything, I did not want cancer to dictate my priorities, or to steal from me the one thing that I was proud of—the thing that proved I was capable. In a forgotten place deep inside my heart, I knew I couldn't be timid anymore about my body or what it needed to be healthy again. I believed I was boldly lifting two middle fingers directly in cancer's face, and from the outside, that's probably how it looked. But in fact, I was hiding. During all of those hours training in the mountains in preparation for my first Himalayan climb, I was hiding. I was also seeking. Looking for connections that I had lost during years of striving to achieve and to prove myself. During that time, I'd lost the connection with my body, with my spirit, and with my husband. Fighting cancer reminded me that I was strong enough to stop ignoring the messy things in my life that were within my control to repair.

. . .

You learn a lot about people when crises unexpectedly invade your life. I thought I knew my husband, but after twelve years, I realized I had missed and conveniently ignored cracks in the vital foundation of our relationship. My intense ambition to prove I was enough and my need to control everything and hold everyone around me to that same standard to create an outwardly perfect life pushed me to exploit even the tiniest weakness in his character—like a persistent drip that turns a crack into the Grand Canyon. I realize now that I'd felt this early in our relationship, when his insecurity was just a faint fracture. And I'd let my ambition and drive and need for perfection harass it repeatedly until it spread into a haze of ineptitude that surrounded him. As our relationship progressed, I could feel this imbalance between us, lurking and deadly, but too easily muted by our collective cocktail consumption. In the beginning, excessive drinking had been as much a part of my life as his. We'd drop friends who didn't drink. "What would we *do* with them?" we'd ask each other. We'd bypass post-hike lunch spots if there wasn't a neon beer sign in the window. Weekends at the lake house began and ended with drinks. After cancer, I'd started to think of my body differently—as something I'd been entrusted to look after, to care for. With this new outlook, weekend binges felt egregious.

For the first time, I acknowledged I was embarrassed when he passed out at dinner parties and a martini glass slipped through his loose hand and crashed onto the carpet. I was ashamed when my argument wasn't compelling enough to persuade him to stop driving drunk.

Divorce and excessive drinking were familiar to me. Those summer afternoons spent with Dad in taverns were the first time I'd felt the pain of realizing that someone I loved was unreliable. Except then, unlike in my marriage, I'd felt useful, naively believing I could get Dad home safely. But in my marriage, I'd been swirling in the gray area of knowing I couldn't ignore my husband's drinking, or be the only source of strength in our relationship anymore, and not knowing what to do about it. So I hid. In the mountains.

CHAPTER 6

14,301 FEET

Mountains felt tangible; I could understand them. I could decipher the terrain ahead of me and skillfully move through it. I could encounter a climbing route and work out the puzzle of holds and movements to get to its top. The more my marriage slipped from my fingers, the more I searched for comfort in dense forests. The more I sought peace atop snowy, desolate peaks. The more I found wonderment beholding the magnitude of a rock face. But still, I could not deconstruct and put back together the conundrum of my marriage. It felt like loose Jell-O. I knew it wasn't right that there was a vodka-filled Nalgene bottle under his side of the bed, but I hadn't been strong enough to do anything about it yet. I'd needed to immerse myself in the mountains to build enough strength to act on what was in my heart.

Unwilling to let cancer deter my goals and still uncertain about how to fix my marriage, I stuck to my original schedule and traveled to Nepal in August as initially planned, five months after surgery. My first glimpse of the Himalayas' pristine summits from a cramped airplane sent a wave of awe through my body. In every direction were snowy peaks skirted by verdant forests. Save for the ribbon of smog, the Himalayas felt like a peaceful mountaineering playground.

Walking to Manaslu's base camp was a five-day adventure. Every day presented a mix of impoverished villages, proud Buddhist stupas, and amiable Sherpas. Near base camp, I walked with the other climbers who had joined the same expedition into a deep valley, flanked from afar by unnamed snowy peaks and studded with the stone huts of yak herders. Their children toddled down the hills to greet us on the trail, yelling *Naaamaaastee!* with cheery voices. When they arrived at the trail, they folded their grubby hands into perfectly peaked prayers under their ruddy chins. They each wore thick layers of dark-red jackets and pants, making them look like cuddly dolls.

Standing on the trail beside the children, digging in my backpack for the colored pencils I'd brought from Seattle for just this purpose, I was stunned by the difference in our lives. A girl with long scraggly hair moved next to me, her intense dark eyes engrossed by whatever I was about to pull from my backpack. I wondered how her life would unfold. Would she venture from this valley to experience the traffic and smog of Kathmandu? Would she fly on an airplane? Stand in line at Starbucks? Earn a college degree? I didn't feel sorry for her, wanting no more for her life than what it was destined to hold. I was struck by the simplicity of this valley and its people, and I longed for more of that in my own life. Thoughtfully, the girl selected two colored pencils from the bundle. A red one and a gold one. She nodded her head to me and scurried back to her house.

Two days into the trek to Manaslu base camp, the team made a detour to an ancient stone monastery at the end of another lush valley. As we approached, I saw its colorful prayer flags ruffle from its peaked roof to the hillside. Adjacent was a squat, square stone building, home to the solitary monk charged with caring for the monastery for a two-year stint. From outside, I could hear the faint mumbling of his prayers. My fellow climbers and I were shy about interrupting something that felt so sacred, so one of the Sherpas cautiously opened the wooden door a crack to peek inside. Although we'd interrupted his prayers, the monk eagerly welcomed us, nodding a head of knotted hair and smoothing his thick purple cloak as we stepped across the stone threshold. I ducked as I entered his living quarters: a single room for sleeping, cooking, praying, and studying. Smoke from a slow fire wisped up its center chimney. Though we didn't share a language, two of my climbing partners and I followed the monk to the fire, still hunched over to avoid the low stone ceiling. We mimicked his movements and sat cross-legged on the dirt floor. This was the first time I'd heard the melodic chants of Buddhist prayer, and I wasn't sure how to respond, so I closed my eyes and let the smoke and prayers meander over me. The monk paused to offer tea and *nak* cheese, then resumed his prayer. The Sherpas came inside to join us now, and one of them mouthed the word *blessing* when I looked at him curiously. I straightened my back, intending to take this more seriously. After more prayer, cheese, and tea, the monk rose, and we followed him out into the crisp air. He took my hands. Suddenly, I was afraid of this tiny enrobed man. But I met his fierce eyes, and he spoke to me in Nepali. I felt like he'd said something very serious for which I should be grateful, so I nodded and offered my only Nepali word: *namaste*.

Miles down the trail, I asked one of my Sherpa teammates what he'd said.

"He felt your heart, *didi*."

I looked at him with raised eyebrows. He clarified, "He told you that the home of your pure heart is in the mountains."

I'd left Seattle to climb Manaslu with a head full of questions. I hadn't been certain I could continue with my marriage, I didn't know if I was invested in my career anymore, and I wasn't sure whether my mind and body were strong enough for a Himalayan peak. Just the notion of my heart being at home in this wildly beautiful place was enough to quiet my concerns.

Once we reached base camp, I settled in with my teammates. Each morning, I woke to a mug of warm, sweet milk tea and never-ending awe at the Himalayan peaks that surrounded base camp. I climbed on comfortably steep snow and learned how to fold into a multicultural expedition team. Though I had trained judiciously and studied Manaslu's route and risks, I was skeptical about whether I could do it. So I attempted to ease my self-inflicted pressure to summit by aiming only to climb above 8,000 meters and to use bottled oxygen.

After nearly a month of climbing, the expedition was called off due to conditions on the climbing route. I achieved neither of my goals, but what I gained on the icy slopes and grassy valleys of my first

Himalayan attempt was more important than a summit. I learned there was a way to regain my power—to grow from the bad decisions I'd made, the things I hadn't said, and the times I hadn't stuck up for myself. The monk had given me an answer: the home for my heart was in the mountains.

Two months after I returned from Nepal, one week after a forty-fourth-birthday realization that my husband's attempted sobriety had failed, I grabbed my running shoes despite the frigid December rain and headed for the neighborhood trails. My mind was thick with the failure and shame that my marriage was ending. When I crested the last hill on my return, I saw my husband, forlorn and soggy. I had been avoiding this conversation for months, maybe years. I'd held it with me all the way to Asia and back, but I couldn't keep it to myself anymore. We walked together on the muddy trail, retracing the route I'd just run. Sweat began to slide in icy rivulets down my back.

"I feel like neither of us knows how to fix things," I started.

"I think we haven't tried together; we've only been to therapy once together. You just keep doing your own thing."

He was right, and I knew it. But I'd already decided in my heart years ago that I couldn't make our marriage work. It had gotten away from me. Even with guidance from two therapists, Tarot cards, and long, teary conversations with my dog, I didn't know how to fix it, and I could no longer satisfy the ache I saw in his eyes when we met. As we walked that day, I could feel the heat from his body next to mine, walking side by side slowly up the rocky trail. I couldn't look at him, but I knew he was crying. Yet I couldn't find the empathy to comfort him.

"I just feel like I'm always taking the lead, like I'm the one making all the plans and doing all the work and you just tag along. I want a partner—isn't that the point?" I said.

He said that alcohol had stolen his motivation and that he could get it back. I said I was sorry.

During the awkward pauses in our talk, I stared down at the mud squishing under my shoe with each step, and I still couldn't look at him. A strong desire to run rose up the back of my neck, like a force pushing me forward. Instead, I stopped.

"What do you want to do?" he said sadly.

I looked up at the mossy cedar trees all around me, some of them swaying slowly in the wind. I wondered what all those trees had witnessed in their lifetimes, what was held in their sturdy trunks. I thought about everything that Lord Hill Park had meant to me and how ironic it was that this conversation was taking place there. My husband and I had first discovered this park the day that we returned from our honeymoon. Although by that point we had lived in the neighborhood for more than a year, we'd never walked up the hill to explore it. That day, we'd wandered around for hours, lazily exploring, making love in tall, sunny grass at the park's highest point. Over the next ten years, I would walk all of our dogs there, run countless miles on the rocky, muddy trails. I would be attacked by angry owls, rescue an upside-down horse in a rocky ravine, and decorate a cedar stump with trinkets from my deceased pets. Most importantly, this park had been a healing sanctuary when I'd recovered from breast cancer.

I gathered my mental stoicism and finally turned to face him. "I want a divorce."

Then he walked one way, and I ran the other.

CHAPTER 7

597 FEET

I did not intend to climb Mount Everest. The highest mountain in the world hadn't held a lavender-inked entry in my pink notebook. Instead, I'd intended to avoid the crowds and commercialization and hone my skills on other challenging Himalayan peaks. Cancer changed that; it granted me the perspective that life is fragile and fleeting. "I'll probably want to climb it one day—why not do it now?" I told wide-eyed friends over Thanksgiving dinner in 2015 with a carefree shrug. I couldn't be flippant about this decision, though. It was *Everest*, after all. I would have to live in the unforgiving air above 8,000 meters, known as the "death zone," for days. I would need to ask my body to perform with less than a third of the available sea-level oxygen that I breathed every day in Seattle. And I hadn't even made it to the death zone on Manaslu. I didn't have any reference for how my mind and body would perform above 8,000 meters. I needed confirmation that there was potential in my embryonic plan.

"I'm thinking of climbing Everest in March," I said to Scott at the end of 2015. I'd learned by now to casually plop these comments into our conversations and then let the unease settle into my stomach while I waited for his reply.

As usual, it was short and to the point. "We can get you there."

"March of *2016*," I said. Just to be sure.

"You respond quickly to training."

"I have reconstructive breast surgery scheduled at the beginning of March."

"We'll focus on pre-hab until then. I really think you will be ready."

A lot had happened in the year that Scott had been coaching me. He'd helped me come to trust my body after cancer. And because plans to climb Manaslu had been temporarily up in the air, he knew my husband wasn't enthusiastic about my Himalayan pursuits. Our partnership and his support had become a key element in my pre-expedition checklist.

I hung up the phone, confirmed with an online search that pre-hab meant ramping up my fitness before surgery to speed up recovery, and sank cautiously back in my chair, not wanting to disturb my brain while it absorbed the conversation. *Holy fuck, am I climbing Mount Everest?*

There was just one little problem—or, rather, seventy thousand little problems. I couldn't afford it.

After weeks of financial origami, I walked into a conference room at my office and closed the door. I took a deep sigh, slid into the plastic chair, and called my bank.

"Hi, I'd like to borrow seventy thousand dollars to climb Mount Everest." I squished my face into a strained wince and waited for the person on the other end of the phone to realize that I had less than twenty-four dollars in my checking account.

Instead, I heard a woman's cheery voice say, without a hint of hesitation, "Let's see what we can do." I swallowed the threat of tears, amazed and shocked at how things were lining up for me and growing more confident that the path opening before me was the right one. With the bank's help, I watched my account expand larger than it ever had, then quickly shrink back to double digits when I handed over the funds for the climb. In truth, I hadn't had a backup plan in the event that my bank wasn't so accommodating. But lately, stepping forward without a clear path felt more comfortable, and I'd begun to notice intersections in my life—sometimes as simple as comments from strangers—that made me feel like I was being pushed forward, toward Everest and a life with different priorities.

In the coming weeks, I revised my pink-notebook plan to include quitting my job, getting a divorce, and borrowing $70,000. Three things that probably shouldn't happen simultaneously.

More than a few people who loved me dearly believed I'd lost my ability to reason. At our monthly happy hour, my closest friends and I sat as we usually did, at a high-top table in Seattle's residential wine country, replaying the highlights of the last month of our lives. Lives that used to intersect naturally at work—now our friendship mostly revolved around monthly gatherings like this one. My departure for Everest was just two months away, and I was restraining myself from oversharing my plans and preparation, but there was something about the air between us that smelled like an intervention.

Kara looked at me with concern. "I'm worried about you. I mean, I love you and . . . I don't know, I just want you to be sure . . . you're making a lot of big decisions right now. I know you're determined. I just don't want you to regret anything."

There is no logical response when your closest friend feels like you're about to jump off a cliff and can't see your safety net. "I know," I told her. "It just feels like I'm doing the right thing, I don't know why . . . I know it all seems crazy. But it just feels . . . *right*."

She frowned at my answer, and I frowned back, trying not to let tension build.

"What if you waited a year until you're totally done with cancer and your divorce is final?" Jeri offered.

In our circle, we'd joked about what dog breed each of us would be. Kara would be the bulldog because of her tenacity, Jeri the golden retriever because of her love for everybody, and I the German shepherd because of my courage.

"What's the rush?" Jeri finished.

The rush was that permanence is a farce. All our stuff—our bodies, our relationships, the porcelain ballerina figurine from your grandmother that you've cherished your whole life—could be taken away from any of us, at any time, without warning. But our accomplishments— the good ones and the ones we'd like to forget—remain knotted to us.

Even when our minds are too brittle to remember them. I didn't want to look back across the expanse of my life, however long or short it might be, with regret. Cancer taught me that life is short and fickle, and that money and hard work and supposed health are not immunities. Cancer taught me that to reach for less than I am capable of is to deny life. But telling my closest friends this felt too know-it-all-ish then.

My friends were right, though; it was *a lot*. It did feel heavy, even to me. Even when I was confident I was steering my life in the right direction. In the space of four months, I had filed for divorce, had reconstructive breast surgery, put two houses on the market, watched my almost-ex-husband get fired, buried a beloved dog, buried a beloved cat, borrowed an obscene amount of money, and quit my job to climb Mount Everest. Despite all the pain and stress and uncertainty, I kept moving forward, not knowing another way. I knew I couldn't ignore or fight the changes in my life. I needed to pay attention to them, to accept and learn from them. To feel them completely without ignoring or hiding. There was a tangible shift inside of me that compelled me—it was a sense of letting go of not only the stuff but also the outcome. The change didn't feel novel or unexpected; it just was. At my very core, I knew I was making the right choices. The decision to reclaim my life didn't feel outrageous; it felt scary, yes, but also as natural as walking on a peaceful wooded path. And even though there were moments of affirmation, where acquaintances at work would look at me with curiosity and tell me I looked different, it was difficult to explain my certainty to people that I loved and respected, because they couldn't feel my security and confidence.

I felt like I was freeing forgotten pieces of myself. With each decision, each thing I let go, each time I stood in my truth, a forgotten piece of genuineness floated to the surface like a bubble released from melting ice. Some of those bubbles had been frozen since childhood. They had been stuck there since the first time a parent ignored a perfect report card or forgot to pick me up from school.

While I sat casually at a restaurant with my best friends, enough of myself had been freed to know that I would regret more years spent in an unrewarding career. I would regret staying in a marriage that no longer fulfilled me. So I let go.

"I just don't want to have any regrets," I finally answered in a small voice. "Who knows what'll happen next year. It's kind of cool to think about rebuilding; when else do you get a chance to do that in life?"

Jeri and Kara just nodded, their faces a mix of pain and affection.

I convinced my sister to drag her son and my father to Chicago to meet me during a layover en route to Kathmandu. For my family, traveling by train from the small farming community where I'd grown up (and they still lived) to downtown Chicago was an anxiety-inducing trek that required multiple phone calls, texts, and itineraries to coordinate.

"You just walk out of the train station and look for a taxi," I told my sister, already giving up on describing how to use Uber.

"But what if there aren't any?" she wanted to know.

"There will be, I promise."

In my mind, our meeting would be a warm and celebratory send-off. Instead, we sat awkwardly in plastic chairs welded to dirty tables in a deserted downtown deli. My sister asked what I would eat on the mountain, and I could tell she was nervous and unsure what to say. I wanted to displace the awkwardness, but what do you say to your family members when you're about to fly to a part of the world that they have never seen? To attempt something that they can only imagine? I sensed the space between us growing, and I lacked the ability to close it.

"Want something to eat, Lis?" Dad was the only person who abbreviated my name to one syllable; it felt like a secret language we shared.

I looked at him, almost eye to eye. He looked old to me, the wrinkles on his face appearing deeper, his hair nearly gone. He seemed slight, leaner than I remembered.

"Sure," I told him. I wasn't hungry, but eating would pass the time. He slid me an aging tuna-salad sandwich and chips as he held back the persistent wheeze that he attributed to adult-onset asthma, though I suspected it was from years of smoking Kool cigarettes. I looked across the table at Sara to see if she found his wheeze concerning, but I couldn't catch her eye. She was wearing baggy jeans and a shapeless men's T-shirt, her long, ropy hair twisted into a carefree bun on the top of her head, her smooth, round face still sporting a sprinkle of freckles across the bridge of her nose. In her lap, she picked at her already truncated fingernails, and I could tell she was anxious. Not just about me, but about leaving her farming community for the chaos of Chicago.

"You feel ready?" Dad wanted to know. His fingernails were the same shape and length as Sara's, and I wondered if her habit was learned.

I knew he was asking about more than Everest; since I'd blown up my life during the last four months, he had been silently skeptical during our weekly phone calls.

"I'm going to pause my career," I'd told him during a phone call several weeks ago. Because "pause" sounded better than "quit the highest-paying job I've ever had, the one I spent years achieving."

"Agh!" he'd said, like someone had just punched him. "You sure you wanna do that? It seems so . . ."

He hadn't had to finish; I'd known what he was thinking. I was the sole college graduate in my family, extending even to cousins, and he had always been proud of the independence and lifestyle that a solid education and successful corporate career had afforded me. *Lisa's traveling to Paris for work*, I'd heard him say to church friends. *Last week she was in Orlando. She and her husband bought a lake house. A ski boat.* I knew I'd let him down now. I knew that, by his measure, I was failing now.

"I just, you know, I really want to climb Everest. I'll get another job."

I knew he was still disappointed, but we didn't talk about any of that now, in the deserted Chicago deli. Instead, we exchanged unemotional comments about what I would wear, how cold it would be on the summit, the length of my flight to Kathmandu.

This familial exchange wasn't atypical. Even during big moments like the death of a family pet or the announcement of their divorce, my parents had always struggled to express their emotions. I'd surmised at a young age that my parents' marriage was an attempt to legitimize my mother's pregnancy, and they'd stuck to it for eight years before the lack of trust and commitment was more than the thirtysomethings could repair. The day Dad told me they were getting a divorce, he came to the upstairs bedroom that I shared with my sister and sat cross-legged on the shaggy carpet. I could tell that he was sad. It must have been gut-wrenching for him to walk up the stairs of a house he'd once been so proud to live in with his family. I wondered how the decision had been made that he would be the one to tell us. Did he want to do it? Did Mom tell him he'd do it?

Sara was in her closet, and I was lying on my yellow Holly Hobbie bedspread reading a Choose Your Own Adventure book. Although the room was large, neither of us liked sharing it. Our beds were on opposite walls, each pushed against the heavily knotted wood paneling so that they could be as far from each other as possible. We were both stubborn, neither wanting to relinquish the entire room to the other. So our unspoken compromise was to create solitary, make-believe worlds in our closets. Dad would often slip short notes, written on scraps of paper with a pencil, under our closet doors. *I always did like you the best*, they most often said. I didn't know until I was an adult that we'd each received them.

His voice sounded drained and weak when he asked Sara to come out of her closet. Dad had grown up in Illinois, only leaving the rural central part of the state for stateside military service during the Vietnam War. For him, stoicism was a perfected trait, likely a generational one passed down by the men in his family.

"You girls are going to move into a different house with your mom." The words fell out of his mouth like he couldn't keep them there anymore. He must have known he was hurting us, but he didn't have the ability to tell us any other way, wishing instead that he could ease us into this announcement, warm us up to the idea, maybe even make it sound like a fun adventure. *You get to have two beds, two Christmases, two sets of neighborhood friends.*

It was just as well that he didn't attempt to sugarcoat it. My predominant emotion had been relief. I didn't care how many Christmases I would have. I was relieved their fighting would no longer wake me up in the middle of the night. Strange women wouldn't knock on the front door, asking nervously if my dad was home. Mom would no longer throw things.

Familial stoicism fostered emotional space; it taught me to maintain that space to not be bothersome, to be "good." It taught me to be independent, too. And it taught me to bury my voice and emotions so deeply that it would scare me when they reached for the surface. As a kid, I got good at being good, so adept at remaining quiet and studious that I felt invisible. Invisibly yearning for their acceptance, yet unable to communicate it with anything other than perfection. And now, climbing mountains.

Sitting in the empty deli in Chicago, I felt there was so much for Dad and me to share, to explain, to love about each other, but then, like most times, everything was hibernating under the surface in some impenetrable place that neither of us could access. After an hour of small talk, he looked at his watch, the same cloudy-faced Timex he'd worn for decades. "Better get you going."

Sara, her son, and my father walked me to the busy street to hail a taxi. Everywhere, people were in hurry, businesspeople stepping quickly with trench coats flapping behind them and cell phones stuck to their faces. *This is the last time I will breathe sea-level air,* I thought, and I wanted to stop to savor it, to relish the feeling of comfort and safety. The taxi came too quickly. Sara hugged me hard and whispered, "Don't die," in my ear with a nervous giggle. I opened the taxi door and turned back to catch Dad's eyes. They were blue like mine, a gift from his Irish ancestors. Neither of us could turn our private whirlpools of emotions into words, so he just nodded his head in acknowledgment. I did the same and got into the taxi.

CHAPTER 8

4,380 FEET

A s I drove away from my family, I wondered if they believed I was
ready. Did they believe my mind and body were prepared to com-
petently endure the challenges Everest would present? I wasn't even
sure myself. I'd committed to climb Everest just four months earlier. It
was true I'd made that decision fresh from the slopes of Manaslu. But
I hadn't even summited Manaslu, and my body and mind had been
through more stress than I'd ever endured. In the months since my
mastectomy, despite additional surgeries, I'd learned to trust my body
again. If I'd been in the best shape of my life before Manaslu, now I
was a beast. Before, I'd carried forty pounds 4,000 feet up Mailbox
Peak. Now, I could do it twice on a Saturday morning. Local peaks that
I'd first climbed in two days I now summited in a single push. Most
weekdays included a pre-work cardio session and a post-work strength
session. I'd studied videos and thoroughly read the diaries of other
summiteers. I'd spoken to some of them personally and asked each the
same series of questions that I hoped would illuminate the difference
between success and failure. Their collective experiences confirmed
that mountains, especially those that nearly pierce the stratosphere,
are unpredictable. Some of my fellow climbers had experienced deep

compact snow etched with steps on the 45-degree Lhotse Face that leads to Everest's Camp 3, while others climbed featureless blue ice. Some ascended the Khumbu Icefall with the aid of just a few aluminum ladders. Some described the icefall as an unending maze of undulating ice and rickety, unstable ladders. The subtext of every conversation was that Everest is hard, cold, and unforgiving. These conversations confirmed that success on Everest—and all Himalayan peaks—couldn't be reduced to a formula, and that mountaineering didn't come with guarantees. The most important thing I could do, I decided, was to control all the things I could, which boiled down to my fitness, my attitude, my skills, and my gear.

On Manaslu, my team had been thwarted at 22,000 feet by a tenuous ice bulge that threatened to release tons of ice and snow onto the climbing route. I'd lain uncomfortably in a dark tent the night before I intended to climb below the bulge and had listened, between wind gusts, to radio conversations with base camp that confirmed the risk of continuing was too great.

"Bring the boys down," I'd heard the expedition leader say over the radio, officially ending our summit bid. I'd heard my tentmate grumble under her breath. "Really wanted a shot at that," she'd said.

"Yeah, it sucks." I'd rolled toward her, but I was fabricating my disappointment. Though I had trained and prepared, the mountain had made me question my ability and readiness to climb to 26,000 feet. I'd been happy to descend, thinking I just didn't have it in me.

Manaslu had reinforced the idea that physical fitness is only part of the nebulous equation for success in the mountains. A significant portion, especially as elevations increase, is mental. So, in preparation for Everest, I'd studied the habits of Olympic athletes, and eventually devoted time each week to conversations with a sports psychologist. I'd left a Super Bowl party early for our first phone meeting, much more interested in building my own mental toughness than watching other athletes test theirs. I'd been eager to balance my physical preparation with mental, hoping the sports psychologist would help me develop dependable tools to get me through the toughest moments on Everest.

"Know why summiting Everest is important to you," she'd

recommended during our first session. "Write it down and be able to draw on it when things get tough."

I'd been stumped. I'd never actually devoted any mental energy to deciphering why climbing was important to me. Ten minutes into our conversation, I'd felt completely unprepared.

"It keeps me in shape?" had been my first superficial answer.

"You don't need to know right now," she'd said gently. "Schedule some time every day, even just ten minutes, to really think about it. Brainstorm words and phrases, if it helps."

I'd known I needed to dig deeper. I'd known that climbing 45-degree ice and starving for oxygen for weeks would require more. So that evening, I'd sat at my desk, blank notebook and purple glitter pen at the ready, but I'd still had trouble coming up with more than:

Climbing forces me to examine who I am.

I like to accomplish difficult things.

It gives me confidence.

Each sentence had felt more like a question than an affirmation. There had to be more to it. I knew the reasons existed; they were just too many layers deep for me to excavate them. So I wrote, and I visualized with all my senses, but I couldn't piece together anything that felt sufficient. Eventually, I'd shifted my mental training to daily visualizations, watching myself confidently climb through the Khumbu Icefall, preparing for the summit in a dark, frigid tent at 26,000 feet. I saw myself standing proudly and humbly on the summit, confident about the descent. I also created hypothetical plans for overcoming each thing that scared me about Everest. *What if I'm cold? Fatigued? Ill? What if I run out of oxygen? Lose a glove? Drop my rappel device?* My home-office walls were cluttered with pastel note cards for each scenario and bulleted plans to overcome them.

Maybe because my mental strength had been bolstered, I'd also made the calculated but risky decision to undergo multiple breast-reconstruction surgeries during the five months between climbing Manaslu and Everest. During my final post-operative appointment, my surgeon looked at me with a wry grin.

"You sure you need to climb that mountain?"

"Unless you tell me I can't."

I'd been up-front with Dr. Welk from the beginning about my

Everest plans, and though he frequently told me that I was potentially crazy and urged me to consider a more reasonable sport like golf, I needed his blessing to feel confident about what my body could endure.

"Well, I don't exactly have a point of reference." He shrugged and looked at me over the rims of his glasses.

"You just call me if anything weird happens." He handed me his business card. "And don't die!"

As I boarded the plane that would take me from the US to Asia, I took with me not confidence but wary trust that I had done enough.

I arrived blurry-eyed and jet-lagged in Kathmandu a day later, on a sti-fling morning, 364 days after a bilateral mastectomy removed all of the cancer from my body. Standing in the baggage area of the Tribhuvan International Airport, I could feel the hard kernel of strength that cancer had left behind. Standing there, sticky with sweat from twenty hours of travel, I instantly felt the chaos and dirt and exuberance of Nepal's capital city rush over me. I was grateful merely to have made it that far, and I wanted to meld into the excitement, to flow with the hustle of sweaty bodies squeezing politely against one another and to share in the exchange of hand gestures and uncommon words—but I had a job to do. Despite all my preparation, the odds of me sum-miting Mount Everest in 2016 were not high. I hadn't climbed above 8,000 meters before, the mountain's overall success rate was less than 50 percent, and, due to deadly avalanches and earthquakes that had collectively claimed the lives of thirty-eight climbers, no one had sum-mited in two years.

Though I didn't let myself relax into the energy around me, I did take inventory of what had changed in my life since I'd stood in this airport five months prior. I felt unencumbered now; I had wiped the slate clean: no job, no husband, no pets, no money. Just a singular goal to understand whether I could endure the tests of the world's highest mountain. I pushed my overloaded luggage cart through the mass of people frantically collecting their own parcels: well-worn duffel bags like mine, square suitcases wrapped in protective plastic, slender boxes encasing TVs. My blond hair and fair skin made me unique in this group, and as I moved, I repeatedly scanned the crowd for other for-eign travelers laden with duffel bags and climbing dreams. The closer

I got to the exit without talking to another climber, the more comfortable I became. Maybe because I was fatigued from twenty hours of travel, but more likely because I still felt uncomfortable calling myself a mountaineer, I didn't want to explain to a stranger who might be more experienced than me that I was attempting Everest. I didn't want to feel the reddening burn on my cheeks when I recited my climbing résumé. I wanted to avoid the awkwardness of the comparison that would come next. I wanted to inconspicuously meld into this crowd that didn't look or sound like me. I kept pushing my duffel-bag-laden cart forward, apologizing with *namastes* and head bows as people made a path for me. Finally, I recognized Garrett Madison, the expedition leader, towering over the crowd near the airport's exit door. He was standing casually, wearing jeans and a black T-shirt, and looking lean and muscled, like a mountain guide. A familiar smile snuck from the corners of his mouth when he spotted me and my cumbersome load, and I was relieved—not just at the familiar face, but at feeling shielded now against unwanted questions from unknown climbers. I'd known Garrett for many years, and though we'd made plans to climb together in the Himalaya, the pieces hadn't fit together until now. The years of intermittent meetings to chat and plan had been an interview of sorts, for both of us. I'd become comfortable with his casual leadership style and appreciated his tendency to assess a situation before directing. I knew that, although he was equally comfortable in a tuxedo and a down suit, the mountains were his home and helping others achieve their mountain goals was his passion.

"Heeeyyy, Lisaaa. You made it. How was the trip?" His sentences always started like a song. I angled my luggage cart through the crowd to meet him. We hugged casually, like I was meeting him for a drink in Seattle instead of embarking on the hardest climb of my life in Kathmandu.

Garrett introduced me to Aang Phurba, and he shyly shook my hand and dipped his head. As the team's lead Sherpa, he carried the title of sirdar. He was slightly taller than me, and I'm five foot three. His black hair was raked straight back into a short ponytail, and wisps of wiry mustache framed his smile. Aang Phurba took the handles of my luggage cart and nimbly navigated into the airport parking lot as Garrett and I trailed behind, me trying to focus my exhausted mind on Garrett's updates about the whereabouts and arrival times of my fellow teammates. I was already confused about how many Jeffs were on the team.

CHAPTER 9

17,598 FEET

Two days later, the whole team assembled, and I met the men I would climb Everest with (turned out there was only one Jeff). There is a natural judgment that occurs when climbing teams composed of strangers converge for the first time. It's human nature to assess capability and experience with the intent to separate the weak from the strong. Aside from me, my climbing team consisted of eight men from the US, India, Argentina, England, and Canada.

For our first team lunch, we sat at a long metal table on an airy patio, temporarily shielded by tall leafy plants from the chaos of honking scooter horns in Kathmandu's tourist district. I didn't know how I'd rank against these guys; they all seemed more prepared and experienced than me. Some were attempting Everest for the third time (having been stymied in the two prior years by natural disasters). Some of my teammates had been as high as 21,000 feet to Everest's Camp 2. I'd climbed higher, but on a lesser Himalayan peak. What made me think that I could summit on my first attempt? Though the conversation at lunch was chummy, I sensed a macho vibe that left me guarded and shy.

"What'd you do for training, Lisa?" Jeff Glasbrenner from Arkansas wanted to know. Of the team, he appeared to be the most leanly muscled and athletic, and I felt more competition than curiosity in his question.

"I did a bunch of hiking with a heavy pack," I told him, too embarrassed to mention that I'd mimicked the Khumbu Icefall's treacherous ladder crossings in my backyard and overlooking how I'd worked for months with a sports psychologist.

I knew I was answering the question not just for Jeff but for the rest of the men seated at the table. I already assumed they thought less of me—that I was too small, too inexperienced, too whatever, to summit. And my downplaying wasn't helping.

"You'd better have done more than that for Everest, girl." Jeff's angular face, topped by spiky brown hair, tilted toward me with a raised, scrutinizing eyebrow.

I sensed in Jeff, though, a no-nonsense comrade, like he knew I'd done more. I sensed he, like me, was attuned to underestimation. Jeff had lost most of his right leg in a farming accident when he was eight. Later, he and I would talk about that lunch at the airy restaurant in Kathmandu and how we both believed that the rest of the team had put us in the same *will not summit* category. A category that we were both so uncomfortable occupying that we trained harder, pushed further, set the bar higher. Jeff and I had adapted differently to shouldering the weight of doubt, though. He was candid, highly competitive, and intense, whereas I was more comfortable flying under the radar so I didn't heighten expectations. Jeff's competitive force, however, was so strong that he only wanted to be surrounded by the toughest teammates and take on the toughest challenges.

At the time, taking my first guarded steps toward team building with these men, I didn't recognize my protective impulse to present myself as less than capable. Then, I couldn't see how much effort I'd given to my campaign to fly under the radar, and how it eroded my credibility, my femininity, and my spirit.

Days later, we'd just begun the nine-day walk from Lukla to Everest base camp when I got a view of Everest for the first time. It felt unreal, like a photograph. From where I sat at 8,300 feet on a wooden bench atop the Hotel Everest View's stone patio, mountains extended in jagged patterns to both edges of the horizon. Their slopes held snow except for the steepest chunks, from which exposed rock shone black in the sunlight. In the back, shorter than the rest of the peaks only because of perspective, a hearty plume of snow blew off Everest's summit. I could not comprehend how I could possibly move my body from that comfortable patio all the way up that colossal mountain and back. It felt utterly impossible.

Everest's potential first summiteer, George Mallory, famously quipped to a *New York Times* reporter in 1923 that he wanted to climb the world's tallest peak "Because it's there." In the same article, he went on to say that the challenge of Everest is a part of "man's desire to conquer the universe."

I gazed hard at Everest's summit now and thought back to the assignment from my sports psychologist to understand why I was here. Though I knew that I didn't want to conquer anything, I felt like my reasons were mostly superficial: *I like pushing myself physically and mentally; climbing makes me feel strong and accomplished.* Now that I was face-to-face with Mount Everest, I hoped there was more to it than that.

Garrett slid next to me on the bench and interrupted my introspection.

"What do you think, Lisa?" he asked with a wide grin, seeming carefree in his plaid shirt and rolled-up hiking pants, like he was in his element.

"I don't know," I said, wide-eyed under my sunglasses. "It's huge! And really far away."

As the expedition leader, Garrett had personally evaluated and confirmed each team member's experience. He'd carefully considered whether we could work well as a team when things got tough. He and I had met many times in Seattle, where he'd patiently answered all of my questions about the route, the risks, the gear, the other team members, and my readiness to attempt the world's tallest mountain. Now, we were all relying on him to interpret weather reports, to collaborate with other teams, and to ultimately determine when, and if, we would attempt the summit.

"Ooh, you'll do great up on the hill, Lisa. I know it. You're one of the strongest."

I scrunched my eyebrows and looked back toward the mountain. This would be Garrett's ninth Everest summit, so he knew what it took to climb and return safely, but I still doubted my place on this team enough that I had a hard time trusting his wisdom and assessment of my abilities.

During the rest of the twenty-mile trek to base camp, I slowly realized, though, that he was right—that I had as much or more experience than many people on the team and that I had trained more thoroughly. And, if I allowed honesty to overcome doubt, I realized the trek so far had been easy for me. That was no measure for how I'd do on the mountain, but I felt strong, and my body, though healing, had not let me down.

The remainder of the hike to the 17,500-foot base camp followed a familiar pattern. Each day we'd walk toward base camp, sharing the well-worn rocky path that gradually gained elevation with other climbers attempting Everest or other nearby peaks. Everyone seemed to have a job: Nepali porters whizzed by me with heavy, bulky loads on their way to various base camps, sometimes carrying towering stacks of plastic chairs and hard-sided suitcases that seemed out of place in the mountains. Yaks—shaggy, surly creatures adorned with ribbons and brass bells the size of my hand—carried the heaviest loads and commanded a wide berth on the trail. I also shared the trail with climbers and Nepali climbing Sherpas. Our backpacks were light as feathers compared to everyone else's loads. By midafternoon each day, we'd arrive at the day's destination: a teahouse where the proprietor's family provided warm drinks, hearty Nepalese food, and an occasional warm shower.

On the ninth day of trekking, I noticed a steady procession of yaks without the burden of loads passing me in the opposite direction. Their Sherpa handlers smiled with bright *namastes* as our paths crossed. Each seemed pleased to have fulfilled his obligation to deliver generators, potatoes, kerosene, eggs, mattresses, or any number of other base-camp essentials.

"Almost there," Aang Phurba said, walking next to me, as he pointed to the yaks' bare backs with a grin.

"Are you excited?" I wondered.

Aang Phurba's grin grew to reveal short teeth, and then he danced in a tight circle on the trail next to me. I laughed back at him.

Like Garrett, Aang Phurba had summited Everest multiple times. Over his mountaineering career, his responsibilities on commercial expeditions like this one had increased from porter to skilled climbing Sherpa to sirdar. As sirdar, he held a leadership role on our team and would coordinate the Sherpas' work to carry loads of food, oxygen, and supplies up the mountain. And he would accompany one of us to the summit.

"How many times have you been here?" I wanted to know.

"This year is number four," he said with a grin.

Aang Phurba's career in the mountains had made him an affluent thirty-year-old. He had an apartment in Kathmandu and a family home in the village where he was born. Today he, unlike many Sherpas, looked like a well-outfitted mountaineer. He wore new running shoes and modern mountain clothes and carried a new backpack.

In a few minutes, we hiked up a small rise in the trail and the scattered curve of base camp's hundreds of tents came into view.

"Welcome!" Aang Phurba said, skipping ahead in quick bursts while I ambled up the rocky path.

I imagined that it must feel like coming home for him, that he would be reunited with friends from all over the world whom he only saw in the mountains. For me, seeing the bright colors of base camp for the first time felt like a chapter closing. The ease of trekking was behind me. Now, the work would begin.

CHAPTER 10

26,200 FEET

Högh-altitude climbing involves multiple "rotations." These forays up the mountain, usually to the next highest camp, force a physiological process that creates more red blood cells. These additional red blood cells swarm our blood vessels and carry the extra oxygen that our bodies need to survive at elevations where the ambient oxygen is considerably less than our bodies are accustomed to. Each rotation concludes with several days at base camp to rest, recover, hydrate, and eat. The whole process of climbing and then returning to base camp is called acclimatization. Following this process of climbing rotations on Mount Everest meant that I would climb from base camp to Camp 1, spend the night, then return to base camp to recover the next day. Several days later I would climb from base camp to Camp 1, then higher to Camp 2, where my team and I would sleep for one night. The next morning, we would return to base camp for another recovery period before repeating the cycle for a third time to Camp 3. Rotations would culminate in a summit rotation, which was strategically timed during a multiday window of stable weather. On Everest, this weather window typically occurred near the end of May, during a narrow slice of time after jet-stream winds leveled off and before moisture rose from the Bay of Bengal in the Indian Ocean to begin the annual monsoon season.

After we settled in base camp for a few days, and before our rotations began, we all had to prove we were competent at basic mountaineering skills like rappelling: lowering ourselves down the mountain with a rope. We also had to demonstrate we could ascend with the aid of a fixed rope using a traction device called an ascender, as well as cross a ladder with crampons strapped to our boots. I had executed these skills many times, memorizing the stitching on my boot that needed to line up with the ladder's rung to ensure perfect placement, modifying my ascender to make it easier for my small hands to open and close it. And while I knew this practice exercise was necessary, I was hesitant.

After spending many miles of the trek to base camp together, a teammate named Stuart noticed my reticence while we sat side by side in the snow lacing our crampons. He was tall, lanky, like a mountaineer, with a fair complexion and a strong jaw. Two weeks ago, when I'd met Stuart in Kathmandu, I could tell by the methodical way he folded his restaurant napkin and by his wrinkle-free shirts that he was meticulous and organized, two traits I appreciated in a climbing partner. There was nothing more maddening than sharing a tent with someone who was constantly searching for a misplaced glove.

"Never pass up an opportunity to build mental toughness, Lisa," Stuart said, and jabbed me in the shoulder. Stuart would know about mental toughness. He'd run ultramarathons in the Sahara Desert, and if he summited Everest, he would be one of a handful of Canadians to have topped the highest mountain on each continent.

"You're right, I know," I told him, even though I had done my best to simulate Everest's technical challenges by suspending myself in a backyard tree and walking on an elevated aluminum ladder in my dark garage. "This is as close as I'll get to practicing climbing Mount Everest," I told him, and finished passing the flat strap of my crampon through its buckle and confirming its security with a sharp yank. "It's just, you know, the judging." I knew I had signed up for this, and I knew I could execute all of the skills Garrett was assessing. But the scrutiny made me self-conscious. And sometimes when I was self-conscious, my brain stopped working. Once, traveling to the Netherlands, a very serious-looking immigration agent asked me if I was traveling alone. And I, hyperfocused on producing the right answer, said *no*. He looked over my shoulder with a raised eyebrow before I caught my mistake.

"Eh, make it a game," Stuart said. "We should be able to get some great photos, too." He stood, adjusted his helmet, and stomped his crampon points in the hard snow.

I moved on to checking my harness, starting with its square metal buckle, ensuring that the webbing that formed a belt around my waist was threaded through the metal plates, folded, and then threaded through a second time from the other direction. This "double backing" would prevent the webbing from slipping through the plates and off my waist if I fell. Next, I surveyed my ascender, the handheld cam-driven device that I would tie with a cord to my harness and use to attach myself to the anchor ropes that were "fixed" to the mountain above base camp. Once I'd double-checked my gear and asked a teammate to check mine as well, I followed the rest of the team through the requisite obstacle course at the edge of the Khumbu Icefall. I slid my ascender up the climbing rope and simultaneously kicked the steel front points of my crampons into dense, steep ice. I passed my ascender and safety carabiner through snow pickets and rigged my rappel device so that I could slowly lower myself back down the steep ice face. The movement of my body in alpine terrain was just starting to shed the mental awkwardness of insecurity when I decided to rappel off the back side of an ice cliff next to the obstacle course. It wasn't that high, and it was rigged for rappelling, but I misjudged the distance to the ground and slid ten vertical feet, landing—*hard*—on the ice, flat on my butt. I immediately jumped to my feet, quick to erase the mistake, and felt pain shoot through my butt.

"You OK down there?" Garrett asked from atop the cliff I'd just rappelled.

"Yep, be back up in a second," I said, then grunted.

Fuck! I said to myself, still not understanding the cause of the pain. *Don't do that again.*

Back at camp, I slurped two Tylenol and snuck off to the Everest ER tent at the opposite end of camp, where a very embarrassed Nepali

doctor clumsily examined me and confirmed that I had likely fractured my tailbone.

"Just don't tell anyone," I said, more to myself than to him, as I
thanked him and left the tent.

After more than two weeks together, affinities were beginning to form
within the team. I was grateful to be a part of a smaller group that
generally performed well. Knowing that these men had my back eased
some stress, and it freed up enough mental energy for me to focus on
taking care of myself and building my confidence. My strength felt
tenuous, though. The part of my brain grasping for confidence was just
waiting for one bad day, and I struggled not to let a fractured tailbone
initiate a deluge of failures or create doubt about my strength among
the team.

Affinities aside, or maybe because of them, I was having a hard
time finding my persona as a woman. It had been my experience that
women on climbing expeditions were stuck on a predictable track: you
were an incapable outsider, you were hit on, you outperformed one of
the men or stood up for yourself (sometimes during step 2), then you
were a bitchy outsider. I'd learned this cycle the difficult way and now
generally defaulted to acting like one of the guys. This meant joining
in on the vulgarity and profanity to obfuscate the fact that I was the
only one with boobs. I'd become so clever at this duplicity that men
on other climbing trips had completely undressed in front of me without the slightest outward appearance of bashfulness. For the first time,
pretending felt insincere. I was tired of stepping into the dining tent
to a huddle of men ogling what I could only imagine were provoca-
tive photos of someone's Tinder date. I didn't want to know how many
women someone planned to bang during their layover in Amsterdam
after this climb. I didn't care to pass their cell phone across the dining table so they could impress teammates with a photo of their ex-
girlfriend posing in only a down jacket. I found it degrading, insulting,
and inconsiderate. Yet, just like when the man had insulted me by
calling me *kiddo* during a board meeting, I played along. I passed the
phone. I laughed at vulgar jokes. I ignored the woman screaming inside of me who knew it was wrong. Because I did not know how to

express my offense as a woman—for women—without appearing vulnerable. In my mind, there was no space between femininity and vulnerability. If they'd asked me what they could do differently, how they could be more inclusive and considerate, I'm not sure how I would have responded. "Stop being assholes!" would have likely blurted from my mouth. My feelings hadn't been clear then. They'd felt like a disorienting mix of acceptance of their behavior and nonchalance. I'd wanted to be seen, but I hadn't wanted to stand out. I'd wanted these men to have my back, but I didn't want the expectations to be different for me; I didn't want the load to be lighter. I'd wanted to be accepted and included but not disrespected. Unable to untangle the mess of emotions, I withdrew to my only coping mechanism: hard work. I resolved to climb hard, to climb perfectly—without vulnerability.

After nearly a week of organizing and practicing skills at base camp, it was time to begin our first rotation onto the mountain. On the south side of Mount Everest, this meant climbing through the notorious Khumbu Icefall. I'd been staring at the icefall from base camp and had watched the slow movement of other climbers snaking through it one afternoon. This giant jumble of ice blocks slowly slides down the side of Everest and can shift as much as ten feet per day. To inject some safety into climbing through the icefall, climbers generally move at night, when temperatures are lower and the ice blocks are more stable.

I was standing on the flat rocks outside of the dining tent, waiting for the rest of my teammates to make their final preparations and adjustments before climbing into the icefall for the first time. It was two thirty in the morning, and there was a spread of stars in the April sky like I'd never seen before. Tiny, twinkling specks of light saturated the vast, inky blackness with such randomness and clarity that it felt artificial.

"Incredible, huh?" Andrew, our base-camp manager, said as he stepped next to me with a steaming metal cup of coffee in his hand.

"So incredible. I never imagined the sky could look like that. It's like constellations are stacked on top of constellations."

In addition to looking after camp operations, Andrew Tierney joined the team to record our climb with an array of GoPro cameras that would eventually turn into an Emmy-winning virtual-reality documentary. His infectious giggle and easygoing demeanor made him easy to like, and I appreciated having someone to talk to who wasn't overwhelmed by the task of standing on the summit of Everest.

"Stay safe up there, 'K?" he said while we were still looking up at the stars.

"Yep."

Climbing through the icefall was like meandering through a giant bowl of misshapen ice cubes—ice cubes the size of apartment buildings that were constantly moving and shaking. Even though it was the middle of the night, I heard the frequent groan of ice blocks shifting against one another and the persistent crack of ice breaking and collapsing. I felt the dark, stale air escaping from the depths of crevasses. Slowly, daylight illuminated the ice, and I began to realize the tallest blocks were more than a hundred feet above me. I felt like I was inside of Mount Everest, and I was wholly insignificant.

At dawn, near the middle of the icefall, one crack was louder than the rest and was accompanied by a thunderous *thwaaack*. I felt the ice shift under my boots. I'd never been in an icefall before, but I knew it was serious. I didn't have a plan, though; ice collapse hadn't been on my list of things to plan for. So I screamed, grabbed the closest person, Phurba Rider Bhote, and waited to be swallowed by Mount Everest. Phurba Bhote, who was fifty-nine years old, had summited Everest nine times and refused to clip the leg loops of his harness. He started to mumble a Buddhist prayer and grabbed the prayer beads around his neck. He seemed to think this was serious, too. I thought about a cross-stitched message in my backpack, a memento from my aunt. *Be Careful*, it said in lavender thread. Huddled together, we waited, tiny specks in a mass of ice chunks, and listened. When nothing else shifted or growled at us, we forced deep breaths and continued climbing.

Three hours after leaving base camp, day broke, and Phurba Bhote climbed ahead of me, satisfied I could navigate the rest of the icefall on my own. I found it eerily peaceful to be alone on the side of Mount Everest.

Near the icefall's terminus, I encountered a man struggling to climb up a ten-foot cube of vertical ice. He repeatedly slid his ascender up the rope, expecting it to grab, and each time it slid smoothly back down. From where I stood on the floor of the icefall, I could tell that ice from the rope had accumulated on the metal teeth of his ascender, making them ineffective at gripping the rope and providing enough support to stop him if he slipped on the vertical ice. In frustration, he let go of the handle, and I watched as he reattached the ascender and then saw it fall off the rope and dangle from his harness.

"What the fuck?" he said. "This ascender's shit."

Watching him struggle was excruciating, and though this was my first icefall, I knew better than to stop in the middle of it.

"It's just iced over," I yelled up at him. "If you whack it on your axe, the ice should clear."

He shot me a cold look and continued futilely sliding the ascender upward. Another climber joined me at the bottom of the ice block and shouted, "Hey, mate, you got ice in your jumar."

"Thanks!" the man yelled back, and he hit the ascender hard with his palm and climbed upward.

The man standing next to me looked up and shook his head. "Too bad the only key to entry is a bank account." I agreed with him, thinking that you shouldn't be here without experience. But being ignored by the climber still stung.

Terrifying ice collapses notwithstanding, I found the process of climbing through the icefall invigorating. I would not recommend it as a tourist destination, but I enjoyed the challenge of testing my body and skills by ascending and descending unpredictable, house-sized blocks of ice. It felt rewarding to assess the texture of ice and to identify the chunks solid enough to support the tips of my crampons' steep points. And it felt affirming to test my mind by crossing the aluminum ladders that straddled the black depths of crevasses. Even though the route was laid out for me, it felt good to solve the puzzle of safely moving my body through Mount Everest's giant maze of ice. Ascending the icefall gave my confidence a boost—small, but enough to feel like I was on equal ground with the guys. And it was rewarding five and a half hours later to ascend the final rickety ladder leading to sunlight and the flat expanse of the Western Cwm. Cwm, pronounced *koom*, is the Welsh word for "valley," a name aptly given by George Mallory to this glaciated stretch, sandwiched between the slopes of Nuptse and Everest's west shoulder.

That afternoon, I lounged uncomfortably in a shared tent at 20,000 feet, contemplating how I had spent as much time feeling overheated in the mountains as I had feeling cold, and that even as a kid I'd preferred Illinois's frigid windy winters to its stifling humid summers.

There was no escaping the heat that day, on Everest's infamous oven.

"Holy hell it's hot in here, Lisa," my teammate said.

"I know. Ninety-two according to my watch."

"I'm gonna strip down a bit if you don't mind, Lisa."

"Sure, go ahead," I told him. "If you hand me your sleeping bag, I'll throw it on top of the tent with mine, and maybe the shade will cool things off in here."

I slid out of the tent in my thin boot liners, tank top, and climbing pants. Cool air radiating from the glacier was a temporary relief, and I straightened my back to inhale the mountain air while savoring the rare feeling of sun on my bare skin. *This is what you came for,* I thought, *to feel this close to the wildness of nature.*

I spotted a teammate taking his final steps into camp, searching for an available tent.

"Oh, wow. Good to see you made it up here, Lisa. Good for you ladies," he said.

I knew this was his attempt at a compliment, but the inference to me was that he hadn't thought I could make it to Camp 1—that he hadn't thought a girl could make it to Camp 1.

"*Thanksss,*" I said, hoping he deciphered the edge in my voice, and I pointed to an open tent.

Though his words infuriated me, I didn't tell him what was boiling inside my brain, which was that I didn't want to be good for a *girl.* I want to be *good.* And even though my superpower was to downplay my ability, I didn't want the expectations to be lower. This was one of the things that drew me to mountains, I realized. They are equalizers. They don't care about gender or fortune. We were all taking the same test, and mountains don't grade on curves.

I crawled back inside the tent with a tightness in my chest and a quickened pulse. The heat inside was stifling, and I wanted to strip down to my underwear like my teammate but felt self-conscious. Not because I was uncomfortable with my body, but because lounging in my underwear with a man usually wasn't something I did casually. And now, I hated every man in the universe for being able to lounge casually in their underwear.

You're wasting energy on stress, I told myself. I finally took my pants off and threw them into a pile in the corner of the tent. Thankfully, my tentmate didn't seem to notice, and I liked men slightly more.

Weeks later, after the expedition, in a taxi in Kathmandu, my tent-mate's face would be close to mine, expectant, when I turned to face him.

"I'm sorry. I just . . . you know. I think of you as a brother," I told him, refusing his kiss.

"But I thought . . . because in the tent at Camp 1 . . ."

"I'm sorry," I said again, not sure what I was sorry for.

Over the next two weeks, we'd climb through the icefall and beyond, all the way to Camp 3, each time forcing our bodies to acclimatize to higher and higher elevations. Each time through the icefall was different. Each time the monstrous ice blocks had shifted, becoming more tangled, crumpling more aluminum ladders and anything else they desired. Climbing through the icefall, the most dangerous part of Everest's South Col route, six times was risky, but it was still far fewer trips than most Sherpas make, who climb through it repeatedly to carry provisions to higher camps for climbers like me. In recent years, expeditions like Garrett's had begun to helicopter gear and oxygen above the icefall to improve safety for the Sherpas on their teams.

By the time our summit rotation began, twenty days later, doubt and illness had reduced our team from nine to seven. Like those of my remaining teammates, my body and mind had slowly acclimated to the stress and intensity of living more than four miles above sea level. My resting oxygen saturation had increased from the low 80 percent range to almost 90 percent, a reading that would have rendered me hospitalized in an intensive-care unit if I weren't on Mount Everest. I had also—thanks to thoughtful gifts from base-camp trekkers—found a hospital-grade, no-rinse shampoo that finally solved my greasy-hair problem. But I was still working on moving quickly with a heavy pack. As a team, though, we were moving faster through the now familiar sections of the route. And my mind was accustomed to focusing only on thoughts essential for my safety, like consuming enough calories and making smart decisions on the sketchiest sections of the route. It was a marvelous thing that my mind could adapt in this way, and when I lay in my tent and reflected on a challenging day of climbing, I realized that there were many moments where I had been in the flow and hadn't needed an explicit plan to jump over a crevasse or to find purchase for my crampons on steep ice. During these moments, I was deeply present. *You are doing this,* I told myself. *You are fucking climbing Mount Everest.* I now realize there was just a glimmer of confidence in that thought—that I was starting to accept the notion that I was stronger than I had let myself believe.

I hadn't grown up believing I was strong—physically or mentally. I don't think many girls raised in the middle of the US in the 1980s grew up believing such a thing, either. Though I secretly aspired to be strong, there were times, when it counted, that I felt inadequate. In high school, the best summer job, as far as I was concerned, was lifeguarding at the local pool. It was fully staffed by high school students; we mostly walked around the pool, checked season passes, and blew our whistles at kids who forgot the no-running rule. During one of my shifts at the deep end of the pool, a man dove off the high board into twelve feet of water and didn't resurface. From my chair, I could see his body curled on the blue concrete bottom. I blew my whistle in the prescribed cadence, dove down to the bottom, and tugged at his limp arms until my breath drained, but I couldn't move him. I surfaced and clung to the gutter of the pool, panting and useless while the other lifeguards brought him up and revived him. There would have been no way, I now know, that my seventeen-year-old body, ninety pounds of nonmuscle, could have carried him through twelve feet of water to the surface (I think they teach you that in lifeguard class), but I'd never forgotten the useless, weak feeling I felt that afternoon, watching my teammates succeed where I'd fallen short.

. . .

As I sat in my base-camp tent and readied myself and my gear to attempt to climb to the top of the world's highest mountain, I sifted through a stack of cards and letters from friends. The glittery images and bright patterns seemed foreign now, and their words and encouragement released emotion that I'd been intentionally suppressing. I came to the pink butterfly-embellished index card I'd written to myself, an assignment from my sports psychologist:

- I am strong.
- I beat cancer.
- I have always been successful.
- Challenges are designed to move me forward.
- *This is who I am*.

I mentally pocketed the affirmations on this card, adding them to the trepidation and fear that I already held in my heart, and hoped that strength would win out when I needed it to.

At 2:00 a.m. the next day, thirty-three days after arriving at base camp, our team of seven climbers plus four guides and seven Sherpas began our summit rotation.

The moment my fledgling belief that I could summit sank the lowest occurred on the flattest part of the southern route, the Western Cwm. *This is just a casual walk at 20,000 feet,* I told myself when I cleared the final ice wall before the cwm's flat valley. *You've been here before. Just a few hills to climb over and a casual walk on a glacier. You've been here before.* But the combination of heat bearing down on me that day and 50 percent less oxygen than at sea level prevented my legs from carrying me forward, even on relatively flat terrain. I focused on the men ahead of me and willed the gap between us not to spread, but I was panting and sweating like a fool, and doing more harm to my body by pushing it than by slowing to a manageable pace.

Just take care of yourself, LT; it doesn't matter who gets to camp first. My brain was in a thick oxygen-deprived fog.

Did you zip your pocket closed after you took a cough drop out of it?

I couldn't remember and reached down to confirm. Nope. Wide open. *Did you eat the cough drop? Where is it? You should pull your buff over your ears so they don't sunburn. They feel hot. You should cover them, but the effort seems Sisyphean. Just a few more steps and you'll do it. Focus on the climbers on the glacier ahead of you; don't let them out of your sight. Then cover your ears. Think about the steps you'll take to do it. Lift the buff from around your neck, up and over your head. Take your sunglasses off first. Then stretch the buff over your ears. Don't drop the sunglasses, and be sure the buff covers your ears. Did you eat the cough drop? You should be eating more.*

Eventually, I paused my ego and sat in the snow. I could see the rocky rib of camp ahead of me but knew I had to walk at least an hour more to get there. Mercifully, a Sherpa walked briskly by and offered me tea. Though I didn't want to drink anything warmer than ice, I accepted. I don't know if it was the sugar, the caffeine, the special yak butter in Sherpa tea, or my restless ego, but something motivated me to get moving again.

"Namaste, bhai," I told him when I stood to continue.

"Strong, *didi*," he reminded me, and continued down the mountain.

As I continued up, I calculated the team's climber-to-tent ratio, determining that I could hopefully occupy the only single tent. *I doubt that the guys are even thinking about it,* I told myself. The luxury of privacy alleviated one small stressor for me, as the only woman on the team: it meant that I could change clothes and pee without burrowing awkwardly into my sleeping bag to hold a plastic funnel to myself and aim its spout hopefully at an open Nalgene bottle. When I arrived at Camp 2, I flung my backpack toward the open tent, marking it, and, in a display of untested confidence, announced that I'd take the single tent. It seemed simple to me, logical.

"Why are you abandoning Stuart like that?" Jeff said as he shoved his hands into the pockets of his down suit. "We're all a team."

I didn't feel like I was abandoning anyone or deserting anything. My sleeping by myself wasn't a sign of disloyalty against our quartet. I just wanted to give myself a baby-wipe bath without worrying about the guy lying next to me seeing my boobs. I just wanted to pee without worrying that I'd accidentally dump a full pee bottle inside my sleeping bag.

I slept alone that night, shivering alone in a three-person tent. The next morning, I did my best to repair whatever team bond I'd fractured. After a team decision in the dining tent during which I explained my rationale, I was admitted back into our team of four. This was the first time on an expedition that I'd stood up for my femininity. I was tired of not being true to myself in order to be accepted in such a male-dominated pursuit. Just like with the guys at the office, I'd intentionally talked like them, joked like them, turned myself into a smaller version of them, and, in the process, paved over the softer side of me. It didn't fit anymore. It was time—time to stand in my authenticity, even if that meant standing alone.

The strain within my little team of four hung around for a few days, as high winds on the mountain pinned us at Camp 2. Though we had timed our summit rotation to match the best weather window, climbing Everest doesn't come with guarantees, even when decisions are meticulously backed by science. The winds above us rendered the mountain unclimbable for the next five days. Each morning, I'd wake, stare at the glistening blue ice of the Lhotse Face, and wonder if I'd have another chance to climb it. And each day, the winds refused to relent, and our potential summit day became more elusive.

On the fourth day, I sat in the sparse dining tent next to Jeff. His knit cap was pulled down over most of his forehead.

"Think we'll ever go up?" I asked, moisture from my breath rising to steam in the frigid tent.

"It's now or never," he confirmed with a sigh. "No way we'll hang here another day. Other teams are already callin' it."

The emotional pull of will-we-won't-we-climb had worn even Jeff down. His normal practical jokes and sarcasm had been supplanted by hyperfocus on the summit. Like he only had room in his brain now for exertions that would lead him to the summit.

I looked around the dining table at all of us burrowed into down suits and slumped over steaming plates of stewed chicken and rice, the same as the night before, and the night before that. I was grateful for the warm meal and the effort to prepare it, but what I wouldn't have given for a vegetable—*any* vegetable.

"*Well*, team." Garrett interrupted my melancholy and slowly rose from his folding chair to stand at the end of the dining table. The dim light in the tent made his eyes appear blacker to me, the effects of living at 21,500 feet showing on his face, too. Like the rest of us, he was no longer clean-shaven or kempt. "Things are looking better up high, team. Winds continue to drop until the twentieth. I think we have a chance to stand on top if we leave in the morning."

The next morning was a beautiful day for climbing. The winds were low on the steep Lhotse Face, and I was able to fall into a rhythm of breathing methodically and moving smoothly with my team. Unfortunately, though, we were climbing toward the wind, and when we arrived at Camp 3 in the afternoon, winds were so strong that movement outside of the tent, on the steep ice, required a tether. I lay in the tent with Billy Nugent and Brent Bishop, two guides from Seattle.

I turned toward Brent. "Think we'll summit?"

He lowered his oxygen mask to speak. "I don't know, winds seem pretty high up there."

I rolled toward the tent wall and realized the tent floor below me wasn't supported by the mountain, since it was cantilevered over its slope. The Lhotse Face is so steep and the ice so dense that tent platforms are created with pickaxes, the sturdy kind used to shatter rock at sea level.

It's going to be a cold night, I thought. I shifted to ease the pressure on my cracked tailbone. I had decided before the summit rotation began that there wasn't any point in toughing it out and had covertly acquired a handful of Tramadol from the team medical kit. My body had enough stress from other sources. Since then, I'd started reminding myself that I was tough every time I felt the twinge of pain in my backside.

A rushed decision to ascend the next morning was welcome, but left Billy, Brent, and me scrambling to shove sleeping bags, food, and gear into our backpacks, all while panting from the lack of oxygen and struggling to consume as much food and drink as possible. Eventually, I was ready and, not seeing the point in waiting any longer, unzipped the tent to peek outside. I saw people moving, but none of the down suits or mannerisms looked familiar. I stepped outside anyway and attached my harness to the fixed line. No point in waiting around at 24,000 feet.

The winds above Camp 3 that day repeatedly blasted me, hitting me with a ferocity I hadn't felt before. Sometimes, the wind caught me midstep and I'd wobble, feebly pulling the rope for stability before falling to my knees in the snow. Each time, I'd recite an affirmation from my pink index card, the ones recommended by my sports psychologist. *I am . . . strong. I am . . . strong.* Then I'd scramble to my feet and continue ascending. Eventually, I learned to recognize the haunting howl of wind moving toward me, and each time I'd lie facedown on the ice and let it blow by. I knew the terrain would ease when I ascended the Lhotse Face and reached a relatively flat section of the route that curled toward a yellowish-brown stripe of limestone at 25,000 feet called the Yellow Band. But when I reached the flat section, it didn't feel easier. I stood in the snow, mesmerized by a glove tumbling down the mountain beside me, into oblivion.

Get it together, I told myself.

Garrett climbed toward me from below. I told him I was tired and thirsty. He astutely checked the gauge on my oxygen tank, telling me to climb slower.

No! I thought. *I need to climb faster.* I could see a string of climbers ahead of me and willed my foggy mind to focus on catching them.

It wasn't until I reached the bottom of the Yellow Band that the correct sequence of synapses in my brain fired and I realized that I was moving slowly and unable to focus because my oxygen tank was empty. I didn't need to check the tank's pressure gauge to know. Climbing the Yellow Band at sea level would have been easy—fun, even. But on that day, standing at the bottom, looking up at its chunky striations while breathing only 26 percent of the oxygen that my body was used to, I knew that ascending this band might be the hardest thing I'd ever do. When I realized my oxygen tank was depleted, I had a decision to make. I could have sat in the snow and waited for a fresh one to be delivered to me, I could have descended, or I could have continued climbing. It didn't feel good on that day, but looking back, I see that I was beginning to stand in my own confidence. I was beginning to trust what my mind and body could do, and it felt liberating.

Obstacles aren't meant to prevent my success, I reminded myself. For some reason, I left my useless oxygen mask on my face, and I vowed never to let the climber ahead of me out of my sight. I don't know what happened next. I vaguely remember screaming. Screaming like a weightlifter heaving an impossible mass of iron over her head. I do know that I made it to the top of that band without losing sight of Stuart's orange down suit. I'm not sure how long (it felt like hours) it took to climb above the Yellow Band, but I finally spotted Aang Phurba crouched in the snow next to a neat stack of oxygen bottles that he and the Sherpas had cached. I sat in the snow next to him, weak and helpless, while he swapped my oxygen tank. I hated that I lacked the acuity and energy to do it myself. In seconds, I heard the swoosh of oxygen fill my mask and felt the sweet taste of it in my dry mouth. I inhaled deeply and let it flood my lungs. In seconds, my vision brightened and my brain fog cleared.

"Namaste, Phurba bhai," I said.

"Climb on, *didi.*" He nodded upward, and I continued while he waited for the next climber.

The winds and route conditions that day were so difficult that we all arrived at Camp 4 past the scheduled time, and some team members not until after dark. I lay in the tent, sandwiched between Garrett and Stuart, and wondered what would happen next. Outside the winds were high, not threatening to shred the tent, but concerning.

"Are we going tonight?" I asked Garrett.

"No, I think it's better to rest for a day, Lisa," he confirmed.

I lay back with a sigh, relieved of the doubt that I could climb for fifteen additional hours without rest.

Resting at 26,200 feet is a farce. This altitude, known as the "death zone," is the physiological point at which your body is dying more than living. Lacking sufficient oxygen, even if you're breathing bottled gas, your body is shunting blood and oxygen away from less vital organs, like your extremities and stomach, and instead reserving them for your brain, heart, and lungs.

I noticed my whole body shaking, even with my down suit on, and even inside of my minus-40-degree sleeping bag.

"You gotta get those wet clothes off, Lisa," Stuart said, quickly identifying the problem.

This time, I didn't care about modesty, and I stripped down and replaced my wet base layer with a dry version, then redressed in my down suit and buried myself in my sleeping bag. This sounds like a simple task—undressing and redressing. But at 26,200 feet, with a fried mind and cold hands, it likely took me close to an hour.

Eventually, I lay flat on my back, closed my eyes, and visualized the climb to the summit.

"Did you swap your socks, Lisa?" Stuart wanted to know.

"Yep."

"You want a Bounty bar?" Stuart asked.

"Nope, I'm good."

"How about an Ambien?"

"Will it make you be quiet?"

"Most likely."

Though I was mightily annoyed, I still appreciated Stuart looking after me in the world's most inhospitable place.

Early the next morning, Stuart and I would share an oxygen mask when mine became faulty and I awoke to confusion and gasps. When my brain had engaged enough to understand that I'd run out of oxygen again, I'd rolled to my side and reached behind my sleeping bag to check the gauge on my tank. Empty. I couldn't do the math, but I knew it wasn't possible to burn through a full tank overnight at a low flow rate. Something was wrong with my tank. The thought of wiggling out of my sleeping bag, putting my boots on, and wandering from tent to tent in search of a spare oxygen bottle made me even more light-headed.

Stuart just handed me his mask. "You breathe for fifteen minutes, then I will," he said. I don't know a bigger word than *grateful*, but I felt it that morning for Stuart's kindness.

Our rest day at 26,200 feet crept by like a film that's been set at half speed. Climbers able to venture outside of their tents ambled slowly while holding a metal oxygen bottle. I did a perfunctory yoga pose, stumbled to the edge of camp, traded wet wipes for more food (because

I couldn't get enough), and generally marveled at this barren wasteland. All around me were the tattered remains of tents from previous expeditions, stains on the snow from tea and who knew what else, and littered oxygen bottles—debris left behind because it was too dangerous to climb up again just to retrieve it. Before the sun faded below the horizon, I walked to the beginning of the climbing route and looked up at the black rock of Everest's triangular face. I traced the crooked line of the route above me, the steps I would take.

"Namaste," I said, and dipped my head.

CHAPTER 11

29,032 FEET

Are you ready to climb to the top of the world today?" Garrett asked, lying next to me in the tent, flicking on his headlamp.

I'd never thought someone would sincerely ask me that question. Never. Not climbing the trees in my childhood backyard, not struggling to make good grades in college, not grappling to unearth my femininity in my twenties, not even while fighting cancer.

I couldn't respond to Garrett; he likely thought I hadn't heard him or was too engrossed in organizing myself to notice his question. But I heard him. The tears welled in my eyes so abruptly that they drowned the words.

I was ready. I knew I was. I knew that all the challenges of cancer and the heartache of divorce and clawing my way out of childhood had led me to this exact moment. And I knew that I had everything I needed to be successful. I wasn't scared or unsure. I was ready, and I knew.

I left camp at 9:30 p.m. and climbed all night, fully enveloped by the darkness above 26,000 feet. I marveled at constellations so bright I believed I could reach up and touch them. Above me, I watched a ribbon of light from other climbers' headlamps slowly ascend. *That's where I'm goin'*, I told the stars. I felt in perfect harmony with Mount Everest, like we were working together to achieve a common goal. And I could not get the song "The Yellow Rose of Texas" out of my head.

At seven in the morning, I looked up and saw the bright colors of prayer flags, and I knew that I was looking at the top of the world. I just put my head down and kept climbing along the narrow, rocky ridge that led to the summit.

And soon, there was nowhere else to climb.

I sat in the snow next to a pile of prayer flags that flapped slowly in the wind. I didn't celebrate. I changed my oxygen bottle, and I asked Stuart to take a photo of me.

Then I walked to the opposite edge of the summit and knelt. The sky was clear and bright blue, and in the distance were scattered high clouds. To my right, a vision that I want in my mind forever: the vast Tibetan plateau expanding beneath me, flattening from this highest point on Earth to verdant valleys hundreds of miles away. I want to re-member the prayer flags marking the true summit behind me and the way ice crystals floated in the air in perfect balance. I want to remem-ber the way the sun made them shimmer like jewels. I let the sounds of other climbers achieving their dream fade and focused on my final task. *Thank you, Mount Everest, Goddess Mother of the World.* Then I took a moment to send gratitude to everyone who'd gotten me to this point: Dr. Lee, Dr. Welk, Dad, Scott, my bank, the woman who'd hugged me on the hiking trail months ago and said, "You got this, girl." And, finally, me. Then I stood up and began the descent.

That moment of gratitude was all that I allowed myself. I have a no-celebrating-on-the-summit rule. Any mountaineer will tell you that the summit is only halfway. I still had nearly 8,000 feet of snow, rock, and ice to descend to reach Camp 2 before my work that day was complete.

Phurba Bhote joined me, and I was soon grateful for his guidance and experience on the tenuous summit ridge. Thanks to fatigue and the downward posture of facing away from the mountain, most climbing accidents occur during descent, a fact that is reinforced by the view: to the left of me on the ridge was an 11,000-foot drop to Tibet, and to my right an 8,000-foot slope that led precipitously back to base camp in Nepal. Descending the rock and loose snow on the summit ridge while wearing crampons and managing the fatigue of climbing for the past ten hours would be difficult enough, but in modern times, it has become complicated by traffic jams. In a few places along the route on the south side of Mount Everest, there is space for two fixed ropes, one meant for descending climbers and one for those climbing up. The summit ridge is not one of those places; it is harrowing two-way traffic on a one-way road. Climbers have two choices in this predicament: wait for traffic to clear, or unclip, pass the climber moving in the opposite direction, reclip into the safety rope, and continue descending.

I stood near the top of the ridge and saw the route below me packed with the bright colors of down suits. I looked at Phurba Bhote, though he couldn't see the question behind my ski goggles.

"Better luck moving," he said, understanding my quandary, and continued down the mountain.

Gripped with fear, I stood near the point where compact snow, the kind crampon points easily pierce, transitioned to rocks, the kind crampon points easily slide across. I needed a plan before I continued. This scenario also hadn't been included on my list of potential problems to solve. Logically, I wanted to wait for a break in oncoming climbers so that I could descend without the challenge of passing them, but I knew in my heart that waiting was futile. I'd burn precious oxygen; plus, my body temperature would drop dramatically if I stood around at 29,000 feet.

As Phurba Bhote said, descending while passing oncoming climbers seemed like the better of my two horrifying options. So I eyed Phurba Bhote's yellow down suit on the shaded part of the narrow ridge below me and marched toward him. The first ascending climber that I met didn't—probably couldn't—acknowledge me standing next to him. I intended to explain somehow that I was going to pass him, but when I waved my gloved hands in front of his goggles, his position didn't change. He appeared to be too caught up in his own struggles to notice me and mine. I'd have to do this without his cooperation. I reached down to the rope between us—the one fixed to the mountain—and unclipped my safety carabiner from it in one twisting motion, just like I'd practiced in the muddy park at home. Then I reached around his bulky body to the segment of that same rope behind him and flicked the carabiner onto it in one motion. I wanted to lock the carabiner's gate to be extra certain I'd be protected in a fall, but given my position, straddling this unresponsive man, I couldn't. *Don't move. Don't move. Don't move.* I repeated this in my mind, hoping my plea would somehow awaken him. At this point, if he took a step in any direction, or even twisted his body, he'd likely knock me off-balance. I had two pieces of gear connected to the fixed rope, so I wasn't worried about free-falling off the mountain, but I was worried about causing a commotion big enough to entangle other climbers and stress the anchors locking the rope to the mountain beyond their limits. Mercifully, he didn't move, and I took half a step backward without looking behind me, then transitioned my ascender from the segment of rope in front of him to the one behind him. My safety carabiner and ascender were now side by side on the fixed rope. He could move upward, and I could continue down.

I repeated this delicate sequence a dozen times or more on the summit ridge that morning. When my wingspan wasn't sufficient to reach around other climbers, I gripped their backpacks. And when the queue of ascending climbers was thick, I squeezed my gloved hand between their bodies to capture the rope with my carabiner.

My training in flawless execution had come, for me, at a young age. When I was a kid, perfection was often expected. More specifically, presenting myself as perfect was expected. The more chaotic things were at home, the more important perfection became. In a small Midwestern town, church was the grandest stage to demonstrate that perfection. I never felt settled inside a church, including the two-story brick one with a basement that smelled like glue, which I'd attended with my parents as a kid, nor the ones I'd visited with my conventual great-aunts, nor the one I visited in high school, with tall glass windows and deep-purple walls where I enjoyed the informal deference accorded to the preacher's kid's best friend. I had been welcome in all these places, by all of these denominations, but the rationale for my attendance never clicked with me. During dull Sunday-morning sermons at the brick church, I'd sit next to Dad in the long wooden pew and pass the time by drawing 3D boxes with stumpy pencils on the back of the offering envelope, the kind of 3D boxes constructed by drawing two offset squares and connecting their corners with four straight lines. Dad's always looked neater than mine.

Though I didn't understand the necessity of attending church twice per week, it was clear to me that we were required to go. All of us, as a family. Our membership in the church was legitimized by our family's photo in the church directory. This yearly black-and-white publication was printed on thick, glossy pages joined together with staples.

On one church-picture day in the 1980s, I sensed the import of our family's photo and, in preparation, carefully removed the yellow-and-white dress from my closet, the one that matched my sister's exactly except for the collar. I dressed myself quietly, complete with white lace tights. Afterward, I twirled in the mirror on the back of my closet door and then presented myself to my mom in the downstairs laundry room.

"Come with me," she said, and marched me back upstairs to the bathroom.

The problem was that I hadn't tied the yellow satin bow at my waist correctly. I'd left the loops lopsided and sagging at their ends.

Her frown drained the hopefulness from my face, and I watched her reflection in the mirror as her thick fingers, tipped with perfectly rounded nails, pulled my bow apart.

She crouched before me. "Pay attention to this."

Her fingers moved in smooth arcs and circles and produced a symmetrical bow at my waist. Then she pulled it apart with a sigh and yellow satin ribbons fell to my sides. She repositioned me closer to her, and again rings of yellow ribbon flowed and bent into a bow worthy of a church photograph.

I studied her quietly, hoping studiousness would make up for inadequacy, as her hands twisted the knot backward and fluffed the ribbons into perfectly sized loops at my belly.

"There," she said without satisfaction. "Now, your hair's a mess."

The church-directory photo turned out just as Mom had orchestrated—Sara and me in matching dresses, glossy smiles and flawlessly curled hair declaring that our family belonged, that we were wholesome, that we were committed to each other and to the church. The story that the photograph couldn't tell was the strain of striving for something that was perpetually out of reach.

Though I'd tried for decades to chip away at the stone of perfection, I appreciated now that I could draw on it when I needed to—in the mountains, when it is mandatory.

The confidence of summiting Mount Everest stayed with me for the rest of the descent that day and the next. It fueled me to descend alone when another climber needed Phurba Bhote's help. It pushed me to descend the rocky, near-vertical Geneva Spur below Camp 4 via arm wrap instead of rappel. Though faster, arm wrapping forgoes some of the safety of rappelling, as it involves wrapping the fixed rope around a climber's arm, leaning forward to create tension, and walking face-first down a slope.

I felt strong. I felt strong in nature—with nature. I didn't feel like I'd defeated or conquered anything, but instead like I'd respected Everest, had come prepared, and had worked collaboratively with the mountain.

The pressure of needing to prove myself hadn't allowed space for understanding my motivations at the time, but when I'd gone to Everest—when I'd gone to the mountains—I'd needed to dissolve the fog of guilt for failing at marriage, rebuild myself after the helplessness of cancer, and unburden myself from loads of hidden childhood anguish.

When I was younger and hiding in my closet wouldn't protect me from screaming parents, I'd climb the tallest pine tree in my backyard—the one rising above the garage's flat roof—hand over hand, ignoring the scrape of rough bark, until I reached the spot where I could see miles of lush cornfields. The humid wind tousled the sword-shaped leaves into patterns and waves that I believed must be what the ocean looked like. In that spot, I'd press my back against the pine's trunk and stretch my skinny legs onto parallel branches. I'd plan my escape from the chaos in my home. In that tree, eight-year-old Lisa vowed to leave that tiny farming community, deciding to go to college and not look back. And she convinced herself she couldn't be any better at raising children than her parents. I'd needed the clarity of nature then, as a young girl, just like I needed it in my forties. That was the first time I'd felt held by nature, and it rinsed away the confusion and uncertainty and exposed me to the resolve and confidence that resided deep in my core. I'd needed Mount Everest to remember that resolve and confidence were still there.

Summiting Everest became proof to myself—not to anyone else— that I was still capable and strong, even after divorce and cancer. Summiting Mount Everest taught me that things I'd thought were mutually exclusive could coexist, *should* coexist. I could be both feminine and strong. I could rely on my team for support and also follow my intuition. I realized that challenge and growth are symbiotic. One is only more vibrant with the other. It took climbing to Earth's highest point to gain a glimpse of what life could feel like if I understood when perfection could be my ally and when it might be a barrier against the natural unfolding of my life.

On May 19, 2016, I became the 408th woman to summit Mount Everest. And while that was an accomplishment I would forever be proud of and grateful for, I'd known that morning, standing in the sunshine at 29,032 feet, that I was capable of more.

CHAPTER 12

4,600 FEET

Bolstered by the carefree confidence of an Everest summit, I found that Kathmandu seemed different now—the horn honks crisper, the prayer flags brighter, the monkeys ornerier. The nuances of this chaotic city were clearer to me without the burden of safely summiting Everest. I felt different, too. My shoulders naturally stood higher. I was easily making eye contact and starting conversations with shopkeepers.

That spring evening, the air was thick with smoke from burning trash and pollution from the day's commuters. But I wasn't worried about the smoggy air damaging my lungs anymore, nor was I as picky about the cleanliness of the rooftop restaurant. I wouldn't worry about twisting an ankle on the cobbled streets when I walked back to the hotel that night. Those things no longer threatened to ruin months of planning and borrowed dollars spent.

"What'd your fam say about your summit?" Jeff wanted to know while we waited for our entrées to arrive.

I shrugged and took a drink of tart white wine. It wasn't very good, but I didn't care, not feeling picky about wine right now, either.

"I emailed my aunt and uncle. They're excited. Mostly glad I'm safe, though."

"What about your parents, though?"

"I emailed my sister. She'll let them know."

He smirked. "You're not very close, are ya?"

I knew what was behind Jeff's words, and it stung. It also burst my post-summit bliss bubble. He was devoted to his family, and proving what was possible to them was part of why climbing Everest was important to him.

Jeff was right; my family's closeness took the form of texts on birthdays and unsentimental Christmas gifts like soap and tea.

"How much do you talk to your sister?" he wanted to know.

"I don't know? Occasionally?" I shifted in the plastic chair and took another sip of wine without looking at him. "How often do you talk to *yours*?"

"Every day," he said, ending our competition with a victory.

I didn't have a big family, and we'd never been talk-every-day close, but I knew I could do better, especially with Sara. She and I had always been different. As kids, I'd preferred the solitude of books, and she'd preferred toy dump trucks. I'd envied her thick, curly hair; she'd wished hers would behave like my thin blond strands. As we aged, the differences had grown bigger, and she'd focused on children and then grandchildren. My days had revolved around building a corporate career and near-constant training for mountaineering.

As a kid, I'd resented having a younger sister so different from me and had devised sneaky tricks to hurt her. When I was six or seven, I'd calculated that if I removed all the nuts from the swivel on the bottom of her green vinyl dining chair, she'd fall. I stashed the nuts in my white crocheted purse and slunk back to our room, waiting for the call to dinner and the final execution of my cunning plan—which went off exactly as calculated, except for the part where I was spanked and then told to put the chair back together.

Though we had always been different, I couldn't let the guilt of not trying harder to have a relationship with Sara continue to haunt me, so I devised a plan.

"Heeey!" I said the next morning to a teammate, trying to hide my motive for approaching his breakfast table in the hotel's vast, sunny restaurant.

"Morning, Lisa. Wanna join me?"

"No, I'm good. I ate earlier, but . . . could I possibly use your phone to make a call to the US?"

"Yeah, of course."

He reached into his pocket and handed me a slender Nepalese cell phone, which reminded me of a burner phone, the kind criminals use on crime dramas to secure their anonymity. I was grateful he'd been savvy enough to buy it when he'd arrived in Kathmandu months ago for easy communication with his family and business colleagues.

"Just get it back to me whenever."

I was giggling as I walked back to my room, knowing Sara would lose her mind when she answered and heard my voice. *But what if she doesn't even answer?* Before calling, I confirmed it was a reasonable time of evening where she lived in Illinois; then I walked around the square corners of my hotel room searching for the best signal. In the flimsy phone, I entered a sequence of digits that I hoped would connect us. The staccato beeps and clicks were unfamiliar, and I wasn't sure if they confirmed success or failure. I evaluated the Nepali man's voice that I heard next. Was he telling me I was successful? Or that I'd dialed wrong?

"Hello?" I heard Sara say.

"Hey!"

"Oh, it's you. Where are you? Are you still on Mount Everest?"

"No, I'm in Kathmandu now."

"Where?"

"Kathmandu."

"Oh."

The phone cut out and I heard a scramble of words that included *you* and *home*.

"I'm flying to Thailand tomorrow for two weeks," I said, hoping to answer her question.

"Where?"

"Thailand."

"Thailand? Is that far from Kathmandu?"

In the forty-one years of my sister's life, she had spent very little time outside of a driving-distance radius around the rural county where we'd grown up. She could tell you which farmers were planting which crops this season and which insects could threaten the bean harvest, but Asian geography was as foreign to her as herbicide was to me.

"Did you talk to Dad?" I asked.

"Who?"

"Dad! Have you talked to him?"

I stood from the sunny windowsill and walked to the opposite corner of the room with my burner phone, stepping over duffel bags and dirty climbing gear. With my free hand, I traced the dark-red wooden scrolls of a Buddha figurine.

"I did."

"What'd he say?"

I wanted her to answer that he'd said he was proud of me and that I was unbelievably strong.

There was a long pause that I assumed was related to a poor connection, but then I heard a shift—a tremble in her voice when she spoke again.

"He's not doin' so good."

"Why?"

"He told me not to tell you."

"Why?"

"I don't know?"

"Can you just tell me? I'm borrowing this phone and need to give it back soon. I don't know when I'll be able to talk to you again."

Sara's relationship with Dad was different from mine. When she'd struggled with alcohol and drug abuse in her teens, their relationship had shifted from a parent-child bond to one of comrades. That they had always confided in each other more than anyone else was a normal part of our family's dynamic.

"He has cancer," Sara said. "Lung cancer. And they think it's in his spine, too. He doesn't want you to worry."

I let out a sarcastic snort and stopped tracing the Buddha's lines with my finger. *Of course he has cancer. You can't smoke cigarettes for*

*twenty years and then downgrade to pipes for twenty more and expect
your lungs to cooperate.*

"Is he OK?"

"What?"

"Is he OK?"

"The doctor says it's stage four."

My heart felt leaden. "What is he doing?"

"He passed out a couple of times, so he went . . ."

"He went where?"

"He went to the VA."

I needed to understand how two months ago my dad seemed fine
and now he was passing out. I wanted to know what his plan was, and
why he wasn't going to the best possible cancer-care hospital, which
surely couldn't be the VA.

"I'm going to let you go so I can call him," I said.

"He doesn't want you to worry."

I lapped back to the sunny perch on the windowsill—even though
the signal was equally terrible in the entire room—and repeated the
complicated dialing sequence on the borrowed cell phone. Same clicks,
same Nepali voice, but this time, instead of excitement, the voice filled
me with dread and nervousness. Our lives could change so quickly,
in unrecoverable instants. I couldn't go back to the space when I'd
thought my dad was healthy. It was gone.

I heard Dad's voice on the answering machine.

"Hi, Dad, it's me!"

I tried to sound cheery and ignorant of the seriousness of his
situation.

"I'm back safely in Kathmandu . . . um . . . so I wanted to just call . . .
to see if you're . . . to see how you're doing. I'll try to give you a call
back . . . um . . . when I can. I love you."

I tried two more times to reach him before my flight to Bangkok.
Each time, I pictured him looking at the antiquated caller-ID display
on his answering machine and then walking away.

Koh Phangan, Thailand, was a peaceful and serene antidote. For an
afternoon, I let myself pretend that my father wasn't dying. I floated

on my back in the ocean and drank fresh smoothies and ate tropical salads. I also inspected my haggard body for the first time. My face was still parched from sun and wind, but the patches of tattered, ruddy skin on my cheeks had faded to dark pink. By comparison, the rest of my body was pallid. My shoulders still appeared rounded and muscular, but my arms had lost their definition. My hips and legs had given the most to the mountain. Jeans hung loose now. The solid bulges of muscle that had defined my quads were gone. My boobs, thanks to modern medicine and Dr. Welk, had not changed. It was all remarkable, I realized, how adaptable the human body was—what it could endure. That evening, I resolved to call Dad one more time, and if he didn't answer, I would consider his wish granted, continue with my travels, and let him fight cancer his own way. I stepped up to the open-air bar that doubled as a concierge desk.

"Hello, madam," said a round-faced Thai man in perfectly formal English. The metal tag pinned to his floral shirt said *Chard.* "How may I be of help to you?"

"I'd like to make a phone call," I said. "To the US."

Chard's eyes widened and his head tilted slightly.

"Oh, madam. It is very, *very* expensive."

I sighed. "Yes, I know."

"*Very* expensive."

I nodded.

"Who, madam, may I ask, please, are you calling?"

"My father. He's sick."

"Oh yes, I see. OK. I am very sorry, madam."

Chard's hesitation raised my anxiety. International dialing had always been a mysterious formula of hidden number sequences, clicks, and disappointing messages in foreign languages. I'd once stuffed twenty euros in coins in an Italian pay phone only to walk away baffled and unsuccessful.

"Madam, I am Chard," Chard said, extending his hand to me. "How may I call you?"

"My name is Lisa."

Chard squeezed both of his warm hands around mine and looked at me intently. I became nervous. I had no idea how I would pull this off without his help, and I realized then that I would only have this one chance to use the house phone.

"Lisa, it is my pleasure to meet you. May I ask your father's name, please?"

"Terry."

Chard released my hand and slid a small notepad and pencil across the wooden bar to me.

"Please," he said, nodding toward the paper.

As I wrote the digits of my dad's phone number, Chard produced a tabletop telephone, the kind my grandmother had in the 1970s. If Dad wouldn't answer my calls from a Nepalese burner phone, he definitely wouldn't respond to a strange Thai voice on the other end.

Night was enveloping the resort's common space. Behind me, men were lounging in hammocks, carelessly strumming guitars, and women in flowy skirts and yoga clothes sat cross-legged on the wooden floor in loose circles. A dog slept amid the big, overstuffed sand-coated pillows that lined the walls. I heard a man talking about how time was an illusion. His soliloquy was broken by crashing ocean waves.

My interior world felt very different from this place. He was not going to answer, I told myself. I would have to decide whether to come home against his wishes, which I was not even supposed to know about, or to continue traveling with a broken heart.

Chard stepped toward me, smiled weakly, and handed me the phone's receiver.

"Lis?"

My dad's voice released an avalanche of emotion that overrode my ability to speak. There were only tears. Real tears. The thrill of summiting Everest and the fear of losing Dad mixed into a cocktail of emotions I couldn't control. Chard discreetly slid paper cocktail napkins and cold glasses of white wine toward me as he walked by to assist other guests. Between tears, Dad downplayed the seizures that had hospitalized him. "They're just episodes." Referring to the masses in his lungs, he said, "They might not be cancer."

"I'll look for a flight home."

"No, Lis. Keep traveling. Don't come home."

I didn't have a response; I couldn't comprehend what he was saying.

"What would you do if you came home? Stare at me?"

"Dad, it doesn't feel right not to be there."

"Lis, lots of people get cancer."

"Yeah, but they're not my dad."

When I stood from the bar, Chard was already in front of me with a plastic bag of food and a hug. I hoped he saw the gratitude in my face, because language eluded me. I melted and sobbed into his humid flowery shirt.

I followed the pebbled path through the jungle to my bungalow. Along the way, it started to rain—soaking, tropical rain. I stood on the hard dirt and let it run over my scalp and shoulders, let it saturate my hair and tank top. Puddles of it moved around my ankles and long rivulets of it ran off the pointed tips of palm fronds. I crumpled to the mud and cried until I couldn't tell the difference between tears and rain.

Fucking cancer.

CHAPTER 13

591 FEET

Two weeks later, Dad led me through the maze of compact rooms in his aged and sagging house in my hometown, and it saddened me that he looked equally as frail. We took a small step down and crossed the threshold between the front room and the guest room, a space so small I could almost touch opposite walls when I stretched my arms across it. Neither of us spoke as we sat on the scratchy green JCPenney bedspread covering the twin mattress against the wall. Between us sat the reason to enter this room together: a flat Roi-Tan cigar box with tattered corners that once housed Dad's childhood rubber-bug collection. When I was a kid, I'd play with the remnants of his collection, each creature rubbery and faded with age, some of them covered in a sticky patina. Today, when Dad picked up the box, his hands shook. I knew what was inside, and I knew he had spent months organizing it, folding bank statements and receipts into shapes that would fit neatly inside a box not meant for file storage. I knew, also, that today the box held scraps of paper with his jittery all-caps handwriting, the scribbles in the margins meant to help manage his meager affairs after he died.

"What's next?" He was making small talk, averting an awkward conversation. My palms were moist because his question lacked a straightforward answer.

It seemed like a simple question. To the overachieving mountaineer on the receiving end, however, it was the same as asking a new mom when she was planning to have another child. I'd summited Mount Everest less than two months ago, and I would have cleverly avoided providing an honest answer to this question on any other occasion. Today, though, I could no longer giggle and change the subject. My dad's lungs, according to a pudgy oncologist at the VA hospital, were mostly tumor. His multiyear persistent cough could no longer be minimized to an asthma symptom. Just like he needed me to know what was inside the Roi-Tan box, I needed him to know the goals I would pursue after his death.

"K2," I said. "It's the second highest mountain in the world." I knew he would assume that shorter equaled easier.

Dad's fingers slid along the rounded edges of the 1970s-era photos in the Roi-Tan box. His hands couldn't hide decades of manual labor, his short fingers hairy and wrinkled, his nail-biting habit creating unique hiding places for dirt. I wanted to let the conversation drop, but I also needed him to know everything. I was not asking for permission; I just needed him to know.

"It hasn't been summited by an American woman."

Now he knew the stakes were higher.

"It's in Pakistan." My voice trailed off.

Except for military service, Dad had spent his whole life in this small, conservative farming community where success was defined on football fields and in taverns, not on mountains in remote countries. I was an anomaly, and Dad was both proud of me and terrified by my accomplishments. When I began climbing, he'd convinced the local radio station to interview me but was unable to induct me into my junior high school's hall of fame. After he and my mom divorced, he'd lived meagerly, as though he'd put so much effort into building a perfect family that, when it fell apart, he could no longer find the interest to try again. His house was in the sketchy part of town, his clothes from the lost and found at the junior college where he was a janitor. He stuffed his pockets full of condiments each time he left McDonald's.

"I thought you were done climbing dangerous mountains." Dad coughed and avoided my eyes by sifting through a stack of canceled checks in the Roi-Tan box on the bedspread. His voice was gravelly and unsteady.

I should have been better prepared for this conversation, because I desperately wanted him to understand why this was important to me. *I* desperately wanted to understand why this was important to me. But I missed the opportunity to build connection between us and instead said, "There's just one more."

The personal reasons for climbing any peak are as varied as its hopeful mountaineers. As my climbing objectives progressed and I knowingly took on more risk, I lost the ability to clearly articulate why. *Why risk my life in a selfish pursuit? Why travel to remote and sometimes dangerous parts of the world? Why sacrifice savings accounts, dinners with friends, going on dates, and nearly everything fun to prepare my mind and body for something that I have no guarantee of accomplishing and that will benefit no one?*

I often pushed these questions to the periphery of my consciousness and instead focused on more tangible challenges, like actually climbing mountains. Or creating spreadsheets to study the cause and location of each death on K2. But attempting K2 felt too monumental to not understand exactly what this mountain meant to me. The notion of proving people wrong was an insufficient reason for attempting one of the world's most dangerous mountains.

As the second highest mountain in the world, K2 is 778 feet shorter than Mount Everest. For that reason, most assume that K2 is easier to climb. In mountaineering, however, elevation is not a gauge of risk or difficulty, and in reality, K2 and Everest are not even in the same league. The first American team to attempt K2 characterized it as "a savage mountain that tries to kill you." It's not just that K2 is in a more remote and unstable part of the world than Mount Everest; it is also steeper, more technical, and deadlier, with five times the death rate.

The sobering history of K2 was part of its attraction for me. I am not a reckless person; I wear my seat belt, I wash vegetables before I eat them, I look both ways two times before I cross the street, and I study mountains thoroughly before I commit to them. So I was acutely familiar with K2's risks because they were what motivated me. The moniker Savage Mountain, the fact that so many women had died, the inherent challenges of high-altitude climbing, and my desire to be vindicated combined into a hazardous cocktail that I couldn't get enough of, and I didn't know why.

My dilemma lay in articulating this, even to fellow mountaineers. Intellectually, I knew there was a fine line between ambition and recklessness, and I feared I was dangerously and irrevocably close to crossing it. But my fear was met with an equally potent will to achieve despite obvious obstacles.

I glanced over at Dad, but he didn't respond to my insufficient explanation. His skin carried the grayness of illness, and it saddened me to remember that he had once been full of defiance himself.

As a young man, he'd joined the military to absolve himself of a catalog of vehicle violations. Once enlisted, he struggled to comply with the rigid rules and schedules of his battalion, particularly those related to grooming. It was the sixties, after all. When reprimanded for hair that was too long, he acquiesced by cutting only the side that the commanding officer would see during the next inspection.

I knew my desire to test boundaries came from him. Now, I realized that he had encouraged me to climb our backyard trees and that he hadn't punished me for punching boys on the playground when they'd teased me. As sure as he was sitting next to me now, I knew this, and I wanted to reach out to him, to touch his weathered hands and thank him. But I was unable to turn this gratitude into words, having perfected the art of keeping it inside.

One Halloween, when I was an adolescent, our family dog, Turtle—the one I'd ridden like a tiny black-and-white horse—limped into the yard wounded. Shot, somehow. Turtle died that night, on the concrete floor of our garage, wrapped in old blankets. After the life drained out of her, I'd returned to the comfort of my closet, confused and sad.

"It's OK to cry, Lis," Dad told me.

"Why *aren't* you crying?" Mom wanted to know.

I think I must have shrugged my bony shoulders and looked away, confused by their concern. Into my double-digit years, I was a bedwetter. At night, to train me to stop, I wore a bulky alarm on my wrist.

It attached to moisture sensors snapped to my underwear. Just a few nights before Turtle died, the alarm had woken me with a jarring screech. I'd collected my shame and waddled across the brown hallway carpet to my parents' bedroom. I don't remember what my mom said in the dimly lit bathroom that night, but I can still see the look on her drowsy face. I still feel the sting of humiliation as I stood there, half naked, red faced, and heaving with tears. Incapable. My parents, the products of Irish, German, and Russian upbringing, expected Sara and me to behave and be quiet. We'd been raised to not inconvenience adults. As a kid, I'd calculated that this included asking questions, desiring things I didn't have, wetting the bed, and showing emotion.

So Sara and I had largely entertained ourselves. On summer days, we rode our Schwinn bikes for hours up the hill by our house, turning around at the tree designated by my parents. We walked just-harvested cornfields collecting cobs to replenish the squirrel feeder in the cottonwood tree. We gathered caterpillars in a red wagon, saving them from certain death on the hot asphalt road.

Being tiny and invisible became my thing. Even as an adult, I would sit in the back of a car, sweating and racked with nausea from motion sickness, apprehensive about asking the driver to switch positions or slow down.

Sitting on the scratchy JCPenney bedspread, I assumed Dad knew how I felt, and I believed that even without the words he realized I loved him deeply, that I'd forgiven his shortcomings as a parent. And, more importantly, that I was grateful for his stubbornness because it had taught me to be resilient—that I could rely on the independence that he'd given me because it made me courageous.

I looked over at him.

"Want a ham sandwich for lunch?" he said.

CHAPTER 14

758 FEET

I spent the next twenty-eight days shuttling back and forth between Illinois and Seattle, wanting to soak up as much time with Dad as possible while honoring his desire to write the last chapter of his life privately.

"He's like an old dog; he wants to die alone," my sister said as we drove away from his house one afternoon. She seemed less frustrated by his request for seclusion than I was. Maybe because she'd had more time with him in the twenty-six years since I'd left my hometown. I didn't regret leaving—I wasn't meant to stay—but now I urgently wanted to fill in the space created by decades apart from Dad. Yet when we were together, we mostly sat in silence or talked about superficial things like the oppressive Illinois humidity or what I'd eaten for lunch. So, for as long as he'd allow, I'd spend a week in Illinois and then a few days away, recharging in the mountains or alternating time with my ex-husband at our forever-for-sale lake house in eastern Washington.

I was at the lake house one morning when the phone rang. Early-morning phone calls are rarely a good thing. Your sister doesn't call to tell you she finally got that promotion, nor does your high school best

Top: Sara and Lisa before a high school dance. Middle: Lisa and the giant purple backpack on her first Rainier attempt in 2008. (Photo: Darrin White.) Bottom: An early climb in the Cascades. (Photo: Darrin White.)

Top: Near Washburn's Thumb on Denali in 2012. (Photo: Darrin White.) Middle: Pre-surgery chin-ups the morning of Lisa's bilateral mastectomy. (Photo: Darrin White.) Bottom: Ascending the north ridge of Mount Baker in 2015. (Photo: Stephen Coney.)

Top: Puja ceremony on Mount Everest, 2016. Bottom: Climbers exit Everest's Khumbu Icefall.

Nearing Camp 1 on Mount Everest. (Photo: Andrew Tierney.)

Everest summit, May 19, 2016. (Photo: Stuart Erskine.)

Top: Klára and Lisa climb above Camp 1 on K2 in 2018. (Photo: Lakpa Bhote Tikepa.) Bottom: Near the top of House's Chimney on K2. (Photo: Lakpa Bhote Tikepa.)

Top: View from Camp 2 on K2. Bottom: Taking the last few steps to the summit of K2. (Photo: Lakpa Bhote Tikepa.)

Top: The summit of K2 with teammate Semba. (Photo: Lakpa Bhote Tikepa.) Bottom: Post-summit selfie taken at Camp 4 on K2. (This is what climbing an 8,000-meter peak looks like!)

friend call to invite you to an overdue lunch, at five in the morning.

I knew when the first cell-phone buzz jarred me from sleep that Dad was dead. Despite my slumberous state, a potent mix of sadness, remorse, and helplessness settled over me. I looked absently through the bedroom window and listened while the details of his death were explained to me. Outside, the July sun was just beginning to creep along the Columbia River, carrying with it the promise of a sweltering summer day. Outside, the river still flowed south, and the hillside dropping to its banks was still dotted with gray prickly sagebrush. How could the outside world not feel this loss and disruption too?

Two weeks prior, Dad had instinctively asked me to stop my trips home to Illinois to visit him.

"You don't need to be here," he'd said.

I hadn't had a good response. I'd been a reluctant silent observer of Dad's battle with cancer. When the battle had been mine to fight, I'd mostly gotten to call the shots, choosing my doctors and how aggressively I'd fight. Now, I had to let Dad define his own path. Even when I knew he'd receive better treatment elsewhere, even when he stopped eating, and even when he didn't want any more visitors. We'd spoken regularly since the visits stopped, and I'd quickly heard the life drain from his voice, realizing he'd gone to that liminal territory between this life and the next.

The afternoon before he died, I'd sat on the deck overlooking the calm flow of the Columbia River and called Dad. After our normal exchange of niceties, with a frail and hoarse voice, he said, "I love you, Lis," before the phone disconnected.

I'd known when I'd flown home from Kathmandu five weeks prior that Dad was dying, so despite having to witness him deteriorate, I'd barely prepared myself emotionally. All the practical decisions were made, and the paperwork finalized. But in the hopes of sidestepping awkward emotional conversations, I'd let myself focus on pragmatic preparations instead of psychological.

For Dad and me, this had been a comfortable habit. On my wedding day, I'd stood in the upstairs room of an old farmhouse, in my wedding dress, and watched the guests assemble in the flowery garden below. Women in flowy dresses and sandals and men in casual suits meandered between the peonies and dahlias and sipped champagne— and I'd felt calm. Behind me, I'd heard the clunk of Dad's steps moving up the wooden stairs. As a janitor and groundskeeper, he never wore fancy shoes and kept one outdated navy suit in the back of his closet for weddings and funerals. Today, though, he was wearing a rented tuxedo, and I could tell by the way his hands moved when he walked into the room that he was searching for something poignant to say. His reticence instigated my own search for the perfect words.

"You look great, Lis," he said, and I smiled. "You know, I mean, I *hope* you know, I've always been proud of ya, kid."

"Of course. I know, Dad."

He looked down and handed me a wallet-sized hand-laminated copy of a poem by Susan Polis Schutz that he'd years ago clipped from *Reader's Digest*. I didn't need to read it. I'd been carrying a worn paper version in my wallet since he'd first handed it to me when I was a teenager.

I am always here
to understand you
I am always here
to laugh with you
I am always here
to cry with you
I am always here
to talk to you
I am always here
to think with you
I am always here
to plan with you
Even though we
might not always
be together
please know that
I am always

here to
love
you

"Thanks, Dad," I said, pressing the tears back into my eyes with a knuckle. I tucked the poem into the silk bodice of my dress. "I love you, too."

"Ready?" Dad said, and held out a bent elbow.

On my wedding day, my emotions had been a blissful mix of gratitude and excitement, generally easy things to express, and yet I couldn't find the words to tell Dad how I felt. When he was sick, my feelings had been even harder to access. I knew I needed to tell him that despite him not always being there for me, I still loved him. I needed to tell him that even though I didn't understand some of the decisions he'd made, I was still proud of the woman he'd helped me become. It hadn't all been bad; there had been happy moments in my early childhood, memories of family bike rides after dinner and summer road trips across flat Midwest highways. But I had to look hard for them, since they were clouded over by my parents' perpetual fighting. It seemed like my parents had been young and happy—or at least curious—to try this family thing out . . . until they weren't. Like in my own marriage, I would never know if the problems came first or the drinking did. The tension and helplessness of those late-night arguments created in me a desire to run when emotions became too intense.

Which they had now, where I was lying alone in bed without even the comfort of a familiar voice from my cell phone. I needed to run, to move, to feel strong and in control. I needed to feel my body move confidently in nature. And I needed to cry in the only place that felt like home to me.

The Enchantments wilderness area in central Washington is one of nature's most magnificent displays of stunning jagged rock and pristine alpine lakes. That morning, I set out on a familiar trail and let the rhythm of my feet pounding on rock and dirt begin to beat away the grief of losing Dad. I ran faster with each mile, until the fir trees were just blurs on the sides of the trail and the pain of pushing my body met the pain of losing Dad and sprang a wave of tears I couldn't suppress. Finally, I stopped at Colchuck Lake and sat on a chunk of polished granite. Separated from the crowds, I stared, still heaving from exertion, across the lake at the familiar alpine peaks. My body wanted to keep running, all the way to the place where Dad was still alive and where I hadn't failed at marriage. And then I wanted to continue even further, to the place where perfectionism wasn't mandatory and parents didn't forget about their children.

I began mourning both of my parents that day, sitting on that cool rock, feeling the warm mountain sun on my bare shoulders. Though my mom was still alive, the rift in our relationship had pulled me to a place where it felt like she was gone, too. So maybe it just seemed simpler, to mourn them both all at once. The pain of grief made it tempting to romanticize my childhood, to gloss over the ugly patches. But to do that would have been to overlook circumstances that made me stronger and more resilient. From Dad, I'd received a smart-ass sense of humor and the tendency to allay awkward situations with it instead of serious conversation. From Mom, I'd inherited an insatiable quest for perfection and the ability to apply that perfection when it mattered—but also when it didn't. From their combined absentee parenting, I'd developed a wicked independence and a pervasive need to prove myself. Grief felt like a confusing, bereft place, simultaneously bound by the dark corners of loss and disappointment and reinforced with bright pathways of gratitude.

I hadn't been that close to either parent as an adult, so we spoke mostly out of necessity. In the mountains that day, I felt profoundly alone. I felt like it was all on me now.

After Dad died, Sara began calling me on Sunday afternoons, as our dad had. I needed her. I needed a dependable voice when everything else in my life was unknown or newly sprouted from the ashes of divorce, cancer, and death. Our relationship was buoyed by the trust of someone who has seen what you have seen. I realized how alike we were, how we both made jokes when we were uncomfortable, how we couldn't sleep if there were dishes to be washed, how we craved reliability, how we both treated our dogs like furry humans. Most importantly, I realized how strong she was, too.

"I'm scared you might die on K2," she told me.

"I won't do anything stupid."

"If you ask me, the whole thing is stupid. But I trust you."

This time, it felt like I meant it when I said I wouldn't do anything stupid. That summer, I backed off sketchy rock when the thought of Sara losing someone else flashed in my mind. I knew, intellectually, that my parents were proud of me, but with Sara, I felt it. In her, I found the connection I'd missed with my parents, and I finally felt what it is to be forever, irrevocably connected to someone.

CHAPTER 15

4,822 FEET

Amonth after Dad died, I felt like I'd temporarily entered a tiny, elite mountaineering circle, one that I did not believe I belonged in but was happy to inhabit for as long as possible. Our one and only meeting occurred at a schoolhouse pub in Winthrop, Washington. I walked into the familiar rectangular brewhouse and scanned the crowd. Though the slanted early-evening shadows obscured my view, I found the expected mix of outdoorsy hippies, shiny tourists, and long-distance cyclists. I'd spent childhood summers in the North Cascades and knew this crowd was different from the dingy, saloon-door swinging scene down the street. My group was easy to spot: weathered athletic men with grooved hands thick with calluses, sporting casual short-sleeved plaid button-down shirts and oversized altimeter watches. I slid uncomfortably onto an open barstool. Amid smiles and introductions, I assessed the climbing experience of the men around me: multiple first ascents, new alpine routes, double-digit Everest summits. My single oxygen-aided Everest summit via the most common route felt embarrassingly meager. My hair also felt overly styled, my sunburned face too hot, my tank top too skimpy. I was out of my league, but since I couldn't slink under the table, I mentally softened everything about myself. And kept smiling.

Scott had invited me to join his group of mountaineering friends on this summer evening. We'd primarily interacted by phone and had only met in person once before, and I still hadn't attached the smooth, measured voice I was used to hearing during training calls to the clean-cut gentleman sitting in front of me. Scott didn't present as a dirtbag climber—or perhaps this was what a dirtbag climber could morph into with time. Or maybe Scott had never subscribed to the stereotype of forsaking all luxuries and comforts to allow the mountains to define his life. I wondered if, like the protrusive veins on his arms, his exacting demeanor was the result of years on the mountains, or if his exacting demeanor drove him to mountain pursuits.

Scott opened the conversation with a topic I'd hoped to avoid. "What's next, Lisa?"

I cringed at that question. And kept smiling. I knew that for well-meaning friends it was a conversation starter, a logical curiosity, but my self-esteem was an unbalanced coalescence of ambition and diffidence. And in this crowd, I preferred not to talk about my mountain goals. Scott must not have realized how self-conscious I was.

All the men's heads turned toward me, still too sunburned and too styled. There was a momentary communication lapse between my logical brain—which was compelled to supply the obvious answer—and my panicked ego.

"K2?" I accidentally spewed into the folksy pub air with a question mark.

"Really?" Scott's head cocked sideways, like a confused golden retriever's.

Craft beer would definitely improve this situation, I decided, and I swallowed a large volume of it without looking up, hopeful the conversation would drift from me to a new topic. But when I set my glass down on the burled tabletop, three sets of raised eyebrows asked for explanation, and I wished my superpower was invisibility.

"Yeah." *Ugh, why can't I take that back? And also, why* should *I? Why* shouldn't *I attempt K2?* I was a tongue-tied mix of sunburn and self-conscious defensiveness. I knew there were countless reasons why

I shouldn't climb K2, all of which ended with regretful apologies to my family.

Thankfully, the waitress interrupted our conversation. Scott slid his empty beer mug across the table with precision, like it was a chess pawn.

For as many years as Scott was my climbing coach, I'd joked that he'd agreed to work with me because he'd mistaken me for a professional climber. The truth was not that harsh, but I'd still felt simultaneously humbled and inadequate working with someone so accomplished. Neither of us recognized yet—casually sipping microbrews in a pub on this summer night—that this imbalance was unhealthy. My constant attempts to please him were exacerbated by the fact that he had coached me through my fight with cancer and had consequently become an integral and superstitious ingredient to my recipe for success in the mountains.

Whatever dismay I perceived or invented that night in Winthrop faded, and Scott coached me the following winter into the fittest I'd ever been in preparation for K2. To my familiar regimen of hill sprints and hundreds of squats, Scott added climbing in the North Cascades and Snoqualmie Pass. Without the rigid schedule of a corporate job, I could plan midweek trips with friends to South Early Winters Spire, Spontaneity Arête, or Guye Peak. Despite a two-month recovery from a foot surgery to remove a painful neuroma from my fourth toe, I could swiftly ascend steep hills while carrying a considerable percentage of my body weight, efficiently scale crumbly rock, and complete six-finger chin-ups. Through serendipitous events and random conversations, I'd even gained the financial support of a climbing sponsor. Everything seemed to be falling into place for a successful summer climb until, one by one, my climbing team disintegrated, and our climbing permits were withdrawn.

"It'd be just me and you climbing, Lisa," Garrett said over black coffees in a cramped neighborhood bakery when he confirmed the climb was canceled. I gave him my best pouty face.

"I know how much this means to you," Garrett said, seriously. "I get it."

That summer I was renting a house from a mutual climbing friend, having never settled down after selling mine before Everest. Mortgages required jobs, and I didn't have one. Plus, I liked the freedom of living for short chunks of time in Seattle's neighborhoods. Looking after my friend Tasha's feisty cat in leafy Ravenna, house-sitting on tranquil Whidbey Island, renting a sunny condo on exuberant Capitol Hill. Though I'd paid my Everest loan from the sale of the house I'd shared with my ex-husband, my bank account was withering. Dodging rent for two months while climbing K2 had been part of my plan.

"You'll still be the first American woman to stand on K2," he said as I mentally reshuffled the puzzle pieces of my life.

Being the first wasn't the primary goal—safely summiting was. But it was part of what I'd hoped to accomplish by summiting in 2017.

My best negotiation efforts failed to cobble together a secondary team, so I stuffed K2 into the back of my mind; shifted my climbing plans to an autumn first ascent of Tharke Khang, an obscure peak in Nepal; got a dog named Chevy and a boyfriend named Anders; reluctantly took a corporate job; and made plans to attempt K2 the following year.

Thankfully, the 2018 team held together, the geopolitical climate remained stable enough for Americans to travel to Pakistan, and, with Scott's help, I pushed my body to its toughest state yet. Five months before my flight to Pakistan, though, Scott expressed concern about my ability to safely summit K2. In an email, he recounted deaths, rescues, and the unsuccessful attempts of many accomplished climbers, closing with: I do not feel you have any concept of what this is going to be like because your experience is so limited. His words exposed my greatest fear: I was in over my head. I wasn't capable then of justifying my decisions to Scott; I couldn't even articulate them to myself. I just knew that in an unidentifiable place inside of me I felt compelled. I felt pushed forward by an infinitesimal spark that believed I was capable. So I thanked him for his candid opinion and let his concerns drop.

Avoidance worked until three months before my departure for Pakistan, a time when I had space in my life for very few things that weren't related to K2. Each day was a unique puzzle of professional obligations, training, climbing, and relationship maintenance. I felt strain everywhere, and, as a result of constant multitasking and sleep deprivation, I was perpetually on edge, fearing that the smallest imbalance would topple everything into a pile of neglected ambitions.

During a business trip, as I slowly counted walking lunges while carrying one-third of my body weight across the tacky plastic floor of an ill-equipped hotel gym, my phone buzzed with an email from Scott. I had been expecting a response to questions about a new workout he'd given me, but it was clear from the first sentence that there had been a miscommunication. Given his feedback two months earlier, he believed that I'd changed my objective. However, I had categorized his opinion as information, not as a directive. He closed the email with: I think you are letting your ego get the best of you here, frankly. I need to think about whether I want to continue our coaching arrangement. His words felt harsh and unexpected, and my hands began to shake. I let my phone slide onto a weight bench, hopeful that ignoring it would erase the implications of its contents.

I hadn't exactly closed the loop with Scott after his initial concerns because I'd wanted to delay the inevitable. However, I hadn't gained anything from avoidance, and now I felt humiliated and stupid. Even though I'd understood his perspective, I had been unable to accept it. On the spectrum of mountaineering experience—particularly among Scott's contemporaries—mine maybe hovered at midline. As my coach, in preparation for K2, he'd wanted me to continue to advance my skills in mixed alpine terrain, where rock, ice, and snow commingled to create a scintillating high-altitude puzzle with complex solutions. It wasn't that he didn't want me to attempt K2; he believed my aspirations needed to be tempered with experience.

My gut churned, the way it churned when I knew I'd unintentionally fucked up—badly. My brain searched frantically for a way to pull our partnership back together, but I didn't understand how we'd gotten out of sync about my objective. Maybe my ambitions really were outweighing my ability. Maybe I should pay attention when people who cared about me waved the warning flag that I was in over my head.

I was holding back tears when I spoke to my boyfriend that night.

"Why is this mountain so important to you?"

I sometimes hated it when people held up the mirror of logic. I gave him the same bullshit answer I gave everyone else. "I want to be a more well-rounded climber."

I was afraid to look deep enough for the truth because I knew that I would have to answer questions that I had cleverly avoided for years: When would I know where my limit was? Why would I do things that might kill me? What was I trying to prove? I wasn't ready then to answer these questions because I would have had to uncover my genuine motivation. And then I would no longer be able to smile and shrug when someone asked why K2 was important to me. So I ignored and avoided. I let the heat of defiance and ambition consume my insides. It organized and solidified, as fluid as a flame, into the desire to prove myself one more time.

I knew that what Scott had passed on to me was more than how to prepare for safely climbing big mountains. He'd taught me to be my own judge of what I was capable of, and to never let others inflict their boundaries on me.

By the time I returned home from the business trip, Scott had officially ended our relationship. Though my gut had stopped churning, what remained was the sickening feeling that someone I respected didn't believe in me.

It was March, and the constant foggy drizzle in Seattle matched my mood. I needed to punish myself, so I loaded my backpack with a bag of playground sand and headed to the mountains, the only place that felt comforting. Thanks to the miserable weather, I was alone.

The forty extra pounds of sand in my backpack rested uncomfortably on the small of my back and felt like it was slowly abrading the skin there. After several failed attempts to shift the weight to my hips, I conceded and mentally scanned my body for something that felt good. Instead of peace, I found a sharp pain in my left Achilles. Each time I stepped up, it felt like an overtightened guitar string. I added the pain in my foot to the pain in my back plus the misery of 40-degree rain, making a macabre mental calculation to determine whether I was suffering enough to atone for fucking up. I could dump the sand, slowly pour it in the woods—no one else would know—but today's hike up 4,000 feet of slick rock and ice was not about proving anything. It was my penance. After two hours, my soggy slog ended, and I reached the mailbox that stood at the summit. The rain had turned to snow now. I'd been here hundreds of times, but today I felt like I had more to do than tag the mailbox and descend. I turned my back to the wet, blowing snow and pulled a crumpled map from my backpack. I needed to say something, so I forced my cold fingers to grip a marker and wrote:

> I am going to K2. I don't know what will happen there, but I trust that I have a solid understanding of the risks and my limits. I accept that a consequence of my decision could be my death.

I added one more sentence before stuffing the sodden paper into the deepest corner of the mailbox.

> When will I know that I am enough?

CHAPTER 16

520 FEET

We walked separately down to the water, Anders faster than me. I wanted to go slowly, to savor. When I joined him on a tree-sized piece of driftwood, I heard stones rolling under the waves as they came and went. I laid my head on his shoulder.

Anders and I had been dating for barely a year. Though he had sweetly studied high-altitude mountaineering, the risks and dangers were new to him. During our first date at a dank speakeasy on Capitol Hill, he, unlike all the other guys I'd dated, had reacted mildly to my mountaineering accomplishments, and I'd liked that.

"Are you worried about anything?" I asked him now.

"Hmm, no, not really. I know that you'll be safe and smart. I trust you."

In the past year, I had intentionally put myself into situations to determine whether I could be both safe and smart in the mountains. I'd let the achy sting of winter creep into my fingers while climbing frosty rock at Washington Pass, and I'd scrambled my way into un-tenable rock that I could barely descend on eastern Washington's bluffs. With experienced partners, I'd tested my assessment of winter snow conditions on Little Tahoma, Mount Rainier's baby sister. Still, I believed that Anders was worried, that he should have been worried, but didn't want to create more stress by saying so.

"What are *you* worried about?" he asked. "That's the more important question."

I laughed to deflect, but he was looking at me now, and his raised eyebrows wouldn't let me.

We should have had this conversation a month ago, I thought. I shrugged and intentionally looked from the water to him. "You know I don't commit to any mountain unless I understand its risks and challenges." I saw names from my spreadsheet flash in my brain as I spoke:

Dudley Wolfe—1939—altitude sickness / exhaustion

Pasang Kikuli—1939—disappeared

Arthur Gilkey—1953—suspected avalanche

Ali, Son of Kazim—1979—fell into crevasse

Alison Hargreaves—1995—fall

Gerard McDonnell—2008—avalanche

"I know that doesn't protect me against objective hazards like rockfall and avalanches." I let my voice trail off, not even convincing myself anymore.

My response was meticulously crafted bullshit, the same bullshit I'd spewed to Jeri and Kara during our champagne-happy-hour send-off a week ago. They'd both watched me skeptically and nodded slowly, unconvinced, too. I hadn't told them this, but I would need to keep their strength close on K2. I needed Kara's fight-before-flight attitude and Jeri's lighthearted wisdom. And from Anders, I needed a belief that I was doing the right thing.

Because what I wouldn't say to any of them was that what concerned me about climbing K2 was dying—unknowingly trusting the wrong rock and feeling it cleave from the mountain into my gloved hand, my weight shifting uncontrollably from security into the power of gravity. What concerned me about climbing K2 was hearing the roar of tons of loose snow accelerating toward me with destructive ferocity. What concerned me about climbing K2 was believing that I had correctly set my rappel device, leaning backward to trust it, and free-falling into the sky. What concerned me about K2 was someone adding my name to the list.

What concerned me about K2 was failing. I had analytically studied this mountain. I had documented each death and categorized its cause. I had considered the ways I could die and made a hypothetical plan to prevent each. I had trained until my muscles screamed. I had climbed shitty, crumbling rock and sketchy fragile ice. And I had visualized my success.

But I'd convinced myself that my fledgling relationship with Anders could not tolerate the pressure of the truth, so I hadn't allowed it to displace the bullshit. I kept that burden for myself. I knew that even though Anders wanted to understand, wanted to be supportive, he had no idea what this was like for me, what I was about to do, the risks that I was about to take, the decisions that I would make, the things I would see. I had never been the one to stay home while a partner climbed a dangerous mountain in a foreign country. I had no idea what it would feel like for him to wonder where I was, to decipher brief text messages, to study the blog posts of strangers and interpret whether their experiences were the same as mine.

"I'll be proud of you no matter what happens," Anders said, and kissed my forehead. His lips lingered there for a second, but we both allowed the subject to drop. It was too late to dig into the details, anyway, and I didn't want the last few hours that I had in Seattle to be tarnished by tension. I needed the memory of this day to become a haven, so I closed my eyes, lifted my chin toward the sky, and inhaled briny sea air.

The June sun was a brilliant harbinger of warm afternoons at the beach, juicy garden tomatoes, and lazy Sunday hikes. I would miss all those things. By the time I was scheduled to return home, the peak of summer would have passed, and nature would be headed toward autumn. I wanted to take it in, to internalize it, to carry this warmth on my bare shoulders and in my lungs for the next two months. I wanted to remember the feeling of ease. Anders slid his hand in mine and squeezed it. I kept my eyes closed and felt his face close to mine. I would miss his smell, too. I had to leave it here on this beach because carrying it too closely while I was climbing would create distraction. Distraction, like fear, created conflicting consequences in the mountains; some is beneficial, too much is deadly.

. . .

Twenty-three hours later, I arrived in Islamabad, head covered, in full fight mode. I hadn't taken the time to sufficiently understand what to expect upon arriving in Pakistan, but I was certain it would be bad. In my mind, I'd concocted multiple scenarios that involved harassment, ogling, and perpetual imprisonment for having breasts. Ogling notwithstanding, the reality was the exact opposite. The airport was clean and modern, and I was greeted warmly by anyone whose eyes I dared to meet. I slowly let my guard down and allowed myself to be enveloped in a culture that was dramatically different from my own and full of contradictions.

The Serena Hotel in Islamabad added to the paradox; it was an oasis of calm amid the chaotic, unknown city. Garrett met me at the hotel's ornate wooden check-in desk, his smile and lanky frame a familiar comfort.

"Lisa! You made it!" he said with a hug.

"Happy to finally be here," I said, dropping my backpack onto the tile floor. "I think I'm ready for a nap, though."

"Let's get you checked in so you can relax for a few hours. You're sharing a room with Klára. She's already upstairs in your room sleeping."

To the polite front-desk clerk, I handed over the requisite credit cards and identification documents. When my bags were sorted and tagged, I padded quietly across the plush lobby carpets toward the elevator. A duo played on a raised wooden platform, their crossed legs touching as they spun seductive music from exotic string instruments into the grand lobby. Businessmen sat on overstuffed couches, smoking and casually chatting over lattes in delicate cups. There was a ribbon of perfume in the air, too. It mixed with the alluring music, the cigarette smoke, and the humidity. Mountaineers were easy to spot in this elegant scene, and several meandered through the lobby, same as me, pacing like wild animals forced into cages. We nodded in passing, and I was grateful to have an excuse to avoid conversation. I was exhausted and I just wanted to be in my own bubble.

Klára Kolouchová and I didn't know each other, but when Garrett and I had met in Seattle months ago to discuss K2, he'd described her as an accomplished Czech climber who, in her quest to be the first from her country to summit the three highest mountains in the world, had attempted the peak with him in 2016. K2 had felt like a world away then, over glasses of wine in a high-ceilinged downtown restaurant, as Garrett had described the accomplishments of each member of the team. I'd been relieved to hear there would be another woman climbing with me. I was relieved again when I opened the door to our shared hotel room and all I saw of Klára was a wave of dark curls in a pile of pillows, since I didn't think I'd have the energy to be cordial. I wanted our first meeting to go well, since I was counting on us being allies.

CHAPTER 17

1,770 FEET

The next morning, I waited as the morning heat bloomed and piles of overstuffed duffel bags were loaded into vans for transport back to the Islamabad airport. It was only eight and I was standing in the shade, but sweat still penetrated my long-sleeved linen shirt that intentionally covered my shoulders, my neck, and my wrists. Although I had only been in Islamabad for a short time, I would miss it. I would miss the elegant Serena Hotel, with its shimmering chandeliers and thick rugs and the smell of smoky perfume. As I became more uncomfortable in the morning heat, I was reluctantly aware that my accommodations and comfort level were about to rapidly decline. For the next five or six weeks, I wouldn't have the luxury of crisp sheets on a cozy bed, or a warm shower, or salads.

I watched as the men worked, speaking in quick Urdu sentences as they carefully loaded duffel bag after duffel bag into and on top of multiple passenger vans. A man dressed in a casual business suit approached me.

"You're trekking?" he said in English with a polished Pakistani accent.

On every expedition I'd been on, I'd been mistaken for either a trekker or the team physician. I knew this businessman didn't know he was contributing to a common misperception, but his assumption still stung.

"Climbing," I corrected him. "K2." I watched his eyes to see if he was familiar with Pakistan's grandest mountain, and I saw his pupils expand with the same mix of surprise and dismay that I saw every time I told a stranger, and I felt self-conscious embarrassment start to rise in my gut.

"It's the most beautiful mountain. I trekked to K2 base camp several years ago," he said, and handed me his business card. *Umer*, it said in bold letters.

He went on to describe his experience as the most transformational of his life. Then he paused, bored his dark-brown eyes into mine, and said, "You will learn things about yourself that you do not yet know."

I wasn't sure if I should thank him or just acknowledge that he was correct.

Umer reached down to collect his briefcase and offered one last insight. "Do not give up until you are transformed."

While Umer waved goodbye and approached a taxi, I remained standing on the hotel steps. *Don't give up until I am transformed?* What if my goal wasn't to summit but instead to transform into a better version of myself? To learn something about myself and the world around me that created more openness in my heart?

Mountain climbing was such a tangible, concrete pursuit. A climber either achieved it or she didn't; credit wasn't awarded for *almost*. Climbing itself was buried in statistics, hard facts that accumulated over time to prove the character of a mountain: death rates, winter ascents, outlandish "firsts."

What if my goal for K2 was different? Less measurable than failing or succeeding? What if I abandoned the notion of proving myself by achieving another summit and instead endeavored to explore myself, to understand the ways that I could move closer to the version of me that was often buried beneath expectations and fear? This new seed planted by Umer felt curiously freeing, but I was still not ready to lessen my goal. Could I really allow myself to believe that I didn't have to summit K2?

I couldn't think of a time when I'd ever allowed myself to just try something. Just dip my toe in the water to see how it felt, then make a decision about my commitment. As a kid, I hadn't wanted to just learn to swim; I'd wanted to be a lifeguard. I hadn't wanted to just enter the spelling bee; I'd wanted to be the state champion (which I wasn't, because *mackerel* has two *E*s). I hadn't wanted to just join the high school French club; I'd wanted to be its president.

As a kid, athleticism hadn't been important to me. Being a part of the basketball or track team had been irrelevant; I'd just done it to be with my friends. But climbing that never-ending rope hanging from the middle of the gym ceiling had seemed important. Pressing my sweaty, jute-burned palm against the brass bell hanging next to the highest point of that rope had mattered to me. It had mattered because no other girls could do it (mostly because we had all been afraid of the boys glancing sideways up our shorts as we hung from the coarse strands). Being a part of a team, wearing a uniform—those things had been immaterial to my childhood self. But doing something unexpected—proving people wrong—*that* motivated me.

Proving people wrong hadn't been difficult in the 1980s in the conservative middle of the United States. Girls weren't supposed to be athletic. We could be helpful, we could even be smart, but we were expected to do "girl push-ups" during the Presidential Fitness Test.

I understood Umer's suggestion on an intellectual level; it was the same advice I would have given to a friend. But I was not my friend. I was über self-critical, and the thought of "just seeing how it goes" felt like copping out. It felt like I'd created an escape hatch: *I wasn't really planning to summit; I was just going to "check it out."* There was a small part of me that understood that by adopting this ethos, I would relieve myself of the pressure of performing, of attempting to prove myself. But I didn't trust the part of myself promoting this notion. I had fought too hard—given up too much—to ease up. I resolved to push forward despite uncertainty and doubt. Regardless of what I'd lost or the bad decisions I'd made or the things I'd broken or walked away from. In the back of my mind, I was hoping K2 would make it clear to me—and everyone else—that I'd done the right thing.

· · ·

I was sweaty and scared shitless as I stepped into the air-conditioned van with my unfamiliar teammates and the duffel bags to drive north-east to the Islamabad airport for the flight that would begin our journey to base camp. These conflicting ideas—of just trying versus endeavoring to succeed—were still swirling in my mind, making it difficult to focus on prefatory conversations. I slid onto a bench seat next to Rob Smith, noting that his lanky legs were at least a foot longer than mine.

"How long have you been in Seattle?" he wanted to know. We shared stories about hometowns and agreed that his home in Scotland might have been the one place in the world with weather drearier than mine. His patinated face carried the wisdom of years in the mountains. I was drawn to his calm, quiet spirit. I didn't sense in Rob the usual mountain-guide bravado; he seemed generally interested in me and contributing to a strong climbing team.

"How long have you wanted to climb K2?" I asked Rob.

"It's been a dream, but, you know, not many people get a chance to guide in the Karakoram."

There was refined excitement in his voice as he explained how he'd convinced his wife that he'd be safe, that he'd return home for her and their son. As he spoke, I noticed that his wedding ring was knotted with a worn cord around his neck.

I nodded, appreciating his openness, and reminded myself that guiding on K2 is different from Everest. It's different from most mountains. Not that Rob wasn't capable or interested in helping if it came to it (I was confident he had been involved in more rescues than I could imagine), but we were all going to be on our own up there. I believed that I couldn't embark on a climb like K2 with the expectation that others would get me out of trouble. Likewise, it was difficult to accept that I didn't know if I'd be able to help someone else. I wanted to believe I could and would. I'd had the mental and physical reserves to help other climbers in the past. But K2 was different. The risks were greater, the unknowns more disastrous. K2, the gem of the Karakoram range, wasn't equipped with the same support systems as the Himalayas. There weren't commercial helicopter operators ready to pluck climbers off the mountain, there wasn't an ER at base camp staffed with a volunteer high-altitude medical team. On the summit of K2, I would be farther from definitive medical care than I had ever been in my life, and in the most dangerous position.

"Must be hard to leave your son for this?" I asked him.

His blue eyes connected with mine, and the corners of his mouth dipped slightly. He didn't have to tell me, or anyone else in this van, what it was like to try to explain to someone you loved that you needed to climb the most dangerous mountain in the world. I wondered if Rob was thankful his son was too young to grasp the seriousness of his endeavors.

"How 'bout your family?"

I chuckled a little. "They're not exactly stoked for me to be here." I didn't tell him that I was grateful my dad had been spared the stress of worrying about my safety.

CHAPTER 18

7,300 FEET

Welcome to Skardu," said the uniformed officer at the bottom of the airplane stairs. He looked up at me over the barrel of his rifle. His eyes didn't catch mine, but a sly smile spread from under his bushy yet kempt mustache. Skardu is the launch point for expeditions to the rugged Karakoram mountain range, and this small village, as Islamabad had been, was heavy with contradictions. There I could wear a bikini at the Serena Hotel's rooftop pool (at least I thought I could—I mean, I *did*) but was to be covered from head to toe otherwise. Here men smiled kindly at me while holding rifles. Even though I didn't understand it, I wanted to take it all in, all the paradox, all the smells and tastes and beliefs that were different from anything I'd experienced before.

After a dusty jeep ride from the airport, I settled into the rustic lodge at the edge of the murky Indus River and then wandered into its garden, which I also wanted to relish: this would be the last time I would take a shower, the last time grass would tickle my bare feet, the last time I would be at ease.

My teammate Jason Black bounded through the swinging glass door into the garden to join me. Once he'd folded his lanky, athletic frame into a metal chair next to me, I asked him about the cycling jersey he was wearing, and he breezed through some of his recent ultracycling adventures.

"Room to your liking?" he asked when he'd finished, his Irish accent thick and rhythmic. He had an angular jaw and wispy brown hair. As we spoke, his eyes darted, hawklike, from me to the garden, then to the river and back to me again.

"Fine. How's yours?"

"These beds are brutal, but you'll wish for 'em up high. Things'll only get tougher from here, ya know. Don't plan for a hot shower in the morning. Tested mine, and it's ice cold."

I already liked Jason's direct candor and appreciated the information he shared. As a team, we were deep into the process of sizing up one another. I didn't think any of us intended to do it, but we were all naturally competitive and, as a result, wanted to identify whom we could trust, whom we could not, who was capable, who wasn't. And the ultimate question: Who would summit, and who wouldn't? It's common knowledge among mountaineers that if you don't like someone at sea level, you certainly will not enjoy their company at 26,000 feet. So I tried to identify early who was positive, hardworking, ready to suffer without complaint.

Jason's experience attempting K2 before put him in the category of teammates that I wanted on my side. He seemed like a gracious, non-ego-driven athlete who genuinely wanted the best for the team and his Irish homeland. I sensed that he was here to test himself and to honor his country, not to check a box.

He eyed my phone in my lap and asked, "You get the Wi-Fi out here?"

Like grass and showers, Wi-Fi was among the comforts that would end after Skardu, and we were all scurrying around the lodge with our phones held to the sky hoping to upload one last post before we were disconnected from the rest of the world.

I told him it was spotty at best, and he pointed to a secret spot in the exterior hallway where it was better. I thanked him and wandered through the roses to try my luck inside.

· · ·

As the sun rose the next morning, I woke to the mournful, melodic sounds of Muslim prayers. They were broadcast over an outdoor speaker, I suspected, and the atonal voice was reverberating off the high banks of the Indus River into the primitive room that Klára and I shared. Since I had first woken to the sound of Muslim prayer in Tanzania in 2014, it had become comforting to me. Even though I didn't understand the words, the slow droning was calming. I closed my eyes and meditated as I lay in the scratchy twin bed.

That morning's breakfast was our first team meal. We ambled in pairs and singles into the lodge's largest room, where floor-to-ceiling windows on three sides framed the muddy, rocky slopes of the Indus River, the same river that would lead us to K2's base.

We were all on our best behavior, I knew, convivially asking questions about hometowns and children, as if we'd just met at a dinner party. I'd been to this dinner party before—we all had—and knew that soon the mountain would expose the rough edges of each of our personalities. I knew that high-pitched laughs and benign chewing with an open mouth would pass by me now, unnoticed, but would become intolerable in a cramped, frigid tent at 26,000 feet. Over runny eggs and muesli, I continued sizing everyone up, wondering who would fill the role of caretaker, asshole, complainer, meanie, comedian, appeaser. I wondered what these people thought of me, and presumed, unfairly, that they believed I was not qualified to be here. That my bank account outsized my climbing abilities. I also wondered which role I would fill within this team. On recent climbs, I'd lost the desire to fit in with the guys, but had also resisted being too feminine, so I was already grateful for Klára, and I was hopeful that we would become allies and that together we could create an alliance against the bro culture.

Mountaineering, especially high-altitude mountaineering, is decidedly masculine. The first woman to summit K2, highly accomplished Polish mountaineer Wanda Rutkiewicz, did so in 1986, thirty-two years after the first man. The stats are similar for Everest, where twenty-two years passed between the first male and female summits. Denali's brochure for the 1969 climbing season permitted women only to go as high as advanced base camp, so long as they were responsible for cooking and did not have aspirations to climb.

Thankfully, pioneering climbers like Arlene Blum didn't accept that women were inferior or incapable of achieving high-altitude summits. Given this history, I didn't find it surprising that, among this team, there was a palpable bro vibe—the insular, exclusionary kind that discounted anyone who didn't look, sound, or dress the same. I could already see guys on the periphery of this circle, the ones who didn't quite fit the bro mold, striving to be included, laughing awkwardly at inside jokes that they didn't get.

I felt as outside of this group as I had in the Philips office eleven years ago. Climbing mountains hadn't rectified that isolation. It couldn't have, I knew now, because the barrier resided within me. What I gained in consolation was more important than entry into an elite club that thrived on conquests. It was true that defiance had provoked me to try mountaineering, but it hadn't led me where I'd hoped. I had never been admitted to the club. Instead, I'd gained something greater, something deep and inherent that wasn't dependent on fitting into a mold.

Rob sat amid the backslaps and hyperbole, his pointy elbows perched on the table, his big hand wrapped around a flimsy metal spoon as he ate porridge. He seemed to be taking everything in, observing, cataloging, not participating—and not judging like me. For this, I admired him as the team's elder. I tried to do the same, to acknowledge but not to control. So I stared down the long wooden table toward the calm, chalky flow of the Indus River. I was already struggling to prevent this dynamic from distracting me, and I knew that I must ignore it. I had to push to the side everything that I couldn't change. Just like I couldn't control the weather on the mountain, I was not going to become less sensitive to exclusionary behavior or more open to the positive aspects of their personalities, and they were not going to drop their bro-ness. Not in the next month, and not in K2's intense environment. Both would likely become more pronounced, not less. I knew that if I let the distraction gain even a minuscule foothold, it would build and grow and eventually consume massive amounts of my mental energy. Energy that I needed to keep me focused on safely climbing K2.

"We're going to walk into town in a bit," Klára said as I cleared my breakfast plate. "You need anything?"

I didn't, but I was hoping to steal a few private moments with her to gain her perspective on the team's personalities and dynamics. I let the members of the team who had visited Skardu before lead our dusty excursion to the commercial district, past mule-drawn carts full of ripe tomatoes and drab storefronts with scrawling Arabic print, their shelves stocked with dusty electronics. I was aware that we were watched constantly and blatantly by the Pakistani men sitting on sidewalks, the men tending to vegetables, the men driving by on motorbikes in tattered Western suits. Sometimes, I successfully caught their eyes peeking at me from under a traditional pakol wool hat as I walked by, and the look I got in return was hollow. I didn't know what they thought of me, but it felt unnerving. Klára seemed to move effortlessly in Pakistan, her long legs striding confidently, her head covered neatly in a scarf, hiding her wavy black hair, somehow managing to look both athletic and fashionable while speaking confidently to men who wouldn't look at her. We dashed across the cobbled street from one partially constructed cinder block building to the next, searching for last-minute supplies that seemed crucial but weren't. Though I had surgically decided what to carry with me to Pakistan, the novelty of food and toiletries in exotic packaging made me second-guess my decisions. *Of course I need Pringles. How could I have forgotten to pack them? And I definitely need body oil. My skin is going to be extra dry on the mountain.*

"Oooh, hey! There's a pastry shop at the end of the next block," Klára said with a wink. I was in.

I managed to make it back to the lodge with just a bag full of pink-iced pastries and a bottle of nonalcoholic beer. That afternoon, the whole team posed on the high grassy bank of the Indus River for a group photo, all of us smiling and hopeful in our street clothes, not yet transitioned to dressing like climbers. As I took my spot in the front row, at the end of a long line of Sherpas, I told myself that I was small but mighty, too, just like them.

Klára and I spent the rest of the afternoon savoring warm bottles of almost-beer in the lodge's garden, a refreshing treat in a country that eschews alcohol. Behind us, the Sherpas were picking shiny red cherries, laughing and wobbling on each other's shoulders to reach the ripest ones. I picked absentmindedly at the label of my beer, trying to decipher its Arabic script. Klára settled into the metal chair beside me with a satisfied exhale.

"How you settling in?" she wanted to know.

"Yeah, good. Anxious to get up there," I said, gesturing to the air. "Part of me wants to know what'll happen up there, you know? I think I'm worried about rockfall. How bad is it?"

I had attempted to assess the likelihood of an errant rock dislodging itself from the mountain and crashing into me, but my studies had been theoretical, dependent on meager online data. I knew that in the first seventy years of serious K2 climbs, up until 2008, there had only been two recorded deaths from rockfall. Yet it seemed to be at the top of everyone's list of concerns.

"It's unpredictable like no other mountain." Klára let out an exasperated sigh between words. "K2 rocks—I don't know—they bounce and bounce and when you think you know where they are going, they . . . zoom! . . . go somewhere else completely."

I watched her long arms as she described the erratic nature of the rockfall she'd seen before. She had spent more time on this peak than nearly everyone else on the team. I imagined the relationship she had with K2, the heartache it must have caused her. So far, she was constantly cheery, but I knew that under her carefree smile there was a bedrock of grit and determination. I wondered if I could muster the energy to attempt K2 multiple times.

"In 2016, it was just like *poof*!" she continued, and expanded her arms into the air. "Camp Three was gone. Our tents, oxygen—all of it—gone. Like it was never there."

My sunglasses met hers, and I imagined her eyes were dark and serious behind them. I knew she was talking about the avalanche that ended the 2016 climbing season.

"We were lucky no one was up there," she said absentmindedly, like her mind had scrolled back to that day.

"Shit" was all I could say.

The tally of deaths by rockfall in my spreadsheet was low, but her description confirmed my general unease about things that were trying to kill me on K2 that I could not control.

"Hey! I brought some nail polish," she said. "Wanna give ourselves pedicures?"

"I did, too!" I said, and popped up from the metal chair to retrieve the tiny bottle of fuchsia polish that I had hoped would make me feel girly despite the harsh environment I was about to enter.

We stretched out in the shady grass, comfortably sharing stories about our lives on separate continents as women and as climbers. I wondered who we would each be when we returned to this calm garden in a month. What would we have seen? What decisions would we have made?

CHAPTER 19

13,335 FEET

A full day of Land Cruiser travel and five flat tires led us to Askole the following evening. This bucolic outpost was as close as vehicles could get to base camp. From here, we became a small, nomadic village of 142, including 120 Pakistani porters, 10 Sherpas, 9 climbers, and 3 guides. For the next seven days, as we walked fifty-five miles from Askole to base camp, we would erect our village each evening and disassemble it each morning. In addition to countless duffels of climbing and personal gear, our ensemble included:

23 drums of kerosene
45 mules
21 chickens
4 goats
1 cow
220 pounds of potatoes
1,400 eggs

The complex logistics of moving a climbing expedition from Islamabad to base camp were overseen by Muhammad Ibrahim, a compact

Pakistani who wore Western clothes and a floppy safari-style sun hat, chunks of thick brown hair peeking out. I asked him about his family, and he wrung his hands as he told me that his wife was pregnant with twins. He smiled easily but shyly as we spoke.

At Johla, the first camp past Askole, my duffel bag that contained the clothes, food, and gear needed for trekking had mistakenly been tagged to go directly to base camp, and I asked Ibrahim if he would help me find it among the piles of drums and duffels also intended to travel there directly.

"What is its color?" he wanted to know.

I explained its details, and he said, "Rest, Lisa, I will bring for you."

"No, I'll help you. I don't have anything else to do anyway," I said with a shrug.

I could tell I'd confused and maybe offended him, but he tilted his head sideways, said, "As you wish," and began walking.

I followed Ibrahim's quick steps over a dusty hill to a wider expanse of dirt and rocks, bisected by meandering trails. Between the trails were short shelters built by the porters for sleeping. To build them, they'd arranged the duffels as shelter walls and secured plastic tarps over their tops with rocks. I realized now why retrieving my bag would be challenging; it had already been designated as building material. I followed Ibrahim as he ducked inside each two-foot-tall shelter, curious to see what was going on inside. He commandingly lifted the plastic aside and spoke Urdu to the startled porters. After a few unsuccessful visits, I became more curious about the porters and peeked over Ibrahim's shoulder to get a glimpse inside the next shelter. Within the small circle, most of the men were making chapati, squatting around small fires and quickly flipping the unleavened flat bread with their bare hands. They shook their heads at Ibrahim politely and looked stunned and confused at me when I peered around his shoulder. I smiled and sometimes said hello, but their dazed looks didn't change. As we walked between shelters, I asked: "Why do they . . . do you know why they don't look at me?"

There was a long pause, and I thought, again, that I might have offended Ibrahim.

"Because . . . you are . . . you are a lady." He smiled crookedly and cocked his head toward me but didn't catch my gaze, the command he'd displayed with the porters seeming to have evaporated now. I wanted him to feel comfortable. I wanted him to know that I didn't subscribe to the same gender roles that he did, that I considered all of us a part of the same team, working in tandem. His soft brown eyes finally caught mine but then darted away again.

I wanted to ask more, about what they thought of me as a Western woman, but the questions didn't make it out of my brain. I was afraid that my ignorance of Pakistani customs had led me into some avoidable gaff. Yet I continued to follow Ibrahim, and he continued to remain accommodating as he scurried from shelter to shelter, finally locating my misplaced duffel.

After a few days, the process of moving as a village became routine. Every morning before seven, we woke; packed our personal gear; meandered to the large dining tent, where there was a flurry of activity as men spoke Urdu, Nepali, and English and efficiently disassembled tents and packed them, along with cooking supplies, food, and gear, into barrels, duffels, and tidy stacks to be carried for the rest of the day on the backs of men and mules and then put back together again in the evening when we arrived at the next camp.

The trek to most base camps generally provided a transition from the comforts of cities to the harshness of mountain life. K2, however, was not like any other mountain. There weren't any teahouses or huts with warm fires and chai; there were only sodden tents and rocks and glaciers and frigid rivers whose silty water rushed above my thighs, plus every type of precipitation. A sunny morning would transition to sleet, then snow flurries followed by rain, and then back to sun before lunch.

Back in Seattle, Anders had appointed himself DJ and sent daily song lyrics via text. I appreciated that they were meant to lighten my mood when the trek became difficult, though on most days, they wormed into my consciousness and required significant mental effort to remove. So far during the trek to base camp, raining men, Jessie's girl, the rains down in Africa, and midnight trains going anywhere had dominated my thoughts. But I appreciated the distraction, because as we progressed toward base camp and gained elevation, the terrain shifted from sand and dirt to every imaginable form of rock. I spent hours walking on rocks buried in sand, grimacing at the possibility of rolling an ankle every time my foot slid off a hidden stone. There were also hours walking in deep, crunchy gravel that transitioned to slopes of loose talus, then back to sand for a few more hours. Occasionally, the day was punctuated by giant boulder fields, which contained meandering cairns that marked a multitude of possible paths. The best form of navigation seemed to be setting sights on a resting porter and generally walking in his direction.

At each camp, Klára and I shared a tent. I was thankful to be able to change clothes without the burden of discretion and to lounge in my underwear when I was too lazy or hot to do otherwise. I was also thankful for the strong plum wine she had carried from Prague.

On our fourth day of trekking, we left behind sand and wild rosebushes and transitioned to the moraine of the Baltoro Glacier. I would not see plants again for nearly a month. The terminus of the Baltoro Glacier that we were walking on was strewn with loose rock, but seeing signs of glacier felt like progress, and after twelve miles of walking, we arrived at Urdukas Camp.

It had been a difficult day of cold, then hot, rain, then hail. Finally, sunshine and blue skies revealed the Trango Towers' steep granite faces.

"It feels like we're in the mountains now," I said to Klára while we inflated our sleeping pads.

"Won't be long and we'll see the mighty K2. And tomorrow we'll meet the Baltoro," she said, peeking out of the tent's nylon door.

All of my clothes were wet from the morning's rain, and I shifted priorities from inflating to strategically laying out the wettest pieces so they would capture as much heat from the sun as possible before it set.

"Hey!" Klára interrupted my organizing. "There's a hose over there." She looked at me with mischievous eyes, but I didn't get it.

"Where?"

Klára pointed to a concrete perch at the edge of camp, behind it the Trango Towers rising into the late-afternoon sky.

"How good would clean hair feel?" she asked.

In the past three days, I'd transitioned from tourist to mountaineer, giving up modesty, soap, and even the makeshift hijab that covered my hair in Skardu.

"Ooohhh, yes!" I said, and evaluated our potential shower from my side of the tent. There was a Pakistani man squatting at its edge, rinsing the concrete slab with a short length of hose.

"I think they just slaughtered a chicken there, though," I said with a grimace.

"I don't care, I'm doing it." She giggled, grabbed a towel, and bolted out of the tent.

I was hesitant as I found my towel and rummaged through duffel bags for shampoo. I knew that more than a hundred sets of eyes would be on us, and that all those eyes belonged to men. I'd been careful to regard Pakistani culture and norms so far, and I didn't want to offend or make uncomfortable any of the Pakistani men working to help me trek to base camp. When Klára stepped out of our tent with loose, wavy hair, I surveyed camp. One of the bros had taken off his shirt while he set up his tent. If he could brush aside modesty to be shirtless in front of the whole camp, why couldn't I wash my hair?

I was confident that all eyes were on us as we washed our hair and legs and arms at that scenic concrete perch. I was also aware that our actions were shocking to some; I could tell by the extra-wide berth we were afforded on our walk back through camp to our tent. I also knew that feeling clean hair dry in mountain sunshine was exquisite.

The tumultuous weather included snow for the first time at Goro 2 Camp. On our fifth morning, I woke to several inches of wet, heavy snow stuck to the tent's roof.

Any team is only as strong as its weakest member, and our weakest cohort, in terms of preparedness for snow travel, were the porters. We were completely reliant on them, too, because we were not prepared to carry our own gear to base camp. There were now fifty porters on the team; the rest had been relieved of their duties because their loads, like kerosene and flour, had been consumed or because they'd delivered their loads to base camp already. This morning, our porters didn't want to walk to our planned destination of Broad Peak base camp. They made about eight US dollars daily for their efforts to carry up to forty pounds on wooden frames that hung from their shoulders on thick, flat rope. I felt like a wimp watching them scurry around rocks and through rainstorms in plastic shoes and traditional long cotton tunics and baggy trousers called *shalwar kameez*. As the sun rose, I could hear tense conversations in Urdu and broken English outside my tent.

Klára stirred in her sleeping bag. "Porter strike?"

"Sounds like it," I said, and snuggled back into my sleeping bag. That the porters didn't want to walk wasn't a wonder; I was not excited to walk in wet snow for hours, either, even with the benefit of water-proof clothes and footwear.

The negotiations continued for several hours, even after the morning's bacon-and-egg breakfast had been cleared from the dining tent. I mentally prepared to rest in camp for the day and wandered self-consciously into the dining tent with a coloring book and pencils. I felt like I should have been doing something more mountaineer-y, like sharpening my crampons, but filling the blank spaces of mandalas with vivid turquoises and purples eased my stress and made me feel just a little bit less savage. Eventually, a gaggle assembled at the opposite end of the long table, and the conversation turned to training. My ears perked up, but I didn't join in.

"Dude, how many ultras did you run before this?"

"Can't remember, like ten."

"Yeah, but how many did you get lost in?"

"Fuck you."

"I remember saving your ass more than once, crying in the woods like a little girl."

The group laughed.

"I was hungover, man. Not my fault."

"What's your VO_2 max?" he retaliated.

"Fifty-four."

"Pussy." Laughter erupted again.

Jason joined the laughter and then deftly elevated the conversation to nutrition. I didn't want to compete with them, but each day, I fought with myself to ignore the difference in our paces.

I knew I'd trained harder and smarter than them, and I knew that I was a more experienced mountaineer than most of them. But I let their bravado and banter fertilize seeds of doubt that had been planted in my mind long ago. This doubt, and its twin, insecurity, had pushed me to overprepare for every mountain I'd climbed. Every one. And even though it had always paid off, I had never felt confident that I'd done enough. Not ever.

"Best stay humble," Jason whispered in my ear, and squeezed my shoulder with his giant hand when he stood to walk out of the tent.

He was right, and downplaying my ability was my superpower. After summiting Everest, I'd scrolled through Facebook comments, and most had boosted my esteem, but one's initial dismissiveness stood out:

> Congratulations, Lisa. When I met you in Kathmandu, I thought there's no way she can summit that big bad mountain.

Among the team, there seemed to be a spectrum of reasons for being here. At one end were the career mountain athletes like Klára and Jason, whose commitment to the goal of K2 hadn't wavered despite avalanches and deaths. In them I sensed a hint of old-school climbing for national pride. In my view, the bros occupied the opposite end of the spectrum. To me, they seemed more interested in thrill seeking and bragging rights. I believed that I fell somewhere in the middle, but closer to the non-bro side. K2 had been summited by many Americans, including the first woman, Vanessa O'Brien, in 2017, so I didn't feel the draw or pressure of being the first of my country to accomplish something, like Klára or Jason. Like the bros, I was there to prove something. However, it was primarily myself I was trying to impress.

Many mountains reveal themselves to climbers slowly. Everest remains a windblown rocky peak on the distant horizon for most of the trek to its base camp, and on the Nepalese side of the mountain, the summit itself isn't revealed until its final camp at 26,200 feet. The Savage Mountain, as K2 is commonly referred to, reveals itself much more harshly. After fifty-four miles of walking, a left turn on the Baltoro Glacier abruptly shifts the landscape from modest snowcapped peaks to one solitary mass of rock and ice and snow. The rest of the walk to base camp, as well as the camp itself, is dominated by just one thing: K2's steep, uninviting slopes. At least that's how it usually works. This year, dense clouds and daily snowstorms kept the mountain from view for the whole trek. Clouds couldn't obscure K2's presence, though; I knew she was there, lurking and waiting to test me. I was unable to silence the voice in my head that repeatedly told me I was outmatched. I didn't know whether I could deliver what K2 demanded. And I didn't know that this mountain, more than any other I'd climbed, didn't care about me and remained unaffected by my wishes, my goals, my preparation.

Seven days after leaving Askole, Jason strode next to me on the trail. "Nearly there, Lisa." He nodded up ahead. His long legs ambled in solid movements over the snow-covered stones. I forced my lips into a weak smile.

"Feeling the elevation now, eh?"

I nodded without looking up, too focused on managing my breath and not twisting an ankle.

"Just over that wee rise there, we'll see Broad Peak's base camp, then K2's."

"Thanks, Jason," I finally mustered between inhalations.

"No sense in hurrying, anyhow, just to stand around in the snow," he offered.

As we continued toward camp, Jason stepped aside for porters, newly freed of their loads, to pass as they descended. Each time he offered a hand in thanks. "Tremendous strength, those guys. And humble beyond."

I began offering my thanks, too, though not every porter accepted my hand. However, those who did shook it with gusto, their skin thick as leather gloves. I appreciated that Jason recognized and respected every member of our team.

I was grateful to arrive at base camp, but there was little celebrating. Despite being at 16,300 feet, the sky had unleashed thick wet snowflakes all day, so the team huddled under umbrellas and took turns setting up tents.

The nomadic strain of trekking had made me excited to settle into base camp, but our haphazard campsite wasn't as cozy as I'd imagined.

I dedicated my afternoon to sorting through wet gear and fixing my tent fly so that the ceiling wouldn't leak. There was already a stream of water running diagonally through it, so I created a pool at one corner to hopefully contain it. With the home repairs complete, I turned to sorting clothes according to moisture content. I usually packed all my clothes in waterproof plastic bags, but sometimes they could get bulky, so this time, I'd stuffed my pants into any available space in my duffel. While that had made packing more efficient, the only dry pair of pants was a pair of wool long underwear. Everything else was wet and cold, some things so wet I had to wring them out. I stretched a cord across the tent and started hanging things, eventually realizing that body heat was the only tool I had for drying anything. So I pulled on each pair of cold, soggy pants, crawled inside my semi-damp sleeping bag, and shivered for a few hours until they were dry enough to wear.

Nothing on this mountain was going to be easy. Nothing.

CHAPTER 20

16,300 FEET

There was a party planned at K2 base camp, though it wasn't an ultracompetitive Crazy Eights card game party, nor a swear-word-only Scrabble party. This party was different because it mattered. It had intention. It was called a puja (pronounced "pooja"), and we were throwing it in honor of the mountain. This party was marked with the same finery as those other kinds of parties, though: there were off-brand candy bars, partially carbonated Coca-Cola, statues made of butter, bottles of American whiskey, and a bright Buddha poster wrapped in cellophane.

That morning, I'd sat with the Sherpas, our plastic lawn chairs forming a neat row as we squinted in unison over the steam from our warm drinks toward elusive K2 and wondered if she'd finally peek through the clouds today. After I sat down, Aang Phurba tugged my elbow and smiled.

"Auspicious day, *didi.*" He pointed with a long fingernail to the Buddhist calendar on his phone. Since we'd summited Everest, Aang Phurba called me *didi*, which means "older sister," even though I continually tried to convince him of my youthfulness, despite being many years his senior.

"Puja today?" I couldn't see Aang Phurba's earnest eyes behind his sunglasses, but I knew they were beaming. He nodded to confirm and shuffled into the dining tent to spread the news.

Holding a puja ceremony meant we could start climbing.

I looked across base camp and noticed Mingma Tenzi Sherpa, a badass Nepali climber and lama preparing to lead the puja. He sat beneath flapping prayer flags in meditative silence. I'd climbed with Mingma before, so I knew his solemn expression hid a gold tooth, and that somehow, he always appeared put together, his shirt always tucked neatly into his climbing pants, his hair always trim, his boots always clean, his round face always shaven. In a month, he would confidently climb with only the protection of a belay across the deadliest section of K2's Abruzzi Ridge to fix the route for the rest of us. Today, his offerings and prayers would float from base camp to K2's residing deities and request that we be allowed to climb safely. Climbing before receiving the mountain's blessing is considered inauspicious, so I had mixed feelings about this day; it meant that I could stop *thinking* about climbing K2 and actually start climbing K2, and that reality stirred fear in my gut. A very large part of my brain and body wanted to stay in the comfort of just thinking about climbing K2.

As puja preparations continued, K2 remained mysterious. Throughout the morning, fluffy white clouds grew and then dissolved on her slopes, obscuring a full view of the challenges that awaited me. After twelve days of travel and waiting—and, even though I was at the base of my goal, about to begin ascending—I had still not been able to see and absorb the mountain in person. Her continued elusiveness made me feel detached from this beast of ice and rock that had consumed my thoughts and priorities for years. I wanted to ease into this endeavor, to get to know K2 intimately before beginning to climb. But this mountain, like all her sisters, maintained control.

After Mingma's meditation, he rose and shook rice from his left hand into the air with three short upward strokes. The flying rice made a connection with the mountain deities and then scattered on the rock at his feet. It was time to begin.

I was sitting cross-legged on the rocks right behind Mingma now. A front-row seat meant sitting uncomfortably for hours in the rocks, though. *This is nothing compared to the discomfort you've signed up for, LT,* I reminded myself. His slow, mumbling chants and methodical rocking soothed me in a place where everything else felt so hard. I couldn't read the Nepali words on the sheafs of tissue-thin paper that he shuffled in his lap, and I didn't know what his chants meant, but I wanted to sit as close to him as possible so that maybe some of his lama-ness would stick to me. Maybe some of his badass mountaineer-ness would, too.

Before us was a short stone altar called a *chorten* that the Sherpas had built when we'd arrived at base camp five days ago. The chorten held all our mountain offerings. In addition to the food and booze, everyone who would climb above base camp had added their climbing gear to be blessed.

"Bring anything that will touch the mountain," I heard Aang Phurba say to a fellow climber.

To the pile, I'd added my ice axe, helmet, ascender, and crampons, since they would be the things that held me to the mountain and pro-tected me from a fall. Tucked in my helmet was a small bottle of Dad's ashes. Since his death almost two years ago, I'd carried him on every climb and sprinkled him on every summit. Sometimes, the coarse remnants of his body floated into the sky, set aloft effortlessly by the wind. Sometimes, they fell straight down in a cascade onto the snow at my feet. I thought it depended on Dad's mood that particular day. I wondered how he felt about being carried to Pakistan, to a country and culture so different from his own. I wondered how he was feeling about being blessed by a Buddhist lama and if I'd have the chance to show him the summit of the mountain that had occupied my mind for years.

I looked back toward our row of tents and caught Mushtaq, our Pakistani base-camp manager, clapping and swaying to the beat as he thumped an empty plastic drum with his bare hands. Next to him the Sherpas tapped their toes and sang. We were in a strange and beauti-ful crucible where multiple religions and beliefs could coexist, where Muslim drumbeats could accompany Buddhist song, all of us united in the pursuit of a shared goal.

Now, I watched Aang Phurba hopping between rocks toward the chorten, carefully correcting some invisible entanglement with the pile of ice screws, helmets, and crampons. I knew that Aang Phurba had done a more meaningful puja in his village before he came to Pakistan. He wore the loose red thread signifying the lama's blessing around his neck. Soon, I would have one, too, tied with a protective knot by Mingma as he wrapped it around my bowed head.

The winds at base camp shifted now, and I closed my eyes and filled my lungs with juniper smoke from the chorten. The earthy smell would pervade base camp until the last climber was off the mountain. Juniper smoke reminded me of hopeful parties like this, and of somber departures from other base camps. Even with my eyes closed, I was distracted by teammates talking and taking photos. I wanted people to be quiet, to stop fidgeting, to take this ceremony seriously.

Klára was sitting next to me and noticed my distraction. She squeezed my knee and whispered, "Don't let them get to you."

She knew more about this mountain and its secrets than most people here, even though they didn't realize it. Her wisdom now was timely; I needed to shift my energy internally. So I let Mingma's steady chanting blur everything except the enormous wall of ice and rock that loomed, partially obscured by clouds, beyond the chorten. I stared back at K2 with reverence. When I'd attempted Mount Rainier for the first time, with my uncle, in the dark tent as we made our final, clumsy preparations for the summit, he'd said, "Remember, the mountain doesn't care." His words had caught in vapor between us.

I knew that no mountain, especially K2, cared how much I wanted to summit, or how hard I'd prepared, or how skilled I was, or how brave I was. K2 didn't care if I summited or not. It made no difference to her if I died.

I focused again on Mingma's words. I didn't know what they meant, but mine meant this: *Please keep me safe. I promise to respect you. Please keep me safe.*

CHAPTER 21

16,300 FEET

The merriment of the puja eventually faded, and with the formality of the ceremony complete, my mood shifted. All the prerequisites for climbing K2 had now been accomplished; I had done all that I could do. Now began the game of waiting for K2 to be ready, too. Technically, that meant we were waiting for winds and snowfall high on the mountain to diminish and for K2 to shake off any avalanche-prone snow that had accumulated near the route. Figuratively, to me, it meant that K2 would not allow us to climb onto her slopes, would not let us enter her bastion, until she was ready. As we collectively waited, K2's readiness and the weather forecast became the primary topic of conversation among the ninety-five climbers from various teams that occupied base camp. Each expedition received daily weather forecasts from one or more of the niche companies that specialized in predicting mountain weather. Several times a day, clusters of climbers met, laptops splayed, to stare at wind speeds and snowfall projections and to debate in multiple languages when the best conditions for climbing to the summit and back would occur.

. . .

I caught Garrett sitting in a plastic chair outside of the dining tent, studying the route through a spotting scope.

"Wanna check it out, Lisa?"

I adjusted the height of the scope and pressed my eye into its cup. Through the high-powered lens I could only see blobs of snow, glistening white like meringue. I passed the scope back to Garrett and asked what I really wanted to know: "How's the weather forecast looking?"

"Hmm, looking good today and tomorrow, then high winds higher up. Aang Phurba and the guys are planning to carry loads. Sounds like the Japanese team is going to set the route to C2."

I nodded, calculating what this progress, this slow inching up the mountain, meant to me.

The Japanese team had been studying forecasts longer than the rest of us, since they'd arrived at base camp weeks before any other team. Betting that climbing conditions would be favorable early, they'd already begun to prepare for climbing by setting the first segment of the route with rope and anchors. All other climbing teams would use and trust their snow pickets, ice screws, and rope. This trust in someone else's work, someone I didn't even know, was unsettling to me. Especially when I knew that Garrett had brought four miles of high-quality climbing rope and barrels of ice screws from the United States. This type of trust is customary in mountaineering; high-altitude expeditions are a mix of teamwork and individual effort, and I knew that ultimately it was up to me to assess and feel comfortable with the route that I would climb and the gear that I would use. No one was going to do that for me; nor did I want them to. I wondered if everyone at camp felt the same, and I suspected that there was a significant amount of blind trust—maybe even ignorance—that just because a rope or an anchor had been placed and everyone ahead of you had used it meant it would be safe. I made a promise to myself not to allow unawareness to create false confidence.

"How you feeling?" Garrett asked.

I shrugged. "I don't know—feels like I'm acclimatizing slowly for some reason. I still get winded walking to the toilet tent."

"You're fine, Lisa. I do, too."

"I just wish there was a way to know when you're ready, you know."

"You're gonna do great, Lisa. You're ready for the mighty K2."

Just like on Everest, I doubted Garrett's endorsement. I doubted that I was good enough for K2. There was no litmus test, no tidy checklist that ensured success on a big mountain. My brain *needed* the tidy checklist, the if-this-then-that guarantee that defined much of my life at sea level. I wanted that here, too. But high-altitude mountaineering didn't follow a predictable formula; there was no room for entitlement at 8,000 meters, and without that security, my mind filled with doubt and played out all the ways I could fail, all the ways I could be inadequate.

I wanted normalcy, so I texted Sara, and she told me about the tomatoes and cucumbers in her garden and the oppressive Illinois humidity that bloomed her hair into a wild tangle. I told her that I was eating frozen jelly beans and wondering how many razors it would take to shave my legs when I returned to Islamabad. I didn't tell her that I was really wondering why I was even here.

Brooding wasn't good for me, I decided. Movement always helped to clear my mind, so I set out to walk through camp. Our section of camp was dotted with matching orange-and-white dome tents, set at discrepant angles in the rocks. It wouldn't make sense to set them in an orderly line, since the ice underneath base camp's rock floor melted so fast that we were constantly moving tents from the low, melted-out spots to higher ground. Our scattered tents made a rough perimeter around the rectangular group dining, cooking, and communication tents. As I ambled through our camp, I heard Nepali music and energetic laughs from the tents shared by our Sherpa team members. Based on the pairs of boots piled outside, I knew that inside several of the men were huddled together, sitting cross-legged, or lying on their stomachs, wearing climbing pants and T-shirts, each of them intent on winning a card game. Most of the other tents that I passed were quieter, and I suspected the climbers inside were spending their idle time reading, journaling, or sleeping. No matter which continent you were from, this was the time that was hardest for climbers. We were all so competitive and accustomed to constant movement and accomplishment that blank time felt awkward and superfluous. I wandered past another tent and heard the faint sound of a movie. Outside, Jason's Irish flag flapped slowly. I continued walking and intentionally looked past the rocks below camp, where I knew the remnants of a slaughtered cow were still being picked over by ravens. I made my way past the last cluster of tents that marked our encampment, and inside the voices were louder, boisterous; the bros were watching movies, too. And, based on the snippets of conversation that I could hear, drinking whiskey.

No matter how we chose to pass the idle time at base camp, we were all basically waiting for the most exciting activity of the day. Three times per day, the thin mountain air at K2's base camp was punctuated with a metal clang. At approximately 7:00 a.m., noon, and 6:00 p.m., a metal spoon struck a metal pot and provoked my fellow climbers and me to emerge from our tents, like animals from holes, and meander in bulky down layers and untied snow boots across the rocky foundation of base camp to the group dining tent.

Tonight, I arrived early and slid the thick zipper of the dining tent's canvas door upward along its track. Inside, the Sherpas had done their best to make the tent cheery, silk flowers hanging in upside-down fountains from the canvas ceiling, plastic lawn chairs arranged in an orderly row along the perimeter of the rectangular table, each with a unique flowered cushion.

It was the centerpiece of the table that was most important, and my reason for arriving to dinner early. Arranged in a jagged row of mismatched glass and plastic containers were condiments from four continents, their crucial role being to turn the unfamiliar familiar. I took on the self-appointed job of organizing the condiment parade. Only I cared about the completion of this task. But more than caring, I *needed* it. I needed it to remove even a small amount of chaos from the waiting and the unpredictable environment of high-altitude mountaineering. I needed to tidy the row, to wipe the sticky sides of jam jars, to venture into the pantry tent and rummage through waist-high blue barrels until I found a replacement for the empty shichimi bottle. Shichimi that my teammate had carried here to Pakistan from his Tokyo home to add the fiery blend of chili pepper, roasted orange peel, and sesame seeds to base-camp meals. He would sprinkle the spices with care even on breakfast porridge. Culinary familiarity was important because the stress of living three miles above sea level elicited a primal downshift in metabolism. To preserve only my most vital organs and functions, my body was methodically redirecting red blood cells from my intestines to my heart and brain. I appreciated my body looking after me in this way; it wasn't that I disagreed that my brain was more important than my stomach. But the result, at a time when my daily caloric demand exceeded 5,000, was that foods irresistible at sea level now had the appeal of wet cardboard. Perfectly symmetrical squares of caramel dressed in rich dark chocolate and embellished with delicate flakes of sea salt? Meh. Ruby tomato jewels that popped like summer sun in my mouth? No thank you. And worse yet, foods like beef, which I eschewed at home, became mandatory for survival.

The sounds of the dining tent's zipper interrupted my meticulous organizing, and I looked up at Khadim Malikpa's ruddy face. Everything about him, save his bushy eyebrows, was narrow, like the edges of his body and face had been pulled tightly together. This was Khadim's first expedition as cook to the Karakoram, and his face was still smooth, not yet rugged from years of mountain expeditions.

"Spaghetti, *didi.*" He gestured toward me with the hefty tin pot between his hands.

I thanked him after he set the pot on the table and raised the lid to peek inside. Khadim stood behind me, curious to see my response to his creation. Thick, pungent steam hit my dry nostrils. As promised, there was pasta and tomatoes, and also striated brown chunks. I frowned at this last ingredient. It bothered me that this "food" had walked with me to base camp, its tiny hooves clicking on the rocks beside me while I fought the urge to reach down and release the frayed rope from its curled horns and convince it to be free—to become someone's pet, even though I doubted that Pakistani pet goats were a thing.

As I was privately debating the merits of eating an animal I'd seen breathing this morning against the need to fuel my body (and embarrassed that it only bothered me when I'd seen the animal), one of the bros arrived wobbly and nearly incoherent, smelling of alcohol. It made me nervous and disappointed, sitting directly across from him at dinner. I didn't realize then that it was not really him I was disappointed in, not really him I was worried might fall over backward in his chair—it was Dad. But without that realization at the time, I would continue to misplace more animosity onto the bros.

CHAPTER 22

21,450 FEET

Sixteen days after leaving Islamabad, the weather had turned in our favor, and it was time to begin climbing. To coax our bodies into surviving in the meager air above base camp's 16,300 feet, we would climb incrementally higher over the next eight days. First to Camp 1, and then to Camp 2, with rest days at base camp in between. This would force our bodies to create more oxygen-carrying red blood cells. It was a delicate process, especially on K2. On other 8,000-meter peaks, multiple acclimatization rotations were accomplished before the summit was attempted. But K2 was different. Every minute spent above Camp 1 was a calculated game of chance with K2, with her rockfall and snow avalanches. These risks were so great that we would complete only one rotation before commencing the multiday climb to the summit.

This abbreviated method made sense to me, but I wanted more time to get to know this mountain before I attempted to climb to her highest point. I wanted her to actually like me and to help me climb safely. I wanted us to work as a team. I felt like a teenager who had moved to a new town and desperately wanted the popular girl to like me. I knew that my survival and ease on her turf depended on her acceptance. I doubted that she ever would, though, and so I had to continue anyway. This was the psychological challenge of mountaineering, where mental strength counted at least as much as physical.

I was thinking all these things as I ambled from the tent at Advanced Base Camp, or ABC, toward the climbing route. Climbing here to ABC yesterday afternoon, I had felt stronger than expected. Yet I knew that I had to let go of expectations about how I thought the climb should go. *Get it together, Lisa,* I told myself, shaking my head to reset my thoughts.

I looked up while strapping crampons to my boots. It was barely light out, but I could see that the slope in front of me was mostly snow, moderately steep, with strands of black rock. Although I hadn't climbed this route before, I had studied it, visualized it, taped pictures of it to my bathroom mirror. But I had not come face-to-face with K2 until three days ago. Clouds had obscured the horizon for most of my time at base camp. Multiple times per day, as I'd walked to the dining tent or washed clothes, I'd stare in the direction of the mountain, but her slopes had remained guarded and abstract. Then, finally, I could connect concepts with reality as the clouds slowly dissolved and brought K2's steep snow-laden slopes into view. Photocopied photos taped to bathroom mirrors hadn't prepared me for the mass of K2 and the presence that she created over camp. Her rocky, icy slopes felt especially uncaring and unyielding. She was always there from that day forward, waiting silently and making me feel tiny and inept.

Here at ABC I was face-to-face with the mildest of those slopes, and as I strapped on my crampons outside of my tent, I reminded myself: *All you have to do today is climb 2,300 feet, mostly on snow. You are ready for this moment. Just focus on today; you've done this before.*

When I started climbing with Klára, the eastern horizon had just started to cast a warm glow on the snow, and I let her pull ahead, content to move at a slow, measured pace up the slope alone. She and I had gotten an earlier start than most of the rest of the team, and I knew that their pace would push past mine. Soon, the pain of ascending steep snow at elevation settled into my body. It was not pleasant, but the familiarity was comforting. This section of the climb to Camp 1 wasn't technical, not even that steep compared to the terrain above. I told myself it was just like climbing familiar Mount Rainier, but my body knew that it was thousands of feet higher than Rainier's summit, and the familiar ache of oxygen deprivation settled in. My lungs felt pricked by a thousand needles at once, every inhalation reminding me that they were inadequate for this endeavor. I wanted my lungs to be bigger, stronger, and capable of capturing more oxygen. I knew that my heart was enduring the effects of climbing at 17,000 feet, too. It was beating faster than normal, fighting to rapidly pump scant oxygen to the parts of my body that were screaming for it. I hoped my brain would quickly remember the strain of oxygen deprivation and diminish its novelty for the rest of my body. Even though I'd told myself that it was smarter to move slowly in this section of the route, I desperately wanted to move faster and was frustrated that my body wasn't acclimatizing quickly. I began to worry that it never would.

My attitude was up to me, and I knew that tortuous mental dialogue about physiological processes that I had little control over would not help me climb this mountain. So I searched for comfort in three words. Each time my right boot kicked into the snow, I said, *I am* and when the left hit: *strong.*

I am.

Strong.

This mantra became meditative. I wasn't certain the words were resonating enough to create a pool of tranquility in my brain, but I stopped ruminating.

About an hour after leaving ABC, short, abrupt shouts from somewhere far above interrupted my introspection. I kicked the steel front points of my crampons into the hard snow to steady myself and quickly looked up, expecting to see a rock tumbling with erratic speed toward me.

Nothing. I focused again on the snow and resumed willful meditation. The yelling came again, but it was too far away for me to interpret, and still I saw nothing.

Yelling in the mountains is discouraged unless it's intended to alert fellow climbers to rockfall or some other hazard. Yelling on K2 is not uncommon, given the amount of rock- and icefall here, but this yelling sounded different. The screams didn't sound like "ROOOCK!" which was the standard call regardless of the falling object. They sounded more intense and desperate.

Then a dark object slid into the periphery on my right. It was a water bottle gliding silently down the smooth snow next to me. The water bottle was followed quickly by a mitten. Even when I heard Lakpa Bhote Tikepa yelling frantically behind me, I rationalized that someone had dropped their pack. Then I heard the familiar sound of Buddhist prayer from Lakpa, and I knew what was coming next. Not a backpack—a person.

Time compressed. Even though climbers were yelling above and below me, everything felt quiet and slow, like someone was covering my ears. He was just a few hundred feet away, so close that I reflexively wanted to run to him, to help him even as he flailed and tumbled chaotically down the mountain. But I knew the mountain had already taken this climber, and there was nothing any of us could do to reclaim him from K2. My breathing was shallow and ragged, and when I looked down, I could see my legs shaking through my insulated pants. I closed my eyes and tried to unsee what I'd just seen.

"Fuck. Breathe," I said into the morning air. *Just breathe.*

Klára and a handful of other climbers were several feet higher than me on the slope, sitting in the snow, all in shock, too. We didn't know who had died. None of my choices for what to do next felt right to me. Equal parts wanted to continue, to retreat, to hide, to cry. I sat with a group of shaken Pakistani men on the exposed rock next to the route. The sun was still rising in the summer sky, and the snow around us sparkled. One of the Pakistanis was mumbling a slow Muslim prayer. I looked at the man next to him in inquiry, who pointed to a nearby pile of rocks. *Body*, he mouthed.

It took a second, but I realized that the rocks were covering the body of another dead climber. Sobering seriousness flushed through me, and my breath went shallow again. K2's geography channels everything that falls from above directly down this snow slope. Everything: rocks, ice, people. I didn't feel like K2 and I were a team. I didn't feel like she wanted me—or any of us—here. I felt like she wanted to flick us all off her back like fleas on a dog. Within two hours of climbing, death had surfaced twice. My intention was focused; I needed to move.

I started up the snow slope and sat in the snow next to Klára when I reached her perch. Her sobs were so intense she couldn't form sentences. I told her to breathe, and to climb when she was ready; there was no reason to hurry today. My emotions were a tangle of sadness, confusion, and shock. I knew that I could not afford the mental energy right now to dismantle what I'd just seen. I was certain of that. I didn't, however, know if continuing to Camp 1 was the right thing to do. But I didn't have the mental capacity to think logically through the options and make a different choice. I hugged Klára hard and reminded her again to breathe. She nodded her head slowly, and I continued upward. As I climbed, rationality surfaced intermittently. *If I'm continuing upward, then my goal today is the same: climb safely to Camp 1. To do that, I must set aside his death, for now.* So I focused only on the basic movements of my body. I lifted one foot after the other and mindfully forced myself upward. That was all that I could do.

That night, I lay uncomfortably in a damp tent at Camp 1, breathing the thin air at 19,700 feet. The space designated for camp was so scarce and steep that any movement outside of the tent required a rope and harness for safety. The tent that Klára and I shared doubled as group storage, the bottom lined with bumpy, soggy nylon sacks stuffed with tents that our Sherpa team would carry to higher camps. I'd given up the notion of comfort tonight, given my undulating sleeping platform, which smelled like soggy nylon. My body ached from today's effort, and I was desperate for sleep but could not erase the vision of a fellow climber falling to his death. Klára lay next to me, flat on her back, too. But we didn't speak. We didn't talk about his death. Every time I closed my eyes, he was there. Through tearful conversations at camp, I'd learned that he, Serge Dessureault, was a husband, a father, a firefighter. Five days ago, we'd celebrated together in base camp, smiling and hugging after the festive puja ceremony. Today, I felt guilty, like I was unnecessarily gambling my life for a selfish endeavor, in an environment where I was unwelcome. But I was too stubborn to stop. I still carried with me the question of *why?* Did Serge know why? Did any of us? Was there a suitable reason that justified risking death to stand on top of a mountain for twenty minutes? Hadn't I used all my might three years ago to fight cancer? Why would I choose to put myself in danger?

These questions swirled in my brain without answers throughout the night.

The mood at camp the next morning was somber. We'd all just witnessed someone with shared aspirations die in pursuit of those aspirations. And even though I had accepted death as an outcome of this endeavor, I now felt like I'd accepted it with brash naivete and reality had altered my perspective. I didn't want to die. No mountain is worthy of that sacrifice. The terrain prevented us from easily moving about camp to communicate, but Klára and I heard bits of conversation and radio transmissions from our tent. She and I hardly spoke. Serge had died rappelling, doing something that we would all do in two days' time. He hadn't made a mistake. The rope had broken. It could have happened to any of us. Perhaps to cope, or to deflect, the conversation outside of our tent shifted from emotional to practical as the day progressed, and a decision was made to replace the current nylon rope, installed just two weeks ago, with the stronger climbing rope that Garrett had brought from the US.

Route fixing, the process of anchoring rope along the climbing route, is an exercise in coordination and trust on big mountains. Typically, one team takes responsibility and the rest of the teams either lend labor to the fixing effort or pay the responsible team for the use of their ropes. This generally works well, assuming everyone is compliant, unless the quality of the work or rope is questionable, which it currently was. Thin nylon, or "Korean rope," was commonly used on Himalayan and Karakoram peaks. It was lightweight and cheap and generally suitable on routes like the south side of Everest, where there was little rappelling during descent. K2 is different, though. Nearly everyone rappels and commits their full weight to cheap, lightweight rope. Plus, the rope on K2 often rubs against sharp rock, further compromising it. It didn't make sense to use low-quality rope in a no-mistakes environment. We'd learned from climbers who had already climbed to Camp 2 that the new Korean rope, which had been in place for only two weeks, was quickly fraying. These reports had spread through Camp 1 and down to base camp, making everyone question its quality. Through conversations with people who'd been climbing with Serge, we learned that he'd clipped into an old rope because the new Korean rope looked more tattered. I spoke to a Spanish climber who had also fallen when the new rope he was descending had broken. He lifted his jacket to show me his bruised ribs. There seemed to be consensus that the new Korean rope installed by the Japanese team should be replaced with legitimate climbing rope—two miles of it. Although this was a lot of work for the Sherpa team, it was the safest solution.

Rocks cracking, breaking, and hurtling violently interrupted my sleep the next morning at Camp 2. When I opened and uncovered my eyes, the bright tent confirmed that it was somehow morning. I knew that I was safe; rockfall was so common on K2 that I could differentiate *concerning* from *interesting* (at least I thought I could). This morning, from inside my shared tent at 21,500 feet, it sounded merely interesting, reminding me that the mountain was in charge, that I was an unwanted visitor here, asking—hoping—for safe passage. Inside my down sleeping bag, I rolled to the opposite hip, temporarily releasing the pain from lying on the other. Klára was curled in her own lump of down to my left, and I was envious that she still managed to sleep.

We were rotating the use of the tents at Camp 2 with other climbing teams, the coordination maximizing the limited real estate here and minimizing the work to carry heavy loads of tents up the mountain. Our climbing rotations were coordinated so that when a team vacated Camp 2, the next team would occupy it later in the day. We would employ this strategy for Camps 3 and 4, too. The previous occupants of this tent had left food and clothes: there was a set of bamboo chopsticks, the thick end painted with a *maneki-neko* cat, and, wadded up in the corner of the tent, a worn jacket from a Russian manufacturer, which I'd used unsuccessfully for a while the night before to level my sleeping pad. Scattered near my feet were Norwegian crispbread crackers. The tent itself was bowed outside of its intentional shape, and it listed dramatically toward the downhill side, Klára's side. The shift was so pronounced that the tent's zipper formed more of a D shape than its intended arc. Yesterday, Klára and I had arranged our sleeping bags and pads on top of the giant slope of our tent's floor. We grunted and giggled and swore in our native languages at our predicament as we tried our best to shift and shim our supplies to create as much comfort as possible. That we could sleep at all was astounding. I reminded myself to never take a comfortable bed for granted again.

Camp 2 rests precariously on a tapered swath of snow, just above a narrow vertical slice in the rock that unlocks the upper mountain from the lower. For decades, a safe route to the area where Camp 2 would be placed and beyond eluded pioneering climbing expeditions, until the 1938 American Karakoram expedition, which set out to scout several possible summit routes for the then unclimbed peak.

Yesterday, as I had climbed the snow and scattered rock leading to this vertical fissure, called a chimney, the thought of it had loomed in my head. I'd watched so many online videos and studied so many photos that it had grown its own persona in my mind. Yet I still couldn't imagine wedging my body into the crack and ascending. Finally, from a relative flat spot in the snow, I had taken a break to check the elevation on my watch. I was close, but when I looked up, all that I could see was an impenetrable wall of jumbled yellow rock. Finally, I saw other climbers on top of the wall; I was staring directly at the chimney but still couldn't distinguish it from the rest of the terrain. In 1938, American alpinist Bill House had stood, presumably, at that same flat spot and determined that the 100-foot-tall crack was climbable. He led the free-climb through the chimney for two hours and unlocked the mystery of achieving K2's summit.

From the flat spot, I watched a Japanese team establish an intermediate camp. I let myself fantasize for a minute about joining them. How comfortable it would have been to rest here, to be out of the wind and snow, to drink warm tea, to relax. But resting wasn't going to get me any closer to the summit.

So I transitioned my ascender to the section of rope leading into the chimney and stepped precariously onto an exposed mound of hard ice, created from the ice shed by the chimney. Navigating the ice mound was tricky, and I repeatedly slammed the front points of my crampons into it but usually found no purchase. I had much better luck resting my front points into the tiny depressions made by other climbers.

The fixed rope that my ascender attached to was meant to prevent me from sliding off the mountain, which it would, but the section of rope leading to the chimney was so high that it hung in the air at the height of my shoulder. I traced it to the mouth of the chimney, which I could now see, hoping that it would lower as it got closer, but it didn't. I felt more like I would have to pull myself, belly up and hand over hand, between the rope's high points—like a spider, inching her way across a delicate web. I knew the rope would drop when the climber ahead of me transitioned off it, but I was unsettled, worrying that when that happened, I would lose my balance and be unable to regain purchase on the ice. I considered switching back to the lower anchor but, in a hypoxic fog, convinced myself that the associated logistics would be too cumbersome.

The risk of an anchor failing was too great for multiple climbers to ascend the chimney simultaneously. So I waited my turn, shaking my arms and wiggling my toes to prevent cold from settling, distracting myself by listening to the muted voices of climbers in the chimney. Or maybe it was the ones on top of the chimney; I couldn't tell, but I doubted their conversations concerned me. What did concern me was getting from here to the chimney. I shifted my focus on the climber ahead of me and studied his movements. I felt like I needed a crash course in how to efficiently transition from the rope that I was on— the one at my shoulder—to the steep one that ascended the chimney. The climber that I was studying was close to a foot taller than me, but the transition between ropes still looked tricky for him, and he didn't have to reach awkwardly across his body to the opposite shoulder to reposition his ascender to the next rope. *How the hell is that going to work?* I wondered. *Breathe,* I reminded myself. *Just breathe. You will figure this out.* There had been other moments like this in the mountains where I couldn't exactly visualize how I was going to navigate an obstacle, and I'd just gone for it, and it had magically worked out, so I was counting on that happening now.

Mercifully, as soon as the climber ahead of me switched ropes enough slack was released, and I didn't lose my balance. My ascender then assumed a more normal position at my waist. I felt instant relief and moved on to the next problem.

Once inside the chimney, I found it didn't seem as daunting as I'd imagined, and I felt protected in this 100-foot maw of vertical icy rock, barely as wide as a man's shoulders. The gray and yellow chunky rock inside the chimney was littered with a vertical spiderweb of old rope and wire ladders. I looked into the deepest part of the chimney, where there was a vein of ice and rotten snow, marred with the remnants of decades of climbing expeditions. The rope left behind was aged and faded by the sun and harsh conditions. Near the entrance of the chimney, I noticed a chunk of hemp rope iced into the rock, so old it had probably been left there by House's expedition in 1938.

The mechanics of climbing the chimney were not complex. I slid my ascender as high as I could reach, then stepped as high as safely possible with each foot while using my hands for balance. In this case, my movement was complicated by the continuous tangle of old ropes and inconvenient rocky footholds that were not ideal for crampons. I followed traces of old rope that had become encased in ice, unavailable for my use. I focused hard to be sure my hypoxic brain was able to discern the best foothold and safest rope for my ascender. With my left hand, I often grabbed a bunch of frayed ropes when there wasn't an obvious handhold. I reasoned that they couldn't all break at once. And, always, I breathed by stopping to take many consecutive, controlled breaths, which felt more like gasping to my lungs and the other parts of my body that were screaming for more oxygen to move upward. I wanted to rest longer, to let my helmet lean against the icy rock, to close my eyes and . . . what? Become a part of the mountain? Iced in like that hemp rope? Climbers who became comfortable with stasis for too long risked safety. So I slid my ascender one more time, searched for safe hand and foot placements one more time, and told myself to breathe one more time. Near the top of the chimney, my internal conversation was interrupted by Lakpa's face, streaked white with sunscreen, peering down into the gap. "Smile, Lisa," he warned before snapping a photo. "You're climbing K2!"

Yes, I was. But this was nothing like the experience of House and his team. In 1938, House free-climbed this crack—in two and a half hours. It was considered the toughest rock climb in the world. The mountaineering community has since honored his pioneering efforts by naming it after him. Those men were true explorers, climbing for national pride, to stake their country's flag on the summit of a peak not previously trod on by their countrymen. Early K2 expeditions included typewriters and employed hundreds of Balti porters. They used heavy canvas tents, not the nylon version I was lying in now. I felt like I was cheating a little bit, like I had it too easy, even though anything tougher than *easy* might have been more than I could handle.

Climbing House's Chimney was hard but felt better than I'd expected. Still grueling, as grueling as climbing vertical rock at 21,500 feet should be. What I hadn't expected to be hard was the snow slope above the chimney. After I exited the chimney, this slope was all that separated me from the shelter of a tent and the rest that I'd been fantasizing about. But my body just didn't want to move as fast as my mind expected it to. I needed oxygen, but there just wasn't enough. So I slowed down, ignored the part of my brain screaming for oxygen, and took deep, measured breaths while staring at my tent and hoping it would begin to appear closer.

I'd struggled for the last few breaths and steps to carry me to a tent—this tent—which was perched on top of the remains of countless other tents from previous expeditions. Now I lay burrowed in my sleeping bag, with a headache, general apathy, and fatigue, and wondered who else had lain in this same spot. Who had occupied the tents upon which mine was stacked? The colorful nylon shreds held the stories of those men and women. What had been their motivations? Had they survived? Had they been scared? Homesick?

Klára rolled over next to me, interrupting my mental review of yesterday's climb.

"Morning, sunshine," she said casually, like all of this was normal.

"Morning, love. Any nightmares last night?"

Klára had warned me about her nightmares when we began sharing a tent weeks ago. *Just shake me until I stop screaming*, she'd instructed.

I'd expected the screams to be muted, subtle. Like a napping puppy. But the night before, sometime in the middle of the night, Klára had released multiple piercing shrieks that had jolted me awake. I'd leaned toward her, dragging my sleeping bag with me, and held her shoulders until she'd stopped.

"You screamed like someone was holding a knife to your throat," I told her now.

"God, sorry, I don't remember anything. Thank you. Sorry."

Vivid dreams were common at high altitude, though mine had

never reached the nightmare level, which meant I actually looked forward to trying to decipher their wackiness. I'd once dreamed that I was at a circus with my grade-school librarian, and she was selling me heirloom soup samples from a leather suitcase.

"How do you feel?" Klára asked, still lying flat on her back with her knit hat on.

We'd barely spoken yesterday, both of us more focused on our own mental dialogue, still trying to comprehend Serge's death. I appreciated that we looked out for each other, even when we were both caught up in our own anguish. It was comforting to know that someone else was considering my well-being.

"Shitty, as expected. My head is pounding, extracting myself from this sleeping bag feels impossible, and I need to poop but have no idea how I'm going to manage that. I probably slept two hours last night."

Klára nodded inside her sleeping bag, and I knew she felt the same.

"Yesterday was hard," I confided in her. "I just don't feel like I'm acclimatizing fast enough."

"Hey, no comparing, remember?" she reminded me.

"I don't know why I let myself get wound up about it. I know better." I exhaled deeply, partly from lack of oxygen and partly from exasperation. "I know it's just me and the mountain, and I know that I don't need any added stress up here, but I hate appearing weak, ya know?"

I knew that she knew. Though we'd been raised in different cultures on different continents, we felt the same strain of competition in this macho pursuit. She knew that she and I were viewed as least likely to succeed. For women mountaineers, competition often came with the added pressure of being questioned for even wanting to participate in such a male-dominated endeavor. And for mothers like Klára, I wondered what extra pressure she must have felt. With two young children at home, this must have been much more difficult for her than for me. I knew that letting competition run out of control was pointless, that it didn't matter who got to camp first, or last. What mattered was safety. What mattered was contributing positively to a team. What mattered was being true to myself. What mattered was finding my boundaries, respecting them, and not crossing them.

"Thank you," I told Klára, holding back tears of gratitude and stress. "So glad we're doing this together."

. . .

Hours later, I was perched at the top of House's Chimney again, waiting my turn to descend, Aang Phurba anchored above me. We were assessing ropes to determine the best one to use for rappelling. Jason was already ahead of me in the chimney and using the most obviously good rope, the new orange one, but I was hoping to speed up the process by using a different one for my rappel. Using a different rope would allow me to rig my rappel device while he was still descending. All of them were crap. Even the one I'd ascended yesterday had bulges of exposed kern from being stomped on with crampons. Had it been like that yesterday?

I struggled to tie knots in the damaged rope to prevent someone from attempting to rappel off it. I wondered how Serge had felt about the rope he'd used for rappelling. Had it looked sketchy? Completely safe? Had the point of failure been far above him on a hidden part of the route?

"That's the god of K2," Aang Phurba said, interrupting my retrospection and pointing to a precarious rock at the opening of the chimney.

"Why did you show me that?" I teased him.

He just giggled. He'd likely occupy his tenuous perch until the last climber left Camp 2 today.

I heard Jason's "OK!" echo through the chimney, confirming that he was off the rappel rope. I reached down and pulled up on it with my index finger to confirm it was lax and ready for me to use.

"My turn!" I said to Aang Phurba as I pulled the rope to my waist and began to rig my rappel device.

"See you later, alligator," Aang Phurba said.

"After a while, crocodile."

"Okey dokey." He giggled again.

"Smoky." I laughed with him.

Seven minutes later, I was out of the chimney.

"Thank you, House's Chimney," I said. "Thank you, thank you, thank you."

"OK!" I yelled up at Aang Phurba, indicating that I was off the rappel rope. "Okey dokey!" he yelled back.

I focused on navigating the sketchy ice bulge and the scattered rock below it. At each anchor, I carefully rigged my rappel device and double-, then triple-checked it. *This is a no-mistakes moment,* I reminded myself every time. *Perfection is required.* I was breathing hard the whole time, a response to the combination of altitude and fear. This was how Serge had died.

CHAPTER 23

16,300 FEET

With our single acclimatization rotation complete, the waiting game resumed. This time the vibe across base camp was more serious. In preparation for climbing higher than Camp 2 in a few days, there were pyramids of green oxygen bottles outside the dining tent and stacks of coiled orange climbing rope that Mingma, Aang Phurba, and the team would use to create the route above Camp 2. We were all slowly, casually getting ready to leave for the summit, which we believed would happen in two days' time.

At breakfast, Garrett announced, "After lunch we're going to the Gilkey Memorial." He was sitting next to me, and he nodded his head up and down with intent as he chewed on a piece of bacon. "You should come, Lisa. Lots of history."

"Hmm, OK, cool, thanks," I told him. I felt curiosity and a melancholy twist in my gut. The Gilkey Memorial is a solemn monument to K2's fallen climbers. It was built in 1953 when, during his team's attempt to rescue him, American climber Art Gilkey mysteriously slid off K2 at 24,600 feet. Though he wasn't the first K2 fatality, Gilkey's life was memorialized by a tin dinner plate stamped with his name and a rock cairn built in his honor. The cobbled stone hillock outside of base camp where Gilkey's plate still hangs has become an ever-growing monument to the lives taken by K2. Today, dozens of plates hang there, along with antique climbing gear, tattered clothes, and bone fragments.

"You going?" Klára asked from my other side at the table.

"I don't know; I'm not sure it'd be good for me to see all that right now. Did you go last time?"

"Yeah, I went. Good to see it. You should hike up there."

I understood Klára's point. I felt conflicted between the importance of honoring the climbers that had come before me and falling into a macabre funk over the very real possibility that Khadim would imprint my name on a tin plate.

"I think I'm going to skip it," I told her a few minutes later. "Too intense for me right now."

Klára nodded knowingly and went back to her pancakes and eggs. At the far end of the table, I heard the bros wagering on who would make it to the memorial and back the fastest. I was eager to let them run off; I didn't need to sit in front of the metal plates and hear them clanking against rock or ravens squawking from their stone perches to honor the men and women who had come before me. I would do it in my own way.

My priority that afternoon was showering, and when it was my turn in the shower tent, I carried a plastic ten-gallon bucket that had originally housed kerosene from the cook tent down the flat rock steps to the tall, skinny fabric tent designated for showering. There was not actually a shower inside, just a weathered plastic chair. With a heave, I pulled the bucket of hot water inside with me. I was out of breath from just that short walk with a heavy bucket. I'd been above 16,300 feet for two weeks and climbed even higher just a few days ago. How could I not carry a bucket of water downhill without gasping for breath? *You're not acclimatizing,* I admonished myself, even though it was out of my control. I stripped down, careful not to drop my dry clothes on the wet rocks as I hung them on a thin cord stretched between the tent's upright poles. I was not really sure how this was supposed to work. But despite the grime on the outside of the bucket, and the cloudy water on the inside, I wished I could squeeze into a seated position inside the bucket. Standing would have to do, I decided, and stepped into the hot water, then laughed at myself standing naked and cold in a bucket of murky water inside a thin nylon tent at 16,300 feet in Pakistan. *What are you doing here, Lisa?* In lieu of an answer, I reached down for the plastic scoop floating in the bathwater. I desperately wanted my hair to be clean. Hair washing at high altitude is tricky business, though. Ideally, it's sunny enough for long enough that it will dry completely and not freeze into a splayed tangle that can't be brushed. I didn't trust that the weather would stay sunny this afternoon, but I couldn't resist the possibility of smelling like a girl again and poured a full scoop of hot water over my head and shoulders.

When I was as clean as possible and the water in the bucket was full of cloudy suds, I stood up straight and looked down at my body. This body. These hips, these hands. These boobs that weren't really mine. I was perfectly vulnerable, standing there, and couldn't resist critiquing what I saw. I couldn't resist doubting that it would be enough for K2. Standing naked in that tent, I couldn't see everything that those legs and feet and heart had given me—and everything that they'd carried me through. I couldn't see that those boobs were a sign of what I'd fought to overcome. I couldn't see that every time I'd asked my body to perform—in the mountains and out—it had. There had been difficult moments, yes, but when it had mattered most, my body *had* acclimatized, it *had* carried the heavy load, it *had* beat cancer. At the time, I didn't recognize that by simply attempting K2, I was implicitly trusting my body again. Instead, I assessed whether I'd lost too much muscle and wondered why I still didn't have discernible abs.

During the camp's last neighborhood reorganization, Klára and I had moved our tents to the edge of camp, away from the clatter of the kitchen tent. She was standing between our tents inspecting her crampons when I walked back.

"Aaahhh! How does clean feel, love?"

"Magnificent," I confirmed, and flipped my wet hair from side to side in an awkward display of femininity.

"Oooh, you know what else you need?" She dropped her crampon and dove in her tent.

"I could use a blow dryer!" I yelled after her.

"No, this is better, I promise." She stuck her arm outside the tent. "My mum bought it for me. Smell."

When I opened the glass bottle, my nose flooded with the exquisite scent of flowers and sunshine and normalcy. I sprayed the perfume all over my face and neck.

"Oh! My god, that's divine." For just a second, I felt like a normal woman in the harshest environment on the planet. "Wow, thank you. Do you have champagne in there, too?"

"Ha! That's for after the summit, love."

"Do you really think we'll start the summit rotation the day after tomorrow?"

"Yeah. The weather looks good, and the Poles said that they're planning to start up, too." She nodded toward the cook tent. "It looks like the Sherpas are getting everything ready to carry up the hill, too."

I didn't say anything, leaning down to pick up a rock for distraction. I wished I could feel as excited as Klára seemed. I wished the confidence I'd felt before Everest's summit rotation would find me.

"You feel ready?" she asked.

"I don't know." To prevent myself from crying, I focused on rolling the rock between my fingertips. Even though I knew she wouldn't think less of me if I showed emotion, I was cautious about any outward display of uncertainty about my ability. "It just seems like my body is acclimatizing slower than normal. I still get winded walking around camp. I don't know what's going on. And I just don't want to race with the dudes, ya know?"

"Why don't we leave tomorrow?" she said simply. "We could have a lovely walk up the hill to ABC, then have a nice rest, and then we start climbing." Before I could contemplate what a change of schedule would mean, she said, "Yes, that's it! Girls go first," and, with a clap of her hands, turned on her heel, and pink pants and black hair became a blur as she slipped back into her tent to pack.

"OK," I said, drawing it out, and turned back toward my own tent. K2 was still staring back at me. "Guess I'm climbing you tomorrow."

Klára's plan was solid. Leaving the afternoon before everyone else would create some space, physically and psychologically, between us and the rest of the team. Plus, spending one night slightly higher than base camp couldn't hurt my acclimatization predicament. The rest of the team would catch up with us at Camp 1, just before the climbing began. Despite a small pang of guilt for not departing with the rest of the team, I knew that this arrangement would start me off in a better frame of mind.

Very quickly, though, the concern over my body's readiness to climb was replaced by panic. I felt an instant urgency to double-check gear and oxygen, to confirm food, to verify that I'd packed everything I needed to stay safe and healthy and not an ounce more. I started by making tidy piles of clothes, food, and gear inside my tent. When I was satisfied with the piles, I scanned through cards, letters, and trinkets from friends and family. There were greeting cards with bright, glittery flowers and encouraging notes on index cards and delicious lavender sachets. But most important to me were the voice recordings that I'd forced my friends to create. Some of them were belly-laughing hilarious, some so serious they aroused tears. Usually, I would save them for summit night, but today I needed an antidote for the uncertainty and doubt. So I watched a two-minute video from my friend Tasha, the kind of friend I didn't have to see every day to be able to count on for a ride and a comfortable bed, without question or judgment, at 3:00 a.m. on a Wednesday when I needed it. In the video, Tasha sang me a song about an underestimated ram with high hopes. The nursery rhyme was silly and powerful. Something about the serenity and vulnerability in her song released a wave of ignored emotions that I would need to leave behind at base camp, since it wouldn't serve me to carry it up the mountain.

CHAPTER 24

21,450 FEET

The next afternoon, a month after I'd left Seattle, my bid for K2's summit began. Klára and I stood on the rocky path that bisected our base camp, wearing bright wool shirts and clunky mountaineering boots that extended to our knees. Inside our backpacks we carried everything we'd need for the next five days that wasn't already cached higher on the mountain. As a pre-climbing custom, Khadim presented us with a plate of roasted barley flour called *tsampa*, which we spread on one another's cheeks as a wish for long life. The rest of the team stood in a standoffish semicircle, and I walked through them to complete the last step in my climbing ritual. I walked clockwise around the stone chorten in the middle of camp three times. Each time, the sweet, woodsy smell of juniper smoke wafted over me and toward the mountain. I knew that Mushtaq would keep the juniper burning until we were all home, and I knew that the smoke would be the last scent of anything remotely festive that my senses would experience for the next week. Where I was going there'd be only ice and rock and the gritty determination of fellow climbers.

Rob joined us—whether out of a sense of duty or not, I didn't care. I was happy to have one more positive personality on our temporary little team. The three of us walked leisurely across the flat snowfield that edged base camp, meandering through the tiny icefall at its nose, taking time to snap photos and marvel at how the terrain had changed since our last foray to ABC. Eventually, we climbed through the icefall and onto a rocky spine, this one leading to ABC and the point where the route takes a sharp left turn onto the southeast spur.

We let interesting rock formations and debris from previous expeditions draw us off the route, curious to examine gear that had been carried by snow and ice slowly down the mountain for decades. Tucked in a shallow rock alcove at the edge of the rocky moraine that hosts camp, I saw a rectangular silver plaque nailed to the stone. The thin plaque was bent at its corners and scratched in places from falling rock. Silently, Rob and I read the bold letters together; then he wandered ahead while I stared harder at the name, Dobrosława Miodowicz-Wolf, a Polish woman who died in 1986, the year I'd turned fourteen. I was grateful for a second, more personal chance to pause and contemplate the seriousness of my endeavor, this time intimately, with only the mountain and a single plaque instead of at the Gilkey Memorial. I didn't want to think about my own memorial, but I did. For several long moments, I sat in the cold brown rock beneath her memorial and stared back down the glacier. *What will happen up there?* I wanted to know. *Who will I be when I return to this place? Was she scared, too?*

"Please give me strength, and guidance, and wisdom. I promise to learn from you," I said. I remembered the letter I'd written before I'd left Seattle. It was still waiting, unaddressed, in a sealed envelope underneath the keyboard in my office. It felt too melodramatic to give it to anyone, yet I felt compelled to write it, to provide some feeble direction to whomever should have the responsibility for tidying the pieces of my life.

Please let Chevy live with Sara but she has to promise to exercise him every day and not let him get fat (I mean it!). Please have a party outside, not a funeral, and play "My Way" (Frank's version, not Usher's). At the end, please give everyone some of my ashes and ask that they take me on an adventure somewhere; it doesn't have to be epic, just fun. And please, please do not let anyone say that I died doing what I loved because while that is true, I would rather be there with you.

That night, Klára and I shared a tent at ABC, and we giggled until we cried about forgetting forks and eating rice with discarded tent stakes that Klára had scrounged from the rocks near our tent. We shared stories from other climbs, reminisced about our lives at home, and decided to stop wearing bras.

"Who needs 'em?" I said. We tossed them in the corner of the tent.

Bonding with Klára felt normal, and though I knew that *normal* was only temporary, it was what I needed to shift my mood and begin climbing with confidence and a sense of camaraderie.

We left camp early the next morning and set our own pace climbing up the now familiar slope that led from ABC to the upper mountain. It felt comfortable this time. This time, I didn't need a mantra to remind myself that I was strong. I felt like I was finally climbing on my own terms, with a small team that I knew had my back. I relaxed enough to let my body and mind do what I'd been training them to do for years: climb. It didn't feel like I was fighting anymore; I left behind the worry of whether my body was ready and instead relied on that tiny spark inside of me that believed I was capable. There was an element of simplicity to climbing this way that was freeing. I didn't have to worry about competing or whether I should bring two pairs of thin gloves instead of one pair of heavy ones. I didn't have to visualize myself climbing K2 anymore because I was finally doing it. This was the same feeling I'd felt on Rainier that first time, ten years ago. Flow, it's called. The same mental space we strive to occupy through meditation.

I continued in this bubble of embryonic confidence until the terrain steepened at 19,500 feet, just below the collection of tents that make up Camp 1. I could see the rest of the team moving swiftly up the hill behind me and instinctively started to climb faster. *It's not a race,* I finally reminded myself, and sat in the snow clipped to an anchor. Klára was already at camp; I could see her sorting through gear and readying the tent. *You'll never be here again; just enjoy it for one second.*

So I sat, eating M&M's, and looked back down the mountain at the glacial terrain that my body had covered the past month. For a minute, I was amazed at myself. Amazed that the same scrawny body that was chosen last for kickball in gym class had navigated all that desolate terrain. She was here, that same uncertain girl—here at 19,500 feet on the world's most dangerous mountain—and she'd earned it.

Eventually, the rest of the team began passing my perch. I continued sitting, reluctant to burst my peaceful bubble, and welcomed them to Camp 1 with an open palm of M&M's. They were all encouraging and positive, and I reminded myself that they were not bad guys. I knew that my bubble of calm, baby confidence was about to end, though. I was grateful to have had a day without the added pressure of competing with the guys, and thankful for Klára's and Rob's friendship. I was grateful for the invitation to leave base camp ahead of the rest of the team. I'd felt like I was climbing with partners who had my back, and perhaps more importantly, I felt like I knew that leaving early was best for me and that I had been strong enough to do it.

At camp, Klára and I assumed the same uncomfortable positions as the last time, only now, because the Sherpas had carried them to higher camps, there wasn't a row of wet tents stored on the bottom of our tent. This time, I was ready for the miserable conditions and poor sleep, and I felt my body start to adapt to the harsher environment, as the familiar cough and congestion that comes with breathing cold, dry mountain air started to settle into my lungs and nose.

We departed Camp 1 the next morning as a team, but soon dispersed on the snow slope above camp. Rocks were beginning to punctuate the snow, a sign that we were entering the steeper confines of rock and ice. After much bickering about overloading the fragile snow pickets acting as anchors, I decided to take a break, thinking I'd rather climb alone than fight about how many climbers should occupy an anchor at once.

"How you feeling?" Klára asked.

"Pretty good, I guess. Glad it's cloudy. You?"

"Eh, I'm not sure," she said.

Klára had been climbing strong since we'd left base camp, and it didn't seem to me that anything could slow her down.

"Are you OK?" I wanted to know, feeling a duty to solidarity.

"Just . . . something's not right, I can tell."

"Not right how?"

"My head . . . maybe my stomach."

"Do you want any meds?"

We were all carrying mini personal pharmacies. Mine was a mix of pain meds, drugs meant to squash gastrointestinal bugs, decongestants, and emergency steroids.

"Yeah, maybe I should take something," she said, and pulled a stuff sack out of her backpack. I climbed up to where she was sitting in the snow and clipped in next to her. Below us, Lakpa, who had been patiently climbing with us all morning, reached into his own backpack for a water bottle. Klára swallowed two Tylenol, and our trio continued. I was more alert now to her movements as I climbed behind her. The elevation forced deep, deliberate exhalations for all of us except Lakpa, who I suspected could run to camp in an hour if we weren't holding him back. The terrain had changed to chunky granite covered with wet, rotten snow. The steeper terrain forced me to begin using both arms and legs in my ever-upward quest, and I was no longer able to merely walk uphill. I was making bigger, more taxing movements with my body, reaching above me to find a wet rock that would support my weight, trusting it, and then stepping up, breathing from the deepest place my body could find, and then repeating the whole process again and again. My crampons scratched on crumbling rock for probably the thousandth time this morning, the sound of metal points grating against granite reminding me that I didn't have the right tool for this job; crampons were meant for snow and ice, not rock. Walking with them on rock is like walking in high heels and greatly increases the chances of a twisted ankle. I wondered how dull they'd become from days of climbing in the wrong terrain.

After another hour of climbing, I noticed Klára slowing above me, and when I reached the rock where she'd paused, I tried to make light of the challenge. "Big step," I said. She didn't respond but made the move cleanly. The weather had changed from harmless clouds to thick gray skies that spat hard kernels of snow. When I looked up again, I saw the bottoms of Klára's crampons and knew she was sitting down.

"Tylenol help?"

She shook her head. There was not enough oxygen for either of us to complete sentences anymore. Every athlete has experienced what she was going through—your mind trying to coax your body to ignore pain in order to perform.

"You can continue," she said.

"I just don't want to get cold," I told her, worried about stopping. "Do you want Lakpa to stay with you?"

Klára shrugged.

"I just don't think it's good to be alone, you know. I think I can catch up to those guys." I motioned to Rob ahead of me on the rock.

"Yeah, go on." She motioned upward with a gloved hand but didn't look at me.

"Need anything?" Not that I had anything that she didn't already have.

Through hand gestures and broken English, Lakpa and I agreed that he would continue climbing with Klára and that I would climb on.

I climbed up to the anchor where Klára was sitting and crouched in the snow to hug her. "See you at camp," I said. I felt her body trembling beneath her down jacket, and I hoped it was from shivers, not tears. I knew that Klára didn't want me to stay with her, just as I wouldn't have wanted her to stay with me if I were climbing slower.

I looked up the route at the challenges ahead of me. The snow, denser now, had become graupel—half snow, half hail. Graupel usually happens ahead of snowstorms, a seasoned climber had told me years ago. On K2's steep slopes, graupel, topped with a layer of fresh snow, will act like ball bearings. Enough weight and just the right pitch of slope can allow the whole mass of fresh snow to slide downward in an uncontrollable avalanche. My mind wasn't thinking that far ahead, though. I was stuck in my own bubble, focused on the hours of climbing ahead of me and chasing Rob's blue jacket above me.

I realized that for the first time while climbing K2, I was cold. Temperature control while climbing is a tenuous game, with so many uncontrollable variables like precipitation, wind, and my body's propensity to sweat like mad when I was exerting myself and then chill quickly to shivers when I stopped. Today, nearing House's Chimney for the second time, I knew that the temperature would gradually drop as I gained elevation, and I suspected that the snow would increase, threatening—as it melted on my hat and insulated jacket—to saturate everything. I knew that wet and cold at 20,000 feet were a quick recipe for hypothermia. But I rationalized that stopping, anchoring, and digging in my pack for another layer could be unnecessarily wasted time and energy, since the climbing was quickly going to become more difficult in the chimney. Plus, I felt I'd rather be chilled than overheated in the mountains. Nothing stole my energy more than heat.

I pulled the cuff of my coat back to check the time and relied on a plan I'd used before when I wasn't sure if I was under- or overdressed: continue for twenty more minutes, then reassess.

Over the next three hours, the snow built and brought with it a sharp wind. By the time I reached House's Chimney, the last obstacle before Camp 2, I was wearing all the clothes I'd brought with me and still squeezing my hands inside their gloves to keep the blood circulating for warmth.

Before I climbed into the chimney, I turned to look down the route for Klára. The blowing snow concealed most of the route I'd just climbed, and below that I saw only eternal grayness. Even the mighty Karakoram mountains were missing. *She's probably right behind me,* I hoped.

When I arrived at Camp 2, six hours after leaving Camp 1, it looked nothing like the last time I'd been there. Dense gray skies and blowing snow obstructed my view, and I could barely make out the outlines of tents. Everything was silent, blanketed by six inches of fresh snow, five more than had been forecast. I wandered from tent to tent, searching for an open space, finally sliding in next to Rob with relief.

"Welcome!" he said. I couldn't tell if his cheeriness was real or fabricated. I'd climbed with people before who got energized when the mountain was giving them all she had; maybe Rob was one of them.

"Fuck!" I said back as I unlaced my crampons in the tent's vestibule, and Rob laughed. I imagined he could see my wide-eyed exhaustion and relief at finally getting a reprieve from the wind and snow.

"Pretty spicy out there today." I sighed, trying to shake the snow and ice off my jacket and backpack, then throwing them in the tent and collapsing on top of them, still wearing my boots. I wanted to relax for just a minute but knew that if I lingered too long in wet clothes, I'd spend the next three hours shivering inside my minus-40-degree sleeping bag.

Rob had shared enough tents with women to know the routine and to recognize that privacy was welcome, so he rolled to his side away from me while I started the process of replacing wet clothes with warm, dry ones. Climbing brings out modesty in me that doesn't exist at sea level. Maybe it's my overall self-consciousness or the lack of showers. Undressing at 22,000 feet with cold hands in a cramped tent is not a simple endeavor, especially when trying to preserve that modesty. Multitasking and conserving energy are key, so when I found the collapsible water bottle in the bottom of my backpack that functions as a pee bottle, I decided that now was the ideal time to use it, rather than waiting until I was cozy in my sleeping bag, lacking the motivation to move. Using a pee bottle in a shared tent is primarily acrobatic, as clothes, body parts, and bottle must be simultaneously perfectly positioned for success. It's also part mind-over-matter desperation, as it feels unnatural to pee in a bottle while squatting in a tent six inches from a relative stranger. I am usually successful, but there had been some embarrassing high-altitude failures. I knew that Rob didn't care and I was making a bigger deal out of it than was necessary. But I quietly shimmied my climbing pants off, moved to kneeling, gave Rob an update lest he unsuspectingly rolled to his other side, wiggled my underwear down, and noticed that my period had started—two weeks early. I dropped my head and laughed to myself. I was not in control of anything anymore.

I knew that allocating energy only to the things I could control was an important skill now, more important than at base camp. Now every bit of energy that my body could summon needed to be focused on getting me safely up and down K2. I couldn't spare any energy to worry about how much snow would fall or how my body would respond to the austere environment that I'd chosen as a proving ground. Without another thought, I reached into my backpack for the emergency tampon that I carried for this exact surprise. I knew it wouldn't be enough, but I'd deal with that later. Now I'd get warm and dry, eat and sleep. I'd carried that emergency tampon in my pack for probably three years, not because any climbing course I'd ever taken had suggested it, but because I'd found myself in a similar predicament on Manaslu, and a considerate Norwegian climber had tossed me a handful of tampons and said, "Ladies gotta look after ourselves up high. Your body'll do what it will up there. Never leave base camp without 'em."

Rob and I did our best to settle into camp. We melted snow for tea and our dehydrated meals, inventing outlandish stories about the unnaturally blissful people on the meal's package. I stuffed everything in my sleeping bag that I didn't want to freeze: pee bottle, food, clean socks. Eventually, K2 brought us back to her and our conversation meandered to the steady patter of snowflakes on the tent. Occasionally, one of us would reach up to smack the nylon walls and ceiling with the back of a hand and wait for the released snow to swoosh down to an ever-growing mound on the ground. Each time we cleared the snow off the tent my heart sank. The collective forecasts that had been studied at base camp called for an inch of new snow today, but there were at least eight inches now.

"How do you feel about this snow?" I asked. Rob had years more mountain wisdom than me, and I wanted to know if he was as uncertain about our prospects for summiting as I was. He rolled toward me in his sleeping bag, his face grooved from a career in the mountains, to which K2 had added a fresh layer of sunburn and stubble.

"Eh, our forecasts missed this snow, and the boys say there's more of it up high."

Mingma and other Sherpa and Pakistani members of our team had joined efforts with their counterparts from other teams to finalize the route to the summit. Together, they climbed first and worked as a team to install the rope and anchors everyone else would rely on to summit.

"I just worry about avalanches," I said. "For all of us."

"Yeah, they're in the teeth of it," he said knowingly but without concern, like he'd been in their position before.

I was still not sure what Rob's assessment of our chances was. Maybe he didn't want to speculate. Maybe he'd been in this position enough to know that it didn't matter, anyway. I decided that everyone was likely waiting to see what the morning would bring and that I was wasting precious energy on something I couldn't control. As I drifted off to sleep, I tried to imagine Mingma and the other men I'd befriended on this mountain, huddled together in tents at 26,200 feet, knowing the job ahead of them required unflappable strength and bravery, knowing that they were risking their lives to make ours easier.

When I woke the next morning, before I wiggled my knit-cap-covered head out of my sleeping bag, I realized that everything felt softer and muted, and I knew that the tent was enveloped in snow again. It felt comforting in this snow cocoon. Like a tiny bastion of cozy in an otherwise harsh environment. But my heart sank at the accumulation. *No way we're moving today*, I thought, and closed my eyes again. I knew that I should crawl out of my sleeping bag, blow the effects of inhaling cold, dry air from my nose, add a layer of warm clothes, lace my boots, and wander outside to find a discreet toilet before the rest of the camp woke and discretion became scarce. I knew I should, but altitude breeds apathy, and the effort to dress and then walk through two feet of fresh snow felt Sisyphean.

"Garrett bhai, Garrett bhai," I heard Mingma's voice say on the radio that hung from the tent's ceiling.

"Hellooo from Camp Two," responded Garrett.

"Garrett bhai, Garrett bhai, much snow at Camp Four. More than one meter. Over."

"Copy, Mingma."

"Very deep snow, Garrett bhai. We try fixing but climb maybe only one hundred meters. Very difficult climbing. Over."

I heard the conversation from my snow cocoon and involuntarily squinted my face hard at Mingma's report. I knew Rob had heard it, too. We both knew that unstable snow conditions above Camp 4 would stop progress for all of us. While waiting for conditions to improve wasn't ideal, it was possible. We had enough food and fuel. What we didn't have was enough good weather.

Mingma's radio communication triggered a multicamp, multilanguage radio conversation aimed at comparing forecasts with actual conditions and coordinating climbing schedules. Even if we decided to climb to Camp 3 today, we'd be without tents if the team currently occupying Camp 3 wasn't able to climb to Camp 4. Likewise, if the team ahead of us chose to descend but we didn't, there would be a traffic jam at Camp 2. We were like links in the same chain, now, moving slowly upward. Garrett closed the radio conversation with a request to Mushtaq that another cow be walked from Askole to base camp.

I was not relieved. I was not disappointed. I was mad. Mad at not having an honest chance to measure myself against K2. Mad at the mountain, mad at the uncertainty of mountaineering. Amid the fog of madness, I realized that I wanted this. On other mountains, I had descended peacefully when weather turned or conditions prevented a shot at the summit. Not this time. I realized that whatever seductive lies I'd told myself in Seattle about just coming to K2 to do my best had evaporated. I wanted to stand on this summit. I had come too far, sacrificed too much, and fought too hard to turn around.

I rolled over and looked at Rob. "What the fuck?"

He shook his head. "If the boys can't move, the other team can't move, and we can't move. Just wish we had another forecast. Wish I could ring my buddy Marc in Belgium, see what he says about a forecast."

I exhaled deeply, flopped on my back, and pulled my knit cap over my eyes.

"We caaan!" I shot straight up, shoved the cap back, and reached for my handheld satellite communication device hanging from the ceiling of the tent.

"You know Marc's number?" I asked.

"No, but my wife sure does!"

"Wait, what time is it there? Will he be awake?"

"I dunno, it's worth a shot."

Rob remained calm, but I was giddy. Partially fueled by denial, I was hopeful that Rob's cross-continental communication would end with a weather forecast that allowed for one more day of climbable weather. Just one more.

I used my new motivation to finally exit the tent. Standing for the first time in fifteen hours, I ambled tentatively outside. Two feet of fresh snow blanketed everything in sight. A few meandering footprints marked climbers' movements this morning, and the clouds were high and scattered, a sign that weather, at least here, was improving. Below me, the Baltoro Glacier flowed and gracefully curved through behemoth jagged peaks. It was as if the Baltoro, one of the largest non-polar glaciers in the world, cleaved these mountains. From my perch thousands of feet above, the glacier looked like a ribbon that curved and undulated. It moved so slowly its progress was undetectable, but with such force and determination that it flattened everything in its path.

Above me was the route. The new snow had buried the footprints of yesterday's climbers. I knew my fate was up to K2. Whether I climbed or descended would be determined by her mood. And I still didn't feel like we were friends. *Just one more day,* I asked.

Garrett assembled the team's guides outside of my tent to discuss our options, and I scurried past their meeting into my tent and zipped the door. I didn't want them to know that I planned to eavesdrop. I heard bits of their discussion, enough to know that Garrett was firm in his decision to descend. He summoned the rest of us for a team update and painted a picture of the conditions above us.

"I think it's safest if we descend, guys. We might have another chance in five days."

A few members of the team retreated to their tents to pack. The rest of us—the more stubborn lot—remained standing, mostly staring at our boots in disbelief and denial. I was waiting for a dissenting view to be raised.

"What if we waited a day?" someone asked.

"You're crazy, man. You heard Garrett. No one can climb."

"What's the problem with waiting, though?"

"Our weather window will close," Garrett explained again. "We don't want to be stuck here in a storm."

I was standing at the back of the semicircle of my team and felt the tension rise, like a balloon about to pop.

"You heard Garrett," someone said. "You paid him to lead this team, didn't you? What he says goes. We're descending."

"Just because you're too fucking lazy to climb doesn't mean I'm gonna end mine," said one of the bros.

"Fuck you, man."

"Look, gents." Jason stepped forward and stood solidly between the men, his hands in the waist pockets of his down suit. "If we descend, we'll never come back, it's over. This is K2, and we're lucky for this weather window. Don't count on another. Our climb's over if we go down. If there's a shot in hell, Garrett, that we can wait, my vote is that we take it."

I knew Garrett's pride was pulling him toward the summit, and I also knew that Mingma and the rest of us were trusting him to make the safest decision and that what we did impacted the team ahead of us.

"OK, team." Garrett took over, moving forward to tighten the circle. "Let's rest, get another forecast in three hours, then decide."

I began a vigil of lying flat on my back in the tent and staring up at the flashing green light on my satellite device, like a teenager waiting for a phone call from the cute guy in algebra class.

I took a deep breath and refocused my energy on things I could control, like taking care of myself. I made some ramen and stepped outside to join Jason on a bench he'd carved out of the snow. Even when decisions weren't hanging in the balance, he could not sit still. At every camp we'd occupied, he'd reset his tent platform, digging and hacking at the hard ice to level it for him and his tentmate. He frequently improved the meandering trails between tents. I felt like he was the team groundskeeper.

"Nice job back there," I told him between coughs and slurps of warm noodles. I'd found someone else's broken spork in my tent and had repaired it with athletic tape, so I was no longer eating with a tent stake.

"Ah, thanks, Lisa. You gotta stick up for what you know to be true, you know?"

I was envious that Jason somehow managed to navigate between all factions of our little team—the bros, the Sherpas, the asshole, the girls, the guides.

"Well, I appreciate your diplomacy. Some of us are better at that than others."

"We're all a team," he said. "All fighting for the same thing. How's Klára?"

"I heard on the radio that she's feeling better. She's back at base camp. It was her stomach," I told him. "She's planning to climb back up to meet us."

"There ya go, then. That's another reason to wait."

. . .

Lying in the tent after lunch, I heard Mushtaq, who was managing everything at base camp while we were climbing, mention on the radio that Klára was preparing to climb up to meet us in the morning.

Klára took over the radio conversation. "Hi, Garrett. How's everyone doing up there?"

"Good, Klára, good. Great to hear your voice. You're sounding strong."

"Feeling much better now. Mushtaq and the boys have been taking good care of me. I'm feeling strong, ready to start climbing again."

"Oh, that's great to hear, Klára."

I could hear the hopefulness in her voice as she outlined a plan for ascending quickly from base camp to Camp 2 to rejoin us.

"Oh, Klára, I don't think there's time."

Garrett had had this conversation before. As expedition leader he'd had to deliver devastating climb-ending decisions to hopeful climbers hundreds of times.

Even so, I imagined this conversation was the toughest for him. On Klára's previous K2 attempt, she'd made it above Camp 2 before an avalanche wiped out Camp 3 and everything below, ending the climbing season. K2 was not a mountain you could quickly or easily decide to climb a second or third time, given the amount of money and time commitment involved.

I was crushed for Klára as she made her plea again, and from my tent I heard the hope drain from her voice. I didn't know if she could have climbed fast enough to catch us and still have reserves for the summit and descent, but witnessing Klára's climb end shook me. It all felt so fragile.

I rolled to my side, facing the stretched nylon wall of the tent. I was gutted for her and sad that I wouldn't have her to laugh with and rely on for the rest of the climb. I was happy to be sharing a tent with Rob, and grateful for his mountain wisdom and caring personality. But it was not the same as climbing with someone who got you, who understood that climbing boots weren't made in women's sizes, and that your period might start at the most inopportune time, and that even though we were at 20,000 feet, it was nice to smell like perfume.

I curled into a ball inside my sleeping bag, hugging my knees to my chest. *I shouldn't have left her. I should have just stayed with her.* Maybe I could have pushed her, convinced her to continue despite her stomach pain. Wasn't that the job of a partner? To encourage, support—not to abandon?

I squeezed my eyes shut, needing to block out everything. I wanted to go home. I wanted to feel the comfort of a warm, thick mattress beneath me, not two inches of inflated nylon. I wanted to wear clothes that were designed for women, not miniaturized pink versions of men's clothes. I wanted to smell lavender and cut grass, not week-old dirty bodies and damp nylon. I wanted to walk without being tethered to this mountain. But these were not the things I'd chosen. Those things had been ineffective for proving myself. Instead, I had pushed myself to prove my worth in one of the most inhospitable environments on the planet.

I visualized my last day in Seattle, eating sandwiches made from thick artisan bread, crunching on homemade pickle spears on the Elliott Bay waterfront. Holding hands in the sunshine but not finding the words. That day, I'd stood in the middle of a stand of cedars, the ground beneath the giants barren from lack of sunlight. I'd felt safe, held by this cluster of behemoth ancient trees. It was the same comfort I'd felt when I was a kid and I'd climbed up the backyard pine tree with a book in my hand to sit among its branches and pretend I was the heroine in a great adventure. I wished I could conjure that feeling of solace now, that I could use it to erase the exposed rawness and susceptibility to K2's mood that I felt in this tent.

Excruciating hours later, my satellite device finally buzzed. I wanted to read it like a fortune cookie but instead tossed it to Rob. He raised his eyebrows and pursed his lips, then scooted out of the tent a few minutes later. Summiting was important to him, too. Guiding on K2 was a rare and impressive entry on anyone's climbing résumé.

A few minutes later, Garrett and Rob assembled the team again.

"The weather on the twenty-second looks good up high, less favorable down here," Garrett said. "If Mingma and the guys can move up in the morning, I think we've got a shot. If anyone wants to descend now, though, it's up to you. I'll be sure you get down safely."

CHAPTER 25

24,000 FEET

No one chose to descend.

In the morning, despite more fluffy snow, the train of climbing teams continued inching upward, our team to Camp 3 and the team ahead of us to Camp 4, where they met Mingma's fixing team. All of us hoping that K2's mood would match the improved weather forecast.

Hours after departing Camp 2, I met the technical crux of K2's Abruzzi Ridge route, the vertical jumble of exposed rock and ice called the Black Pyramid. At sea level, I'd been excited to climb this section, hoping its mix of rock and ice would be challenging in a fun way. But today, standing at its base, looking up at the clutter of rope and rock, wearing crampons and a down suit, I felt overdressed and overwhelmed. The Black Pyramid was a 1,500-foot puzzle, and I didn't know where to begin.

Most climbers like the feel of rock; I prefer to climb barehanded even when temperatures drop so I can know the rock's personality. I wanted to feel the rough nubs of granite with my fingertips, to slide my hand up cool, smooth limestone when I reached for a hold. I wanted to hear the hollow thud of weak rock. More than that, I wanted to sense my body moving efficiently, to savor the feeling of interacting with the mountain to climb gracefully. I wanted to feel the give-and-take of my body perceiving the route, understanding it, and then adapting to it by matching my ability to what the mountain required to safely ascend.

This intimate interaction usually created a connection, a bond between me and the mountain. But K2 denied me even this. As I began the climb, my thick gloves, down suit, and oxygen mask created a physical barrier between me and the rock in front of me. I was not able to intuit what she was asking for, and I felt clumsy, unworthy, and isolated.

I let my head drop forward and heard the hard plastic of my mountaineering helmet scratch rock.

"Breathe," I reminded myself out loud.

My gaze traced the orderly confluence of the Baltoro and Godwin Austen Glaciers below me, and I assessed my advancement. In ten minutes, I'd made four inches of vertical progress. Through my oxygen mask, I forced an inhalation and felt sharp mountain air bite my lungs.

I'd trained for moments like this, challenges where mental ability was more crucial than physical ability. Still, the desire to cry rose to my throat, and I reprimanded myself for letting it get that far and then slammed it back down. Not only was crying a monumental sign of weakness, but it was already hard enough to breathe without the futile gasps that I knew would accompany my cries.

Is this all that I am capable of? It was a simple, personal question that I'd posed multiple times in the past month. Before I'd left Seattle, I'd made an agreement with myself that if the honest answer was ever yes, I would turn around. Now, I filled the deepest parts of my lungs with iced air two more times and searched for the answer. I scanned the glaciers again. Though they were in one of the remotest parts of the world, they were inviting, peaceful, known. The prospect of descending felt luxurious. I could do it. It would take effort, but I could reverse my direction on this rope and be back in the relative safety of Camp 2 in hours. Tomorrow I could be back at base camp eating cake. I could take a proper shower and sleep in an actual bed and eat food in a restaurant in Islamabad next week. Or I could keep going, pushing myself harder into the unknown challenges and risks above me. Though my motivations for taking such risks were still murky, I told myself *no*.

No, this is not all.

I felt Aang Phurba on the rope below me. I felt him try to lift my left foot higher to a bread-loaf-sized ledge near my calf. Persuading my foot to move the distance felt inconceivable.

"I'm good, Aang Phurba," I yelled between my legs.

"Step, *didi.*" I knew he was offering help, but I wouldn't accept it.

Ten years ago, on Mount Rainier, I'd learned the importance of climbing in good style, and while some would argue that climbing with fixed ropes and the ascender in my hand didn't fall within the definition of good style, I believe that the choice is personal. I was comfortable with aid from climbing gear but not with locomotion from others.

I was breathing bottled oxygen for the first time on K2, and I took two more deep breaths and raised my left foot to the bread loaf, the steel points of my crampon grating across its smooth surface to confirm placement, a welcome sound but also a reminder that I was dulling their edges—edges that I would rely on to penetrate the dense, vertical ice above me in two days.

Before we'd left base camp, Aang Phurba had crouched on the rock outside of my tent, a smile peeking out from under his scraggly black mustache. "No, *didi*, Black Pyramid short, just one hard place."

I'd scrunched my eyebrows together and looked at him sideways in disbelief. Everything that I'd read about the Black Pyramid told a different story: 1,500 near-vertical feet of icy rock at 23,000 feet. In my mind, the Black Pyramid unlocked the upper mountain; after it, the terrain eases to ice and snow, which is still treacherous, but much closer to my comfort zone.

"No, Aang Phurba bhai, Black Pyramid five hundred meters," I said firmly.

"No, no, *didi*, very short." He lifted his hands from his thighs and moved them together to imitate *short*.

I'd wanted to believe him, to believe there was just one tiny section of rock between me and the snowy comfort above 24,000 feet, but in my heart I'd known better.

I realized that the section I was struggling with now must be Aang Phurba's Black Pyramid—the crux, the segment of a climbing route that offered its greatest challenge. And risk.

As I struggled, I knew that behind and below me was 7,600 feet of frigid yielding air. My brain acknowledged the risk by constricting its focus to just the most basic movements needed to propel me upward: slide, breathe, breathe, step, step, slide. There was only room in my mind for these things. I had visualized this moment; I had imagined the airy one and a half miles below me. I knew that a mistake here, one moment where my oxygen-deprived brain forgot to expertly feed the rope through my gear, would initiate an irreversible sequence of flails and shrieks. I knew it would happen fast, so fast that my brain wouldn't register the sudden freedom of unrestrained movement. The weight of my backpack would quickly attract gravity, forcing my feet above my head and preventing my groping and writhing body from righting myself. My brain would eventually catch up with my body and would flood with adrenaline as it pitched into survival mode. In the end, there would be violence; my body would accelerate into the mountain and break absolutely beneath the power of K2.

I had forced this scenario to live in my consciousness; I'd wanted it there because I believed that denying I could die was disrespectful to K2. I wanted fear to be an accessible emotion because a sprinkle of it would keep me safe, but too much of it—regardless of whether its source was falling or not being enough or being labeled incompetent—would immobilize me.

Eventually, the terrain eased, and the rock became completely buried by feet and feet of fresh, powdery snow. I knew the snow signified that I had climbed the Black Pyramid, that I was safely above K2's crux. I allowed myself to stop, and I dropped a knee into the snow and looked behind me, past the Black Pyramid's jumble of merciless rock. This was my world, jagged rows of sharp black peaks, stacked endlessly on top of one another. Graying sky and feet of sugary snow. I felt insignificant in a vast, wild place and grateful that I'd made it past the most technical bit, into the comfort of steep snow. The snow and the clouds narrowed my focus to just my strained breath and the orange rope leading me upward.

Seven hours after leaving Camp 2, I arrived in a whiteout at the flattish stretch of snow called Camp 3. The mood at camp was focused, with little conversation and lots of activity. I noted that Aang Phurba, who'd passed me on the route after the Black Pyramid, was wearing a down suit for the first time and the same bright-yellow helmet he'd worn on Everest two years earlier. Bashir, a Pakistani high-altitude porter whose teenage daughter endeavored to be a mountain guide, crouched in the snow to tighten a tent's guyline. Everything felt serious now. Perhaps it was because the new snow had muffled everything, but the air felt dense, like it had begun to congeal. Our movements were reduced to only the necessary few, our sentences brief.

This year, Camp 3 was tucked closer to the ridgeline, this placement intentionally higher than in previous years in a hopeful effort to avert any avalanches that K2 might launch tonight.

I crawled inside my tent, still wearing my oxygen mask and dragging my backpack that held its tank behind me. I marveled at the first flat tent platform since I'd left ABC four days ago. Inside, it was spacious but cold. I knew that I would miss a teammate's body heat tonight, but right now I was happy for the space and privacy.

Organization is the foundation of efficiency in the mountains, and I wanted to inspect my gear and clothes one more time while I had the mental capacity. First, I savored a deep inhalation of sweet bottled oxygen and then closed the tank's valve and removed the rubber mask that covered my nose and mouth. Immediately, the frigid oxygen-starved air at 24,000 feet jabbed my lungs and pounded at my temples. It wasn't like I'd just switched off sea-level air; the supplemental oxygen had maybe brought the relative elevation down by 10,000 feet. Still, my brain and lungs responded to the difference. I knew that inflating my sleeping mattress later would be painful.

For now, though, I was focused on organizing, not just to prepare but to calm my rattled mind. My backpack contained only the food, clothes, and gear necessary to reach the summit and return. In the mountains, ounces equal pounds, and pounds equal pain. I'd learned this the hard way early in my mountaineering career when I'd thought that a daily change of clothes counted as essential. I first made a tidy stack of food: dehydrated rice and chicken, soup packets, oatmeal. But I was mostly interested in the sweet stuff because it was what would keep me fueled while I climbed. There were packets of maple syrup and mini candy bars that I'd buried deep in my duffel bags for the past month to prevent them from melting. Next to the candy was more candy, the hard sugary kind that I would suck on to keep my throat moist and maintain a constant trickle of sugar. I'd also brought a bag of savory Pakistani flatbread called chapati, made by Khadim at base camp to Jason's specifications. And the most important ingredient: chocolate-covered espresso beans that I'd delicately push into my mouth from underneath my oxygen mask as I climbed on summit night.

Next to my food, I slowly stacked the clothes I'd wear to the summit: clean underwear, a black one-piece sleeveless fleece suit with a crotch zipper that aligned with the one on my down suit, just in case. I also stacked the same lobster-claw leather gloves that I'd worn to the summit of Everest, a pair of fleece-lined gloves, new insulated socks, and a thin down jacket. My movements to inspect, fold, and stack each piece were slowed by hypoxia as my brain intentionally downshifted my movements to conserve energy. Next, I focused on my climbing gear. I tested the gate of each carabiner to be sure it locked cleanly; I confirmed the handmade leash that attached my ascender to my harness was solid. Finally, I scrutinized my black climbing harness. Its thick, padded waist was old and bulky, obsoleted by newer, lighter models. Even though I'd purchased a lighter version and erased my doubt that it was stronger than dental floss by hanging from it in my backyard tree, I preferred the older model. It was the first climbing harness I'd purchased, and it had been my trusted companion on every climb since Mount Rainier. I folded the harness and stacked it and the rest of my climbing gear inside my pink helmet. The helmet was new and had been embellished with neon puffy paint and glitter during a climbing-girls crafting party at my dining room table. I traced the design—an unconvincing interpretation of Buddha eyes—with my gloved index finger. Outside the tent, my ice axe and crampons were already prepped for tomorrow's climb to Camp 4, where we would rest before the summit, the axe driven vertically into the snow and the crampons hung over its head with their laces loosely tied to the tent's guyline so that I could quickly locate them even if they were buried by snow in the morning. I arranged my clunky outer boots next to my sleeping bag. Tonight, I would sleep with them inside the bag, using my body heat to keep them from freezing overnight. When I put them on in the morning, it would be the last time until after I summited; I'd need them for warmth at Camp 4, even while sleeping.

I sat back in the tent to breathe, satisfied by my inventory and the comfort of familiarity the tidy stacks brought. These were the things I had chosen, tested, and trusted. I knew that it would take all of us doing our jobs to insulate, to hold, to nourish, to breathe, to protect, in order to meet the demands of K2.

I wouldn't have this much space or privacy in a tent until base camp, so, although I'd been waiting to reach Camp 4 tomorrow before taking the tiny luxury of clean clothes, practicality won out, and I stripped down to replace the clothes I'd been wearing for four days with cleaner versions. The act of pulling on my fleece suit felt ceremonious, like I was a warrior preparing for battle. These were the clothes that I would wear to the summit of K2, I told myself. The next time I changed clothes, this would all be over.

Later, Garrett made the rounds to each tent to check on each team member. There were eight climbers, plus five Sherpas, five Pakistani high-altitude porters, and three guides. In addition to Klára, one other climber had abandoned his bid for the summit.

I heard Garrett unzip the outer shell of my tent. "How's the palace, Lisa?" He sounded extra cheery to me, despite the elevation. Somehow, he was still maintaining the same singsong greeting that I'd expect if we were meeting for a drink in Seattle.

"So spacious," I told him, and coughed.

"Ooh, nice, you're all organized." He sat inside, and for a second I wondered if he'd gotten bad news.

"How's the weather look?" I wanted to know.

"Looking good so far. Keep your fingers crossed, though." He bobbed his head as he spoke and reached up with a bare hand to zip the tent closed. His fingers were long and lanky; they'd be called elegant if they had a manicure, I thought. They didn't look like working hands, not like my dad's calloused and dirty hands. My own were less elegant than Garrett's. Squat fingers topped with uneven nails, my cuticles long gone years ago, unable to abide the torment of daily picking.

The faintest of splotches dotted the backs of my hands, and their skin was starting to wrinkle, a change I falsely attributed to rough days in the mountains more than to age. I envied what Garrett's hands knew. I wanted mine to know every jagged rock they'd trust, every slice of ice they'd ascend. I wanted my body to have every advantage it could have.

"You think the fixing team will make it to the summit tomorrow?" I realized I was blasting him with questions, but my brain was in a kind of fog, like I'd had one too many glasses of wine.

"Looking good. Mingma and the boys are ready to go up."

I nodded, still not completely trusting that everything was lining up so well.

"How you feel, Lisa?"

I told him my head was pounding and that I'd like to shower and wash my hair.

"Sleep well. We'll leave about six tomorrow. Let me know if you need anything tonight. You got enough Os, right?"

I nodded. Since I'd run out of oxygen on Everest's Yellow Band and again at Camp 4, I'd meticulously monitored my oxygen usage, memorizing flow rates and consumption, and tomorrow I would write that information on my wrist with a marker, just in case my brain failed to make the calculation at a critical moment.

I was grateful for Garrett's leadership and experience on this mountain. He'd led teams to its summit more than any other Westerner, and had seen K2 unleash her wrath multiple times, so I trusted his judgment and experience. Garrett zipped my tent closed and moved on to check in with the next teammate. *He's not even wearing gloves*, I thought. *How does he do that?*

There was really nothing to do at 24,000 feet except breathe, eat, and sleep, all of which are forced activities. I snuggled into my sleeping bag wearing a down coat, knit cap, and gloves over my fleece suit, and typed seven broken sentences in my cell phone's journal.

getting here hardest thing I've ever done. feet of fresh snow. made it in seven hours! but twenty min behind fast group. orange rope going up and up to nowhere in whiteout. needed and appreciated everyone's strength. Measured sat in tent—53 started Os—70.

Before I'd attempted sleep, I'd checked my oxygen saturation, which was 53 percent. It should have been at least 98 percent to avoid a hospital stay. Alarmed, since no one would know if I passed out right now, I put my oxygen mask on and remeasured: 70 percent. Still alarming, but it would have to do; I wondered how many brain cells I was killing in this endeavor.

With the fear of climbing the Black Pyramid behind me, I felt lighter, more comfortable. I felt a little stronger, like I was taking up a bit more space on the mountain. There was still a lot of treacherous climbing and descending to do, but the stress of doubting whether I could climb the crux had subsided. Yet I was still craving a connection with K2. I'd found it on Everest—the floaty, half-meditative feeling of flow where there was no difference between me and the mountain, and there was no difference between me and the universe. I longed for this oneness, this camaraderie with a mountain that had been a daily part of my life for the past two years.

26,025 FEET

The route between Camps 3 and 4 didn't produce the same anxiety as everything that had come before it. *It's just steep snow,* I told myself. *You've done this thousands of times.*

Dense white clouds obscured the sun, and feet of fresh snow muffled both sound and movement. I was grateful to be alone, feeling insulated, protected, like I was in a mountain cocoon of frozen stillness. I focused on the orange rope in front of me and occasionally traced it upward with my eyes until it was swallowed by the clouds, too. I put so much trust in that rope, following it wherever it led, believing that it was taking me in the right direction and that it would save me if I fell. That rope could have been leading me straight to a cliff for all I knew, not having set it myself and not having enough visibility to confirm its destination. Eventually, the rope led to blurry orange blobs that I knew were tents on the horizon. The altimeter on my watch confirmed my disappointment.

The highest camp on K2 sat at 26,025 feet, just below the death zone, on a relatively flat section of the Abruzzi Ridge known as the shoulder. Collectively, the teams this year had decided to place camp lower than normal, a wise decision, meant to add protection in case of an avalanche. For that safety, though, I would climb several additional hours tomorrow, on the longest climbing day of my life.

The orange blobs gradually became six tents, arranged in two short rows, facing each other. I felt out of sorts here—unwelcome—like I'd shown up at a friend's house unexpectedly. There was still a feeling of separation between me and the mountain, and I was not comfortable here. Although I was breathing bottled oxygen, my brain was still hypoxic, fighting to function on significantly less oxygen than normal. Hypoxia was likely creating the unease, I decided. That and the hazard above me. I couldn't see that hazard now, but I had studied it, watched movies about it, spoken kind words to it.

Most routes on the Pakistani side of K2 converged here at the shoulder, which means that no one is exempt from climbing under this hazard, a looming serac above and to the east of camp. I knew it was up there; it had been embossed into my mind even though I couldn't see it now. I also knew from the spreadsheet I'd compiled months ago that the most frequent location of deaths on K2 was the area just below the serac, a narrow slice of snow pinched between two rock bands called the bottleneck. Climbing the bottleneck was technically easier than ascending the rock bands. Even so, every climber would spend hours beneath the humongous, tenuous blocks of ice that make up the serac. Though thick skies hid the serac from me today, I knew that it was larger than a skyscraper, and that the natural force of the moving snow above the serac was gradually pushing it down the mountain toward me. It was the unfortunate calving of the serac that I'd read about with disconnected interest while sitting comfortably on my sunny Seattle patio in 2008. It had been unimaginable to me at the time that I would be here, in the same position as the eleven hopeful climbers who'd died that day. Though I couldn't see the serac, it was no less intimidating to me. I was not safe here. Everything above me felt bigger and more powerful than me, and I acknowledged that I was timidly asking for safe passage, hesitantly hoping to survive in K2's environment for just a few more days. I couldn't change where I was, though. I had signed up for this risk, for this danger. By ascending this far, I'd accepted that the mountain was in control, and I was hoping she would be kind. My job was to respect her, to take care of myself, and to make smart decisions. Even if I had done my job and she un-leashed tons of angry snow in my path, I would be helpless.

Focus on what you can control. I reminded myself that my sixteen-hour summit day would begin in less than ten hours, so I forced my brain to shift from geography and risks to self-care. I needed to eat and drink and sleep. I was not interested in any activities that weren't related to those goals. The Sherpas were tidying camp, gathering snow for melting into water, and counting oxygen bottles. I began to search the half dozen tents that made up Camp 4. Unzipping the first few, I realized that the team ahead of us hadn't vacated them yet. They were still descending from the summit. Sleep would have to wait. As a team, we carved seats in the snow above the lines of tents to wait.

"How ya feeling, Lisa?" Jason wanted to know when he settled in the snow next to me. He didn't seem daunted at all by the dangers lurking above us.

"Scared as fuck."

He chuckled and searched his backpack for a snack. I did the same. He and I had been surviving on carbs, mostly in the form of Khadim's chapati. I'd been carrying this chapati in my backpack for four days, so it was more like chapati crumbles now. I shoved a gloveful of crumbles in my mouth and looked back at him, my eyes asking for confirmation, even though they were blocked by sunglasses.

"Sounds about dead on," he confirmed, with confidence that I wished I had.

I'd sat in the snow like this many times, on many mountains, not al-ways in queue for a tent, often resting between hard stretches of a climb, sometimes just enjoying warm sunshine on my face and shoul-ders. On my way to Rainier's summit for the first time, I'd sat like this at 13,000 feet in the dark. I'd wondered then what lay ahead and above me. I was scared then, and ten years of climbing and thousands of feet ascended since hadn't changed that; it was the same on K2.

When the team ahead of us reached Camp 4 on their descent, they carried an air of matter-of-factness. They looked strong to me, not beat up by the mountain. I paused my conversation with Jason to study each of their movements. I watched them pack gear, analyzing what they were wearing, paying attention to their conversations. I studied the seriousness of their faces. Looking for their special secret ingredient and hoping that I had it, too. I was awed by them and what they had accomplished.

By early afternoon I'd assumed the middle tent position and lay shoulder to shoulder with teammates. Although I lay between Jason and another teammate, in the warmest position, my body occasionally shook uncontrollably from the cold even though I, like the men lying on either side of me, was wearing all my clothes, boots, and climbing gear. The cost of undressing and crawling into a cold sleeping bag was too great; every movement now was an exercise in conservation, and I was pleased with my decision to change into my fleece summit suit the night before.

"How ya feeling?" Jason asked again.

"Eh, fine, I guess. You?" I said without looking at him, nearly every word punctuated by a cough.

"Same, I suppose."

It had been more than a month since I'd enjoyed the comforts of modern life in Islamabad. The mental and psychological impacts of living in a harsh environment with limited oxygen had shifted the "feeling good" scale. I took a quiet inventory. My brain felt too big for my skull. Oxygen deprivation had made my thoughts viscous, requiring more effort to form them and even more still to coax them to my mouth. My body carried malaise that I could only assume rivaled having gone twelve rounds in a boxing ring. And, though it was buried beneath layers of fleece and down, I knew that I stank. At home, I would have been on the couch binge-watching TV with a bowl of warm soup if I felt this bad, and today, I was preparing for the most physically demanding day of my life.

The weather forecast was verbally passed from tent to tent, and it sounded unbelievably good: the snow had tapered off, and winds at the summit were supposed to be around fifteen knots, the temperature minus seventeen Fahrenheit, which would have sounded horrible at sea level, but at 28,000 feet, those were perfect conditions. I couldn't imagine any reason we wouldn't follow our current plan, which was to leave camp around 9:00 p.m.

I knew my body was wrecked from weeks of climbing and sleeping in a harsh, oxygen-deprived environment, and I knew it was deteriorating faster than it could repair itself. I also knew that at this altitude, climbing had become a mental game. I would now rely on my mental fitness and strength to coax my depleted body into continuing to slog upward. *Everything happening to you right now is normal,* I thought. *So resist the urge to take inventory of what is wrong or broken or hurting and instead prepare for the summit push that will begin in a few hours.*

There was tension in the cramped tent and very little talking. We were all lost in our own hypoxic worlds, mechanically preparing the food, gear, and oxygen that we would need for the next day of climbing. Aside from eating and drinking, I was double-checking the chocolatey, carb-y snacks in the pockets of my down suit and memorizing which food was stored where. The left outer chest pocket was full of chocolate-covered espresso beans, unwrapped so they were easier to grab, even with a down mitten. The left inner pocket held a half-liter thermos, which I would fill with sugary tea before we left tonight, likely the only fluid I would consume for twenty hours. In my right inner pocket were packets of maple syrup, their tabs already partially torn for easier access. My sunglasses were already strung around my neck. I'd replaced the batteries in my headlamp with new ones and tucked another fresh set in an inner pocket so that they wouldn't freeze. I reviewed the oxygen times at each flow rate to be sure I had them memorized and then wrote them on my wrist. I pulled from my backpack the only luxury I'd afforded myself in the death zone: a gauzy dryer sheet. I held it to my nose and pulled in its sweet freshness. It smelled like normalcy. Without looking at him, I handed Jason his glove, and he tossed a tea bag in my lap. Nothing rehearsed, everything efficient. I double-checked my meds, an array of prescription pills meant to slow rising pressure in my brain and lungs if their tissues began to leak fluid due to lower atmospheric pressure. Having witnessed other climbers with edema, I doubted that I'd have the capacity to locate any of the pills if they were needed, but climbing with them made me feel self-sufficient, and I put them in the top of my backpack.

There was one last decision: I hadn't considered before now whether to turn on my satellite communication device. Until now, I'd been sending pings of my location so friends and family could follow my progress. It seemed like a clever way for loved ones to play along at home. But now, in the frozen seriousness of 26,025 feet, I was conflicted, concerned that it could fail and falsely alert my loved ones to an accident—or that it could accurately alert them. The possibilities and consequences were a jumbled tangle in my hypoxic brain. In the end, I held the power button until three beeps confirmed it was on and slid it into the inside of my backpack.

Eventually, the three of us lay flat on our backs, still fully clothed and wearing sunglasses. It was midafternoon. Our faces, terse words, and dry coughs told the impact that K2 had imparted. Our cheeks were gaunt from dehydration and burned from sun and wind, our hair matted and dirty, our eyes wild and needy from fear and oxygen deprivation. We didn't sleep, not really. I tried very hard to think about anything but the struggle and challenge that I would encounter in the next twenty-four hours. The pocket of my down suit also contained a letter, and I read it one final time.

> Dear Lisa—
>
> You are a badass. Don't forget that. Don't forget that you are smarter, and stronger, and more beautiful than you will ever know.
>
> Remember that you grew up in a tiny town in the middle of nowhere, in a place where most people never imagine that they can travel all over the world and see and achieve amazing things.
>
> You have worked hard, your whole life, to get to this very moment. All of the stress and planning and missed dinners and early-morning alarms, and runs in the rain, and cancer, and hikes in steep snow with heavy packs, were meant to bring you right here, on the brink of accomplishing something amazing, that very few people,

and even fewer women, will ever be able to say that they have accomplished.

   Things are going to be hard, probably harder than you know, but believe that you have everything inside of you to tackle those obstacles. Every challenge is designed to get you to the top. Every difficult pitch, low-oxygen moment, sketchy steep ice, is meant to push you forward, it's there to get you to the top and back safely. You are ready now, and all that you have to do is believe. Really fucking believe. And trust the tools and training and techniques that you've practiced and you will succeed. You are stronger than you know, you are a badass.

   Love, Lisa

CHAPTER 27

28,251 FEET

The hardest part of climbing K2 occurs on summit night, another testament to the mountain's cruelty. Tonight, it seemed exceptionally brutal as I coaxed my body from resting in the tent to climbing steep snow in gusty winds. By 9:00 p.m., we were all walking silently upward in the dark, the only sound the Styrofoam-y squeak of crampons in dense, dry snow that broke in blocks and chunks, some as high as my thighs. At first, the terrain felt easy.

You're still on the shoulder, I reminded myself. *Nothing is easy on K2. Your job is to take care of yourself and make smart decisions.*

I took advantage of the relatively mild terrain to shine my headlamp into the night. The blackness that surrounded me was deceptively comfortable, hiding the full enormity of the tenuous serac. I still sensed it, even though all that I could see of it was the glare of vertical ice when I shined my headlamp upward. From behind me, Lakpa shined his headlamp toward the serac, too, exposing more menacing ice. In front of me, Rob did the same, and the ice above us grew. I settled into the cocoon of night until it occurred to me that my headlamp wasn't as bright as theirs.

Your batteries are frozen. I heard my own voice in my head. *But they're brand new. Just focus on putting one foot in front of the other. But they're brand new. It doesn't matter; you have to swap them.*

I didn't want to pull away from my team to replace the batteries, since there was safety in numbers, and I didn't want to be left behind. I also didn't want to appear that I didn't have my shit together. So I continued moving upward, fighting with myself about the best resolution.

Your job is to make smart decisions, I reminded myself finally.

I tried to position myself directly in front of the light from Lakpa's headlamp behind me while also relying on scattered light from Rob's ahead of me, but my field of view was shrinking fast. Mercifully, the terrain remained relatively benign, and I was able to continue this way until, as a team, we stopped for a break at the edge of the shoulder. Vision was more important than eating and drinking, so I removed my helmet, taking care not to disturb the straps of my oxygen mask. I couldn't see the battery compartment of my headlamp now but knew it was not possible to access it while it was attached to my helmet. I ripped the headlamp off my helmet by its lamp. I was going to need light from someone else's headlamp to do this, and no one had time to take care of me, since we were all fighting our own private battles. But I was desperate.

I yelled to Garrett. As the leader, he at least needed to know what was going on. Lakpa unroped and stepped toward me then, shining his headlamp on my dismal situation. Silently, he took my headlamp from me, and I reached into my pocket for the spare batteries, hoping my body heat had kept them warm. With his help, I departed the shoulder with my team a few minutes later.

Get your shit together, LT. Problem solved, it's over, and you can see fine now. Move on.

I focused on delicately reaching with my right gloved hand into the outer chest pocket of my down suit to retrieve a few frozen chocolate-covered espresso beans. When I'd captured them, I rolled them between the fingertips of my thick glove to confirm they were secure, then lifted the bottom of the oxygen mask up and away from my face with my left hand and shoved most of the beans in my mouth. I'd just consumed maybe twenty calories. Repeating this sequence was a welcome distraction and helped my nerves settle and my brain focus on something useful as I moved up the steepening snow.

After several minutes, my headlamp looked dim again, and after several more minutes, I couldn't deny that it was dying. Our rope team slowed, and I wanted to take action to correct the problem, but I didn't have a backup plan for my backup plan. In darkness, I looked ahead and noticed the dots of headlamps to the left of me, ninety degrees from where I stood.

We're at the traverse, came the voice in my head.

The traverse was a narrow path worn into the dense, 45-degree snow and ice below the serac. Climbers must navigate it to reach the steep slopes that lead to the summit on its other side. Each year, the width of the traverse varies; sometimes the ice and snow are so impenetrable that climbers aren't able to walk across and instead shuffle sideways while sinking ice axes and crampon front points into the thick ice for safety. Every year, the mass of the serac blooms above the traverse, and every year below it is thousands of feet of nothing, only frigid indifferent air. The snag of one crampon point or the roll of one ankle, one lapse in focus, would at best leave me dangling upside down on the fixed line praying for the anchors not to fail. At worst, I would die. I had accepted this risk, had prepared for it by visualizing myself safely crossing the traverse. Now, I was face-to-face with it, and when I looked ahead at the traverse, I couldn't see all of it, given my waning light source, but I knew that I was not doing my job if I thought I could cross it with a failing headlamp.

Thankfully, the queue of climbers waiting to delicately navigate the traverse provided an opportunity.

"ROB!"

He turned silently, his headlamp scanning the frozen air above my head. I pointed frantically to my headlamp. It was pointless to explain the saga of the last several hours, even though I wanted him to know that I was not a dumbass and that I had brought extra batteries and that this was a new headlamp.

Rob instinctively removed his backpack and efficiently reached inside to produce three batteries while I fumbled with helmet removal, headlamp removal, and several blind attempts to catch the plastic lip of the battery compartment with a gloved thumb. I heard muffled words come from behind Rob's oxygen mask, but they floated into the frozen darkness before registering with my brain. I reached an open gloved hand toward Rob. He shined his headlamp onto it and method-ically pressed one battery into my palm.

"If you drop this, your climb is over," I said to myself out loud, and exhaled.

In slow motion, I guided the first battery into an empty groove in the headlamp and then repeated the process with the second and third.

I wanted to thank Rob, to hug him. I would have even agreed to pay his kid's college tuition. There was no time for niceties, though; we were standing in one of K2's notoriously dangerous places.

"This'll at least get me across the traverse," I said.

The queue ahead of me slowly inched forward, and with my new visual ability I studied the climbers' movements as they crossed the traverse. They looked like ants walking on the side of a marble. Eventually, it was Rob's turn, and he clipped into the segment of rope that stretched across the span.

Breathe, said the voice in my head. *You've done this thousands of times.*

To protect climbers, our Sherpa team, led by Mingma, had fixed the traverse with multiple ice screws. They expertly screwed the long, hollow pieces of grooved steel several inches into the ice and then strung a continuous piece of safety rope between the screws' heads to create anchors that protected the traverse. What was really being pro-tected was the climber—not from falling, but from falling far enough to die.

My job was to clip into the fixed safety rope using a carabiner and rope system that was attached at its other end to my climbing har-ness. Also, my job was to move quickly enough to limit my time in this deadly place, but not so quickly that I would fall. To improve my speed and accuracy crossing anchors and climbing with the aid of fixed lines, I'd strung climbing rope up my staircase, I'd built faux fixed lines in the mud at a local park, and I'd timed myself crossing anchors while wearing mittens, while wearing gloves, and in the dark. Technically, this scenario was no different from the rehearsal; the motions were the same ones I had repeated thousands of times. But my brain wouldn't let go of the fact that the stakes were much, much higher tonight.

Near the middle of the traverse, Rob reached one of the ice screws. To continue moving forward, he had to transfer his safety carabiner and ascender to its other side. Through the circle of light from my headlamp, I watched him deftly move his gear, then balance on one foot and high-step over the rope to the other side. I had not included gymnastics in any of my practice scenarios.

When Rob had cleared the final ice screw at the opposite end, I stepped to the edge on my side, clicked my safety carabiner from one side of the anchor to the other, screwed its metal gate closed with my gloved thumb and index finger, then tapped the gate and waited for a metal click to confirm it was locked. At this point, my weight, if I fell or if a single ice screw failed, would be safely spread across multiple anchors. But in this configuration, I could not move forward, so I released the locking cam on my ascender with my right thumb and reached forward to move it next to the carabiner on the rope ahead of me. I was less safe now, relying on fewer anchors, fewer points to protect me as I stepped onto the traverse. I had made a different choice than Rob; though his decision to walk *between* the rope and the serac seemed safer, I was not sure that I could step over the rope at the middle anchor. For several seconds I'd hesitated, and then decided that balancing on one foot and high-stepping would not be the safest choice for five-foot-three me.

"You're just walking. You do this every day," I said to myself.

I stepped forward rigidly with my right foot, thinking about all ten points of its crampon connecting with the snow. The path across the traverse wasn't quite as wide as my boot, and my headlamp illuminated chunks of snow crumbling beneath it and falling into the night. I heard my breath more loudly now, fighting with my brain to maintain calm. Eventually, my breathing won, and I took one intentional breath per step while my brain focused like a camera lens on each foot placement. When I reached the ice screw that provided protection for the first half of the traverse, I patted it with my glove and said, "Thank you, ice screw."

On the other side of the traverse, the route took a sharp right turn and continued upward alongside the serac. I sensed the serac now, the way you know someone is standing next to you in the dark.

This sensory-deprivation-induced denial created by darkness helped me ignore the nearly two miles of exposure that still threatened me, now from behind. I focused only on my immediate challenge, which was kicking my crampons hard enough to gain purchase on the 30-degree blue ice beneath me. I bent my right knee back as far as I could without compromising balance and then quickly snapped it forward, hoping the momentum would be enough to stab the two front points of my crampon into the ice. They bounced off. Again. Bounce. The thick glove of my right hand was clamped around both my ascender and the rope, but still I felt the menace of the deadly chasm behind me.

You need a plan, Lisa.

I shone my headlamp downward between my legs and noticed quarter-sized bumps in the ice. I twisted my right hip into an awkward angle and gingerly placed my front points on the ice protrusion. This was the ultimate game of trust; I had no choice now but to hold on and rely on hope in the exact place where K2 had claimed the most lives. I shifted my weight to my right foot and exhaled. I didn't fall. This delicate dance continued mercilessly for what felt like hours, though I had no way to tell.

Gradually, light consumed the dark sky. It was too cumbersome to access my watch under layers of down and thick gloves, but it must have been close to 5:00 a.m., which meant I'd been climbing for eight hours. In the growing daylight, I saw Rob's green down suit kneeling against the slope ahead of me. When I finally approached him, my face was wrinkled in confusion, though he couldn't see it behind my ski goggles and oxygen mask. How could I have caught up with him? And why was he just kneeling there? His oxygen mask was off, and he was fiddling with his oxygen bottle, wearing only thin gloves.

Rob looked up at me, and I saw more pain on his face than just the effects of climbing in the death zone. "I'm fucked," he said.

"Why?"

"I need a new regulator. My spare's a Poisk, doesn't work."

"Can I do anything?"

"No."

"Did you radio Garrett?"

"I can't raise them. I'm fucked, just go."

Nothing had prepared me for this decision, not time spent studying the route or even hours with a sports psychologist. It did not feel right for me to leave him there, struggling. It didn't even look right to see Rob encounter a problem that he couldn't immediately resolve with a cheery smile. I didn't know if *fucked* meant *I'm going to die* or *I'm descending,* and it didn't occur to me to ask. I couldn't access the tools to help Rob.

"I'll tell Aang Phurba when I see him," I said casually, like Aang Phurba and I had a lunch date in an hour. It was all that I could offer.

The mental recalibrations that occur in intense situations are a marvel, a necessary response to ensure self-preservation. Choices that couldn't be fathomable in normal conditions become routine. At sea level, I wouldn't have thought of leaving a man in trouble, a man who, hours earlier, had stood in the most dangerous place on this mountain and helped me, had ensured that my climb could continue. But now, I reached around Rob to move my ascender and safety carabiner past the anchor that he was kneeling at and continued upward.

Ahead of me, it looked like the route eased at a shelf and then continued up more steep snow. When I arrived at the shelf, Aang Phurba was resting in the sunshine.

"Rob needs a new regulator. Does anyone have one?"

"Garrett-*dai* does. I'll radio."

"*Dhanyawaad,* Aang Phurba," I thanked him.

I let the sound of Aang Phurba speaking into the radio fade and fought with the part of my brain that wanted to sit with him and share sweet chai and smiles. If I allowed myself that luxury, I would never continue. So I ignored that part of my brain, remained standing, removed my oxygen mask, and grabbed random bits of food—mostly in the form of sugary carbs—from my pockets to consume as many calories as possible before continuing upward.

I was grateful to be past the blue ice and serac and now climbing in steep snow. I'd told myself that once I got to this point, the climbing would be straightforward. But the tracks from yesterday's summit team plus my teammates ahead of me had created deep unconsolidated snow steps as big as buckets on the slope above the shelf, some so deep that the uphill edge touched my thigh. I stepped up, breathed three times, then stepped up with the other leg, breathed three times. Occasionally, a snow step broke under my weight, and I slid downward several steps with jagged breath until my boot reached snow that would hold my weight. When I had to, I kicked steps into the slides from the climbers ahead of me.

I was not exposed anymore, so my danger of falling was low, but the mental frustration of minimal progress was draining. And I was not relying on physical fitness anymore. All the hours spent running, lifting weights, and hiking with a heavy backpack had been eaten away by altitude. What was propelling me upward now was mental: grit and fear of failure. I knew that if I failed at K2, everything else that I had accomplished in the mountains would lose its value in my eyes. Not because prior summits hadn't been meaningful or I hadn't worked hard for them but because I had set the bar higher. Failure on the world's most dangerous mountain would let the belief that I was not capable enough continue to thrive. Yes, I enjoyed proving people wrong; it gave me a plucky satisfaction. But proving myself wrong was where growth lived.

Despite the unstable, steep snow, it was a perfect day for climbing. Between breaths, I looked up to a crisp blue sky and noticed airborne ice crystals glinting off the sun, floating aimlessly at 28,000 feet in perfect balance. I continued scanning the sky all the way to my left and noticed flecks of red and orange at the top of my field of view. Disinterested, I looked back down at my heavy boots, searching endlessly for stable snow to take them upward. Then my hypoxic brain caught up with my eyes, and I looked again ahead of me, near the line where the sky met the snow, and confirmed that the bright colors were fellow climbers.

I'm going to summit K2.

Every cell in my body wanted to release, to cry, to shed the self-inflicted burden of this mountain. I knew with certainty now that I would summit, but I couldn't allow that release yet; I had too much work to do.

Focus! said the voice in my head. *Do not fucking cry!*

There were still hours of sugary steep snow between me and the summit, but there was no part of me that wanted to quit now.

The first time I stood on top of something with *mountain* in its name, I'd shared the accomplishment with my dad.

"I climbed a mountain today!" I told him over the phone, even though what I'd accomplished was walking up a hill on a well-worn path.

"That's neat, Lis. Good for you. Just keep puttin' one foot in front of the other."

Dad's advice now reminded me that that was all I had to do. One foot. Breathe, breathe, breathe. In front of. Breathe, breathe. Breathe. The other. Breathe, breathe, breathe.

My mantra went on until I reached a windblown ridge that continued to the left.

The summit of K2 is a narrow strip of hard, windblown snow. The steel points of my crampon points squeaked when they pierced it, the same sound my crampons had made walking on Rainier's summit ten years ago. At the opposite edge of K2's summit ridge was a huddle of other climbers, celebrating and taking every variation of photo with trinkets and flags that they'd carried from their home countries. I was not ready to celebrate. To every summit I'd brought a mental list of tasks to complete before I descended, but my list never included celebrating. Today, my list was short: change oxygen bottle, thank the mountain, take photos, say goodbye. When all other tasks were complete, I knelt in the snow and removed my backpack. With thick gloves it was difficult to manage the zippers, but I located a plastic pill bottle that had been tucked in the inner pocket for two years. I wanted this moment to be special; I wanted to say something poignant, but my thoughts were an emotional, oxygen-depleted fog. I clumsily unscrewed the pill-bottle lid and quickly flicked its contents into the air.

From the pinnacle of my savage mountain, the final grains of my dad's ashes floated into the wind above Pakistan.

As I returned to my backpack, I heard Jason's dense Irish accent conclude a satellite-phone conversation with his daughter. "You can be anything you want, never forget." His words drifted over me, settling for a second but not really sinking in. When I stood to shoulder my backpack, he was standing next to me. When we hugged, I felt his body heave, and I knew he was crying. We separated and faced each other, but words and emotions were hidden beneath snow goggles and oxygen masks. I wanted the same release, to be free of the weight of K2, but there was only frozen air and a lot of work left to do. I turned to descend.

CHAPTER 28

21,450 FEET

Descending is a completely different game, a game that, thanks to exhaustion and a climber's position facing away from the slope, claims more deaths than ascending. I let this fact float through my mind as I took my first step from the summit ridge to the powdery snow beneath it. This was the first downward step my body had taken in eleven days. As I climbed down, I would be relying mostly on balance for the first few hours, after which the terrain would transition from snow to steep ice and I would have to add to the equation perfectly executed rappels. I knew that my body and mind were beyond exhausted. They had been singularly focused on my survival since I'd left base camp six days ago. There were no carefree thoughts while climbing K2. I hadn't had the luxury of thinking about email or whether today was trash day since I'd left Islamabad. Instead, I'd relied on my brain to alert me to hazards, to ensure I made zero mistakes, to rig my gear perfectly, to choose the safest foot and hand placements, and to stop me before I pushed too far. All with 65 percent less oxygen than at my home in Seattle, and in a calorie-deprived and dehydrated state. Now, as I descended, I was asking my mind and body for ten more hours of vigilance until I arrived safely at Camp 2, 6,000 feet below.

I mentally reviewed the hazards between me and rest. It started off benignly; I would descend the deep powder on this slope, then transition from walking downhill to rappelling the steep, exposed ice next to the serac, then walk along the crumbling exposed traverse, then . . .

That's enough, I told myself. *Focus on one thing at a time. First, descend this slope.*

I took deep, deliberate breaths and continued walking. Below me, I saw a green blur. After a few more downward steps, I realized that it was Rob, moving slowly and willfully upward, his head cocked awkwardly toward me.

"Awesome job, Rob. Need anything?" Cold and oxygen deprivation slowed my words.

As we passed each other, the air between us remained blank. His body didn't shift from its hunched-over position, and I didn't even know if he'd heard me, hidden behind ski goggles and oxygen masks.

I continued to descend past Rob. I should have been happily surprised, even relieved, to see that Rob had resumed climbing after his oxygen-regulator failure so close to the summit. But it didn't seem like my brain could conjure those emotions in its hypoxic, survival-focused state. Instead, I remained concentrated on pressing one heel after the other into the steep, powdery snow.

Hours after passing Rob, I left the deep snow behind me and again met the steep blue ice that paralleled the serac. When I'd climbed it this morning, it had been quiet, peaceful even, each of us lost in our own solitary bubbles of headlamp light. Now, in daylight, the slope was a shit show of tangled fixed lines and at least a dozen climbers moving in both directions. I stood at the top and peered down, scanning methodically for a free rope and clean line to descend. Although there were two sets of fixed ropes here, they were both being used for ascension. I saw the climbers still hopeful for the summit heaving, stopping, even lying motionless on the steep ice. To my right, I saw Garrett anchored to the slope and attempting to direct traffic. But, given the other climbers' mental states and language differences, he was making little progress. To make the slope safer, he would later attach a third fixed line.

. . .

Still, one climber would die here today.

I had unfortunately been in this situation before, on Everest's summit ridge, where a mistake would result in either an 8,000-foot fall into Nepal or an 11,000-foot fall into Tibet. A mistake here meant a 10,000-foot fall to base camp. So, I knew, I had two options: to wait for hours for the ascending climbers to clear the rope, or to descend and then delicately transition around the upward climbers when we met. Waiting is a death sentence, a hopeless oxygen-wasting game without guarantees. Though Garrett was attempting to help, I had no control over upward climbers. Furthermore, they were no more likely to wait for me than I was for them. Choosing to descend, however, could also be deadly. But moving felt safer than standing in line. I had a choice about how I descended, too. I could arm wrap or rappel. Rappelling involved looping the climbing rope through a metal device attached to my harness and creating friction, then leaning back and walking backward down the slope. Arm wrapping was a different kind of scary, though faster, since it wouldn't involve a rappel device, instead creating friction by wrapping the climbing rope around my arm, leaning forward, and walking face-first down the mountain.

As I was contemplating the best choice, Garrett yelled up at me. "I think you should arm wrap this one, Lisa." He was close enough that I could hear in his cracked voice the strain that K2 had caused.

The part of me that wanted to follow directions and not disappoint people provoked my body to prepare to arm wrap, and I bent forward and grabbed the climbing rope, pulled it toward me, and began wrapping it around my right forearm, laying it over the strips of worn nylon on my down suit, abraded by the friction of previous arm wraps. As I was wrapping, I felt the faint but urgent twitch of intuition.

Two years ago, on Mount Everest, I'd departed Camp 4 full of pride and confidence until, just a few hundred feet from camp, I'd encountered the Geneva Spur, a rock buttress strewn with piles of fresh snow. I'd caught up to Garrett as he peered over the rocky lip to assess our options for descent. Below us were a dozen climbers scattered across the rock, slowly ascending the fixed lines.

"Arm wrapping's the way to go, Lisa," he'd said through his oxygen mask. "We'll run out of Os queuing here."

The thought of leaning forward and walking down the rocky slope while using the rope for tension and friction had struck instant terror in my gut.

"He's fucking crazy," I'd muttered. But before I could verbalize a protest, he was efficiently moving downward. I arm wrapped the Geneva Spur—not as smoothly as Garrett, but I'd made it happen. At the bottom, my apprehension had evolved into confidence. I arm wrapped the whole rest of the route. There are times when mentors see in you more than you believe you are capable of, and you elevate your ability to a place you didn't believe was accessible. The Geneva Spur had been one of those places. K2's 50-degree ice slope was not.

Today there was an uneasy flutter in my stomach. The right-most column of my spreadsheet flashed in my brain again. The highest tally of deaths had historically occurred in this place.

Learn from them.

I told Garrett no, involuntarily, as if the flutter in my stomach pushed the words out of my mouth. Until now, self-doubt had made it hard to hear my intuition, but now it was as though K2 had stripped everything else from me and it was all I had left. I didn't even reconsider my decision, not on this killer mountain.

I let the rope unwind from my arm, reached to my harness's gear loop on my left hip, and retrieved the metal ATC device that would allow me to safely rappel the slope. When the ATC was clipped to the belay loop of my harness, I reached between my legs, grabbed the climbing rope again, and pulled it to my waist.

"No mistakes," I said as I pulled hard on the rope to thread it through the ATC and its locking carabiner, then confirmed that it was rigged correctly. As a final confirmation, I tapped the locking gate of the carabiner with my gloved finger and listened for the metal tap to verify it was locked. Then I looked over my right shoulder, down the slope, and let my gaze drift farther, to the point where ice rolled into air. *That's where I'd fall,* I thought. I didn't look again, to avoid the risk that fear would overtake my ability to move. Instead, I took a deep breath and leaned back to weight the rope and begin walking backward. As I descended, I recognized some of the climbers and, judging by their slow, ataxic movements, wondered if they would make it to the summit. When I saw a man lying facedown on the rope I was descending, I stopped.

"MOOOVE!" I yelled.

He didn't.

"GET OFF THE ROPE!" I yelled again, but he remained motionless.

"Fuck!" I said, frustrated and full of adrenaline. I knew I'd have to maneuver around him. I continued descending the ice and stopped a few feet above him.

"You're lying on the rope!"

I recognized him and was surprised that he'd let himself get to this point, since we'd had conversations at base camp where he'd spoken with confidence and experience. *The mountain doesn't care*—I remembered my uncle's words. I could tell that he was still breathing, and I asked him if he was descending.

"Summit," he said, and raised a hand feebly into the air.

"I think you should descend," I told him. "Summit many hours away."

"No! Summit!" he said. I knew that I could not reason with him. His brain had gone to that myopic place where death was an acceptable cost of summiting.

I inhaled deeply. My maneuvers needed to be surgical. *No mistakes, LT. No fucking mistakes.*

My right hand needed to remain firmly on the rope below my ATC to act as a brake. If it didn't, I would slide first into the man lying on the ice and then, if he wasn't anchored, we'd slide downward together, in a tangle, to the next anchor. I assumed he was not properly anchored and kept my brake hand in place. Next, with my left hand, I reached to my waist, located my ascender, and released it from my harness's gear loop. My ascender was designed for right-hand use, and it was an awkward five-minute struggle to open its cam with the opposite thumb and lock it onto the rope above my ATC. This wasn't a scenario I'd practiced at home. But once it was there, I could release my brake hand and ATC and use two hands to untangle the web of rope and leashes at my waist. After the tangle was dismantled, I moved my safety carabiner to the section of climbing rope at his waist, which left me in an uncomfortable, crouching position next to him, and I reminded myself to keep my feet squarely under me even as I leaned. I was ready now to slide my ascender down the rope as I took two steps downward, kicking my crampon points hard into the ice as I went. I looked up now and knew there were other climbers waiting for this shit show that I was now a part of to clear, but I pushed them out of my mind. I repeated this delicate sequence two more times, pulling hard on the rope to gain enough slack, and finally was able to attach my ascender to the rope below him. Now I could rerig my ATC and continue downward.

"Bloody hell," I said when I was finally free.

I knew that I couldn't relax, however, and soon turned the corner to my left and for the first time, in daylight, saw the traverse. The stoic, glistening serac loomed over it like an angry dictator. It was bigger than I'd imagined, the size of a skyscraper. But I didn't even consider the danger here, not wanting to distract myself with thoughts about the consequences of a misplaced step now. The pressure of high-altitude acrobatics on an icy slope with an incoherent, collapsed man had heightened my focus and shifted trust to myself. I'd walked across this traverse last night; it was no more complex or challenging now, just one foot in front of the other.

When I cleared the final ice screw anchoring the traverse, the logical, calculating part of my brain realized that I'd just descended the deadliest part of K2. I patted the ice screw again with my glove and said thank you. It seemed like a moment worth celebrating now, but the uncertainty of descending 10,000 more feet wouldn't allow any emotion other than gratitude. I had a lot more work to do before celebrating.

Five hours after leaving the summit, I reached Camp 4. As I gathered my belongings from the tent, I realized that it was no longer sunny. The clouds had started to build, obscuring the route above and below me. It felt eerie, sitting alone at 25,500 feet in the clouds, and I was frightened again, and for the first time I felt the heaviness of fatigue in my eyelids, in my muscles.

You must take care of you, I reminded myself, and began eating what was left of the candy in my pockets. I felt more comfortable when I could make out Jason's lean frame descending toward camp in the fog.

"Good work up there, Lisa." Exhaustion made his Irish accent sound extra slurry to me.

"You, too. We're not done yet, though."

"Nope," he confirmed.

As we both resumed stuffing sleeping bags and extra food haphazardly into our backpacks, I felt intoxicated. Jason's normally swift movements seemed slower now, and I couldn't tell if it was him or my brain that had downshifted.

"Shall we?" he asked when we were done, and tilted his helmet toward the direction of base camp. We descended together through the first anchor of the Black Pyramid, and then I urged him to go ahead.

"I want to take my time," I said. "No mistakes, ya know." My statement was slurred because my face was too cold to form words.

"Roger that," Jason said. "See you at camp."

It was too cloudy to see the Baltoro Glacier on its eternal glide toward Concordia, but I sat on a rock and stared in its direction, trying to contemplate what I'd just done. It wouldn't sink in, though; it was too enormous, and my brain was still occupied with survival. But I knew that I'd relied on myself. I'd made smart decisions based on what had been best for me. I felt a tiny, tenuous flicker of pride and relief.

I heard the familiar sound of steel scraping rock as I took my first steps onto the Black Pyramid's patchwork of ice and rock, but this time, along with the sounds there was confidence. I took deep breaths, now to fan this new spark of confidence and independence rather than to calm my fear and uncertainty. Somewhere on the pyramid, the bros passed me, laughing and racing from anchor to anchor. That was their brand of climbing, I decided, and I was not bothered by it anymore, though I knew bravado wouldn't save anyone here. When I finally saw the oasis of tents below me, I sat on a pale rock just above camp and breathed deeply with closed eyes. I was more overwhelmed by what was inside of me than the scene around me. *You just did that*, I thought. *You just trusted the tiny voice inside of you that was squashed for so long but believed you were capable. Don't lose this.*

Eventually, I ambled to the tent that I'd shared with Rob when we were last at Camp 2. Inside, I lay flat on my back, fully dressed, my legs, still wearing boots and crampons, splayed outside the tent. It was 5:00 p.m., which meant I'd been climbing for most of the past twenty hours. Though the pull of sleep was strong, I couldn't go there—not yet. It was still my job to take care of myself. First, I unlaced and removed my crampons, leaving them in the tent's vestibule. Then I lay flat on my back and closed my eyes for a short rest before I set up my sleeping bag and inflatable mattress. Then I rested again. Every time I closed my eyes, I saw ice and an orange climbing rope.

In between resting and undressing, I made a video. It was the first time I'd seen an image of myself in six days. I wasn't shocked by what I saw; the face looking back at me in my cell phone seemed apropos. My hair was matted and sprouting at odd angles, my skin desiccated and crinkled, my lips faintly blue. And my eyes—my pupils were constricted to hard black specks. Later, someone would tell me that my eyes matched those of refugees she'd known. In quiet words, my video began: "I have no words except huge, huge respect for this mountain and everyone who encouraged and supported and believed I could do this. I hope that I never forget this feeling. I hope that the next time someone tells me that I can't do something I remember this feeling. And I promise to share this feeling with anyone who'll listen. Because no one gets to define my boundaries."

Just before dark, the sounds of the tent's zipper woke me. When I lurched forward, I saw Rob's haggard face as he fell inside. He carried out a similar sequence of resting and undressing, resting and eating, resting and gear sorting. He was unusually quiet, and I sensed that he'd had an epic day, so I didn't want to pry. Finally, he matter-of-factly described his ordeal. After I'd left him above the bottleneck this morning with a broken regulator, he'd been unable to find a replacement that matched his oxygen bottle. So he'd screwed his mismatched backup regulator onto his oxygen bottle. The incompatibility leaked critical oxygen and stretched his regulator hose beyond its limit, resulting in not only less oxygen delivered to his brain but also limited head mobility. That Rob had summited—and afterward would spend an extra night at Camp 2 to help a fellow climber—were testaments to his mental and physical strength, resilience, and character.

At seven the next morning, despite my body aching in protest of the past day's effort and the prospect of more climbing, I began the last leg of K2's descent. Rigging my ATC device every time now felt tedious, but I could not let my guard down. I could not become lazy. But I was so, so tired. It was sleeting and alarmingly quiet on the rock below House's Chimney. All around me was wet rock, rotten snow, and ropes so frayed that I was forced repeatedly to choose the least shitty one. Because the orange climbing rope had been used on the steepest, riskiest part of the route, this section wasn't fitted with it, and choosing the safest rope was more terrifying than when I'd ascended—because now, I was trusting my full weight to the ropes. I was misplacing confidence in aged, tattered ropes, I knew, but was without better options.

My body acknowledged the risk by quickening my breath. When I leaned back, weighting the frayed rope, I tried to control this fearful instinct with long, slow breaths and a mantra.

Thank you, K2, please keep me safe . . . thank you, K2, please keep me safe.

My crampons scratched rock, my weight slowly lowered, and I watched wet, frayed rope slide through leather gloves and then the metal slots of my ATC. I wondered how much weight these ropes had endured, and how much more they could. The tension of the rope creaked and, for a second, overpowered my labored breath. I was completely alone, with dense fog and freezing rain dampening all other sounds except the occasional, startling *whiiizzz* of rocks, some as big as kitchen sinks, flying by.

Thank you, K2, please keep me safe.

When I arrived at Camp 1, it was flattened, obliterated by falling rocks and roaring wind. Shards of tent poles, strips of nylon tenting, and random fragments of food and gear littered the ground. I saw battered climbing pants, tins of fuel, and the feathery remnants of a down jacket.

K2 was not done, I realized, and I didn't want to be here. I didn't need to experience any more of her fury. I turned and continued descending, thanking fear for self-preservation.

An hour later, I was wandering alone on the rocky ribs below Advanced Base Camp. I took a short walk to the place where a wall of brown rock jutted inward enough to create an alcove. After a few steps, I spotted the bronze plaque that had triggered my contemplation on my ascent. I removed my glove, kissed my hand, pressed it onto the wet metal letters that made her name, and closed my eyes. *Thank you.*

I wanted to cry. I wanted to leave all the shit and weight of doubt and proving and perfection right here. I wanted to leave it and skip away, light as air, off this rock and into the rest of my life. But the tears welled into unsatisfying globs in my eyes and wouldn't fall. K2 had denied me every satisfaction, and I could only continue to wander through the icefall and onto the flat glacial moraine. Within an hour, I was nearly to my base-camp tent, the one I'd left seven days ago. There was a cold, penetrating drizzle, the kind I was used to as a Seattleite but still disliked. Sodden fog surrounded me on all sides, and even though it would have been difficult to become lost on this strip of rock-strewn ice, I felt tension build in my stomach, and I slowed my walk to search for landmarks. But the ice and rock and fog all looked identical. *How ironic it would be to get lost here,* I thought, and continued plodding on the broken ice and rocks, still unsure. Then I heard the faintest Muslim prayer through the fog. I didn't know the words, but they comforted me, wrapping me like a blanket and reminding me of normal. I let them pull my exhausted, beaten body forward until I met their source, Mushtaq, our Pakistani base-camp manager.

"We are so much happy to see you, Lisa!" he said, and enveloped me. "Congratulation! Congratulation! Congratulation!"

"Happy!" Khadim joined him. "Happy, we brought here cake." Khadim presented his confection with a wide smile.

"You brought CAKE?" I exclaimed with a strained voice, and shoved nearly a whole piece of sugary comfort in my mouth.

Mushtaq would stand in the freezing rain until the whole team had reached the safety of this moraine, greeting each of us with leis, cake, Coca-Cola, and hearty hugs.

Klára walked to the edge of camp to greet me. We hugged, and her hair smelled like soap and juniper smoke. Mine did not.

"I'm sorry," I said.

"It's OK." She swayed and hugged me harder while I cried.

In a year's time, Klára and I would meet back on this moraine. We would run screaming toward each other like little girls. She would pick me up and hold me, like a fireman rescuing a child, with two firm arms. She would summit K2 that year, 2019, on her third attempt.

At base camp, I ate, congratulated the team, and then wandered back to my tent, like everything was normal. I didn't have the emotional, cathartic moment I had been waiting for, too amped with adrenaline and cake to realize that I'd just become the second American woman to summit K2. I'd later realize that it no longer mattered that I wasn't the first, that the order wasn't important; it was the continuation, the progress. As I settled into my base-camp tent, I didn't yet understand that, most importantly, I'd done it on my terms, I had trusted myself, and I had acted with confidence.

Three days later, base camp's tents, stoves, and generators had been dismantled and packed into tidy bundles and blue barrels, and we let K2 have her solitude back as we began walking to Askole, retracing the steps we'd taken five weeks before. I caught a glimpse of Aang Phurba, standing at the edge of camp with his hands in his jeans pockets and a backward baseball cap holding his hair back. His face was more angular now, his cheekbones more prominent, like K2 had chiseled them. His smile seemed to carry more ease now, his laugh quicker.

We took a team photo to memorialize our time with K2. One of the bros bent down to pick up my trekking pole when I dropped it, and I softened—a little. Mountaineering is a unique mix of individual effort and teamwork, and we'd all played a role in one another's accomplishments. I couldn't have made it to the top and back without them.

The mountain had changed, too. Summer temperatures had melted snow, shifted rocks, and created a torrent of glacial melt that rushed though base camp toward the Indus River. For the next three days, we prevailed in our downward march with icy rain, angry river crossings, naps in the fleeting sunshine, quicksand, luxuriously soft kittens that mewed in my ear, and slurps of Jägermeister when my brain and feet needed motivation to continue. It wasn't until I reached the military checkpoint at Askole's perimeter on the third day that I felt tension start to creep from my body and I let my guard down enough to smile and skip like a young girl to the Land Cruiser waiting to drive me back to Skardu, not afraid anymore of blending femininity with strength.

The rugged ride was interrupted by a multihour funeral procession, and for a while, as our vehicles idled behind, I watched the mourners, watched their black mourning dress and dusty sandals walk solemnly up the road. Eventually, our convoy drivers, frustrated by the slow progress, exited their Land Cruisers to smoke cigarettes in the shade. I stepped out, too, to feel the sunshine on my face and the thick air in my lungs. I could no longer see K2, but I looked toward her, past the scrubby bushes and down the chaotic jumble of dirt and rock that made our road. *Why did I do that?* I asked myself again. When I'd been up close with K2, my brain had been too fraught with fear to answer. Or maybe I hadn't been ready for the answer. But here, behind the mourners, I was contemplative, ready to know. *Why?* It was the question posed to many high-elevation mountaineers, the question I'd carried with me on every mountain. My answer was not simple. It couldn't be. The determination, the grit, the hours of solitude, the sacrifices, the sheer expense required a deeper examination. That day the answer was all around me, it turned out. It was in the mourners' march, in the river's constant flow, in the ever-shifting rock at my feet.

I climbed these mountains and took these risks to evolve, to avoid stasis. It wasn't to accomplish. It wasn't to prove anymore.

Umer had had it exactly right: "Don't give up until you are transformed."

15,390 FEET

During the summer of the following year, 2019, I returned to Pakistan. Not with the aspiration to summit anything, but instead to help others reach their K2 goals by trekking to base camp.

The Pakistanis were still gracious, the Serena Hotel still plush and perfumed, and the trail still arduous. But this year the weather was more sun than rain, and on the fifth day, Aang Phurba and I rounded the corner at Concordia, paused, and looked up.

"There she is, *didi*."

Yes, I thought. *There she is.*

We grinned widely and, along with Bashir, marveled at our fortune to summit together last year and arrive back here today. I wished them a safe summit again and didn't envy the challenges ahead of them.

"Inshallah," Bashir said, his light eyes looking wild, and I wondered if he was more worried now than before his first attempt.

I lingered as the men continued onto the broad, rock-strewn Baltoro Glacier.

"Coming, *didi*?" Aang Phurba said, looking back.

"No, I'll meet you at camp."

I sat on a flat rock and stared up at K2. The sun was fading, and

I could see the beginnings of shadows creep across her south face. I closed my eyes and let the image of K2's steep slopes seep back into my consciousness. Now, the emotion of last year's summit finally came.

"Thank you, K2, for keeping me safe," I said between tears.

Without the heaviness of summiting in my heart any longer, all that I felt was gratitude. Not just for a safe summit, and not just for what K2 had given me, but also for what she'd taken. Like a slope overburdened with unstable snow, she'd released from me the need to prove myself with perfection. She'd finally shown me why I'd taken these risks.

Since summiting, I no longer had to grip everything so tightly. Now, when I felt my breath grow shallow from the tension of needing to be everything or prove everything, I released it to her, like a prayer from a flag. In this way, K2 and I had become friends. I trusted that life would forever be messy and mysterious, and that she would continue to erode my hard edges and expose the vulnerable parts. This process would never be complete, and in that there was peace and intrigue.

I stood up from the rock at Concordia, straightened my back, stretched my arms wide, and inhaled deeply. The crisp mountain air flooded my lungs, and it felt like home. I continued walking toward K2, with confidence this time, knowing that she and all the other mountains in my heart were an indelible reminder that I was already enough, that the joy in perfection was fleeting, and that together we would continue to find elevation.

ACKNOWLEDGMENTS

March 21, 2022, Boca Raton, Florida

Birthing this story would not have been possible without the people who encouraged me, who saw through my own doubt, procrastination, and excuses and pushed me to keep going. The book you're holding started as a childhood dream, but found purpose in 2015 when I began journaling about my battle with cancer. I could not have navigated the arduous path from that point to today alone.

Thank you to Dr. Christine Lee, MD, Heidi Dishneau, ARNP, and the rest of the team at Swedish Health Services for literally saving my life.

Thank you to Dior Johnston at First Tech Federal Credit Union for answering the phone that day with love and optimism. Attempting Everest would not have been possible without you and your team.

Thank you to Cheryl Kitashima for not letting me conclude a single financial-planning session without a book update; your inquiries kept me on track more than you know.

Much gratitude to Jeff Huffman at Alcon for thinking outside of the sponsorship box and making my K2 climb possible.

Hugs to Daniel Benitez and Andrew Tierney for your creativity, enthusiasm, and unflappable willingness to lug drones and camera equipment uphill in the mud and rain. Those forays would not have been the same without both of you.

I am also deeply grateful to the men and women who introduced me to the mountains and helped me build confidence. Thank you to Vern Tejas for a solid mountaineering foundation and unforgettable anecdotes. Thank you to Tracee Metcalfe and Brigit Anderson for high-altitude lessons, laughs, and companionship. Thank you to

Garrett Madison for your leadership and friendship.

The effort to nurture my disjointed journals into a manuscript often felt opaque and overwhelming; I will forever be indebted to the women who answered every question, shared wisdom, read every early copy, and taught me the art of memoir with skillful honesty. You're my literary doulas: Johanna Garton, Kristi Coulter, Gail Hudson.

I have unending gratitude to the women at Girl Friday Productions for holding my hand—sometimes both of them—making it fun, and evolving my manuscript into a book. Most especially Devon Fredericksen for serendipitously showing up in my life at just the right moment with mindful patience and deft handling of details. I don't know how you do it.

Love to Anders Westby for always being willing to read early drafts, for believing in me even though I give you plenty of reasons not to, for showing me things about myself that I don't even see, and for your fervent support of the Oxford comma.

Finally, and perhaps most importantly, a sincere thank-you to the people who told me no, who doubted or thought I was reaching too far. Your motivation is the most potent.

Lisa Thompson is a mountaineer, cancer survivor, and sought-after speaker and coach. Growing up in the flat, humid farmlands of Illinois, she relied on adventure as a distraction, always knowing that she'd someday leave her hometown for something bigger. She soon became the first person in her extended family to graduate from college. She worked for twenty-five years as an engineer and in leadership roles at technology companies.

Since she began climbing in 2008, Lisa has summited some of the most challenging mountains in the world, including Everest. She has completed the Seven Summits, reaching the top of the highest peak on each of the seven continents. Through her company, Alpine Athletics, and other platforms, Lisa shares her message of strength and resilience with corporate and private groups worldwide. She lives in Seattle with her golden retriever, Chevy, who loves the mountains almost as much as she does. You can learn more about Lisa at www.lisaclimbs.com.